The Entrepreneurial Arch

As the number of universities offering entrepreneurial programs continues to increase, there is a growing need for a suitable framework for the teaching of entrepreneurship beyond the operational side of the business and the preparation of a business plan. This book offers a fresh approach to entrepreneurship by teaching readers how to discover and create a new firm or grow an existing one, starting from a firm's or team's capabilities. The core methodology is based on the "Entrepreneurial Arch" which provides a more holistic view of entrepreneurship by dividing the business development process into six distinct segments. An important feature of this model is the inclusion of learning units focusing on opportunity identification, business design, and risk reduction before the business planning stage is attempted. Illustrated with various real-world examples, this structured and concise book will appeal to students, as well as to practitioners looking to develop their entrepreneurial skills.

TIMOTHY L. FALEY is Kiril Sokoloff Distinguished Professor of Entrepreneurship and Special Assistant to the President for Entrepreneurial Initiatives at the University of the Virgin Islands. Dr. Faley was an architect and builder of the entrepreneurship program at the University of Michigan, which he helped transform from an unranked program to the number one graduate entrepreneurship program in the nation (*Princeton Review / Entrepreneur Magazine*, 2013).

The Entrepreneurial Arch

A Strategic Framework for Discovering, Developing and Renewing Firms

TIMOTHY L. FALEY
University of the Virgin Islands, St Thomas

CAMBRIDGE
UNIVERSITY PRESS

CAMBRIDGE
UNIVERSITY PRESS

University Printing House, Cambridge CB2 8BS, United Kingdom

Cambridge University Press is part of the University of Cambridge.

It furthers the University's mission by disseminating knowledge in the pursuit of education, learning and research at the highest international levels of excellence.

www.cambridge.org
Information on this title: www.cambridge.org/9781107424821

© Timothy L. Faley 2015

First published 2015

A catalogue record for this publication is available from the British Library

Library of Congress Cataloging in Publication data
Faley, Timothy L., 1956–
The entrepreneurial arch : a strategic framework for discovering, developing and renewing firms / Timothy L. Faley.
    pages   cm
ISBN 978-1-107-07427-9 (hardback)
1. Entrepreneurship.   2. Business planning.   3. New business enterprises.   I. Title.
HB615.F266   2014
658.4′21–dc23
                                                    2014012738

ISBN 978-1-107-07427-9 Hardback
ISBN 978-1-107-42482-1 Paperback

Contents

Figures

Preface

The parable of the blind men and the elephant is well known. Each feels a different part of the elephant and describes that part as though it were the whole animal. One believes an elephant is like a snake as he feels its trunk, another a fan as he feels the elephant's ear, still another a rope as he grasps the elephant's tail, another feels the elephant's side and believes the elephant is like a wall, the last man feels the elephant's tusk and describes the elephant as a spear. Entrepreneurship is described in a very similar way. Some emphasize the business plan; others argue how the business plan is "dead" and it is now all about the business model; still others argue that it is all about financing or growth or passion. Like the blind men, they are all correct and simultaneously all wrong, as they each describe a piece and not the whole.

The Entrepreneurial Arch is the result of my quest to pull all these pieces into a unified description of entrepreneurship. That description has two parts: Business Discovery and Business Execution. Each of those parts has three components. Together the six components describe fundamental skills that every organization wishes it could enhance:

- identifying emerging opportunities (and threats)
- formulating innovative business solutions around those opportunities
- assessing the feasibility of those proposed businesses
- developing a practicable implementation plan from disparate and incomplete information
- identifying, aligning and/or acquiring the necessary resources needed to power the plan forward, and
- driving accelerated growth.

We call people with the above skill-set entrepreneurs.

Some elements are missing. I was originally trained as a scientist and have been involved in all aspects of the creation and commercialization of science throughout my career. Transforming inventions into innovations seemed mystical and unknown to all but a few. Earning an advanced degree in business did not help resolve this mystery for me. Traditionally, the teaching of entrepreneurship has focused on the operational side of the business: How to plan your operations, how to resource your plan, and how to grow your business. Sometimes business assessment and/or business model creation are taught, but this still requires that you first have a specifically defined business. How does any of this help when all you have is an invention or some expertise that you desire to leverage? A big piece of the story seems to be missing. How could we become an innovation world when such a big piece of the puzzle is missing and untaught? We need to teach students how to create differentiated businesses from their differentiated capabilities, building upon their own unique knowledge bases and what they came to the university to study. Business is the vehicle for creating and capturing value from your capabilities. The discussion of how to leverage your capabilities to create value for the world should not start with the vehicle, but with your capabilities. That is what students are passionate about, and that is what they come to the institutions of higher learning to deepen their knowledge about. This was my motivation for developing the Entrepreneurial Arch.

As the elements of the arch became clearer there rose a second and equally difficult challenge. How do you teach this? The traditional way of teaching entrepreneurship uses what some call the apprenticeship model and what I usually call the "mentor model." You take someone with a promising idea and connect them with a mentor who guides them through the mystical process of business formulation and execution. That methodology works well when you have a vibrant entrepreneurial ecosystem to draw upon. However, if your goal is to *create* an entrepreneurial ecosystem in your community, you are caught in the conundrum of needing a robust ecosystem (with a plethora of experienced mentors) in order to develop one. As I talked to educators from Cairo to Kalamazoo, it became clear that this conundrum had to be resolved if they were to have the impact they desired. Not only did the description of entrepreneurship need to be made whole, but addressing how to teach it also needed to be updated. The "learn–do, learn–do" model was the result of that effort. Thinking of entrepreneurship as a learnable skill, and understanding that the foundation of any skill is knowledge, we experimented with programs and courses and experiential learning programs that would deliver a portion of the arch (the "learn") and then allow students to develop those skills (the "do") before acquiring additional knowledge. By breaking the process down into small parts, we were also able to develop coaches for each part. The process overcomes the classic conundrum by creating a pathway to follow in bootstrapping an entrepreneurial ecosystem. I say "we" because no one can teach this range of work on his or her own. I must also admit that the work is not "complete." As John Cotton Dana once said, "Who dares to teach must never cease to learn." I love to teach and I am definitely still learning.

It is my fervent hope that this book will help in forwarding you along your own entrepreneurial journey.

Acknowledgments

I have a long list of people that contributed to this book. As Buddha once said, "When the student is ready, the teacher will appear." I have had the pleasure of many great teachers in my life. I have also been blessed by being in environments that allowed me, and often even encouraged me, to "experiment." (There are, of course, no "failures," simply "experiments" that did not yield the anticipated outcome. It is from those experiments that the most learning is derived.) I particularly want to thank Hank Kohlbrand, Tom Kinnear, Bud Williamson, David Hall, Sam Zell, and Kiril Sokoloff for creating my learning environment. I especially wish to thank long-term colleagues at the University of Michigan, Paul Kirsch and Peter Adriaens, for their contributions. No one would ever quite believe the amount of time we collectively spent in front of white boards debating frameworks and teaching approaches. I also want to thank Dave Hatfield, who encouraged me to keep writing and helped me put structure to the book. As any parent knows, the best teachers are your children and my wife and I are blessed with five great teachers (Ryan, Nick, Alexandra, Kortney, and Matt). And as every teacher knows, students are great teachers and I have had some of the best from all over the globe.

The book would not exist without the diligence and vision of Paula Parish of Cambridge University Press. I cannot thank her enough for her belief in this project. I also want to thank my editor Malu Comboye, who desperately tried to transform my rambling text into readable prose. Not only is Malu a good friend, but a very patient woman, having to read and re-read multiple versions of portions of this book.

Most importantly, this book is dedicated to my deceased mother Maxine and my wife Kelley. Their energy and faith continue to be infectious and inspiring.

Tim Faley
St. Thomas, US Virgin Islands

I   Introduction to the Entrepreneurial Arch

I was sitting on the side of a hill one day when a breeze wafted over me. That's when it hit me – the glorious idea that became my billion-dollar business! My message to you, aspiring entrepreneur, is to go find your hill and feel your breeze.

Does anybody really believe that this is how new businesses are created? Wafts of breezes? We have all heard variations of this entrepreneurship tale before. They may be awe-inspiring, but they are useless to help transform aspiring entrepreneurs into actual ones.

Innovation and entrepreneurship are far too important to be left to a chance breeze. Growth is the number one goal of business leaders and economic developers across the globe. Growth creates value. Growth creates jobs. The world desperately needs more people that can understand how to do both. In short, it needs people that can:

- identify clear opportunities and threats from a confusing, chaotic, constantly changing environment
- formulate potential businesses that take advantage of these opportunities
- assess the feasibility of these proposed business ventures
- create practicable, operational plans for these new business opportunities from disparate and incomplete information
- acquire and align the resources necessary to launch the business (these resources will be both within and outside the organization's immediate control), and
- execute the plans in a manner that drives accelerated growth for their organizations.

We call these people entrepreneurs. Organizations of all sizes and types need entrepreneurs to solve tomorrow's problems. Entrepreneurship is

1

a profession, or at least it should be thought of in that way. A profession is defined by what the professional does, not where they do it. An accountant is an accountant whether they work for PWC or for a small non-profit. The core of what entrepreneurs do is contained in the list above. The myth of entrepreneurship as this magical gift bestowed only upon certain individuals is debilitating. Entrepreneurship needs to be approached like any profession; a serious topic of study which takes training and experience to perfect. There will always be gifted individuals, of course. That is true in any profession. The fact that there are exceptionally gifted surgeons does not preclude the teaching of surgery, or music, or engineering, or any other profession. Entrepreneurship should be no different.

This book describes the Entrepreneurial Arch, a graphic representation of a methodology to develop a new, financially sustainable organization. That organization could be a new line of business within an existing corporation, a startup with high growth potential, a small business, or a non-profit. The methodologies of the Arch can be used to renew or grow existing businesses. The Entrepreneurial Arch takes a capabilities-centric view of business formation. Your team or organization's capabilities form the foundation of the Arch. Moving left-to-right, each segment of the Arch progressively layers on additional complexity. The venture is also systematically de-risked as it moves across the Arch. Make no mistake; this is no linear march to a successful business. The methodology is both stochastic and highly non-linear. It is also specific enough to guide any business through its development, while being general enough to account for the idiosyncratic and contextual nature of new business creation. The critical aspect of the methodology is that it breaks down the entire business creation and launch process into digestible portions.

The Arch contains six segments. These segments represent the fundamental activities I have just described, that define what entrepreneurs do. Every segment is important in the creation of a new sustainable organization. Take out any one segment of the Arch and the entire structure collapses. The Entrepreneurial Arch has two distinct halves,

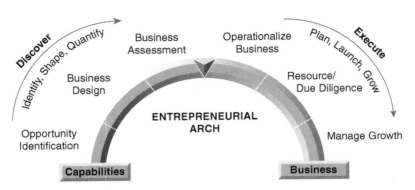

Discover — Identify, Shape, Quantify

Business Assessment

Business Design

Opportunity Identification

Operationalize Business

Plan, Launch, Grow — Execute

Resource/ Due Diligence

Manage Growth

ENTREPRENEURIAL ARCH

Capabilities

Business

• Assets (physical, intellectual)
• Know-how, skills, expertise
• Relationships, networks
• Aspirations, passions, interests

FIGURE 1.1 The Entrepreneurial Arch

as illustrated in Figure 1.1. The left-hand side of the Arch is the business discovery portion. This is an oft-neglected set of entrepreneurial activities. It is not an ideate and screen process (one where you brainstorm business ideas and then select the most promising), but rather one of directed discovery. Just as archaeologists dig to uncover past civilizations, entrepreneurs must be 'futurologists' and dig to discover future ones. Your initial idea is only a starting place on the journey. These are hypothesis-based, data-driven evaluation and reshaping techniques. The right-hand side of the Arch is the business execution side. These are the activities that are most frequently covered in standard entrepreneurship texts. Across the whole Arch de-risking, consistent with each stage of development, is performed on the venture. The discovery segments of the Arch follow a "fail fast" philosophy – determining with as little consumption of resources as possible whether there is an opportunity for you or your organization to create a business in which you can both create and capture value. Once discovered, and appropriately de-risked, you move on to the execution half of the Arch.

Many new businesses try to begin by creating a business plan, the first segment of the execution section of the Entrepreneurial Arch. However, before you spend all that time determining how you are going to execute the business would you not want to know whether that business makes any economic sense? Sadly, I knew of a couple that started a catering/hosting business. Every year they lost money, but they thought if they could just "do more" next year things would be all right. After several years, they performed a quick-and-dirty break-even calculation. They would need to do twenty events a week to break even. The only problem was that, given the elaborateness of their events, they could only do a maximum of six per week. The firm went bankrupt and the couple ended up divorced. Both the economic and the human toll of failed businesses are significant. Had they performed the assessment before launching the business they could have possibly repositioned the company as something that was more viable.

Starting with your business at the assessment phase does not work, either. Before you can evaluate the viability of a business, you have to know what it is you are evaluating. "It" has to be clearly and precisely defined. In short, the business needs to be designed. Before designing your business would you not want to know whether there is a problem worth solving, or an unmet/underserved need in the marketplace, that is aligned with your capabilities? That is opportunity identification. You need every part of the Arch. Skipping segments can lead to disaster.

Most people that are interested in starting their own business do not have a specific business they want to launch. They may talk about their passions and aspirations in the context of a business, but what they really have is a love for something. They love art history, they love helping new mothers through the birthing process. What they really want is to spend their careers getting paid to do what they love. They understand that in order to be paid to do something they have to be good at it. But that is not enough. What they do not know is how to monetize their skills and passions. Showing them how to create a business plan is not going to help them. Showing them how to do a feasibility study is also useless. They are starting with capabilities. They need the entire business discovery methodology (the left-hand side of the Entrepreneurial Arch). Without that, the entrepreneurial potential of individuals and societies will never be fully realized.

The next six chapters of this book will each cover one of the segments of the Arch, progressing from left to right. Elements that are common to multiple segments will be contained in the appendices. The final chapter summarizes the entire Entrepreneurial Arch methodology. The remainder of this chapter provides a succinct view of every segment of the Arch. The book is intended to be used both as an overview of the complete methodology and a reference for each segment.

Each of the segments of the Arch will leverage the individual or organization's capabilities. Capabilities are defined very specifically in this book and include four distinct areas: Assets (physical and intellectual), know-how/skills/expertise, relationships/networks, and aspirations/passions/interests. It is the nexus of these four areas that produces organizational opportunity.

One skill that you will use in every part of the Arch is the ability to view both the big picture and the small detail. While strategy focuses exclusively on the big picture and operations focus exclusively on the details, successful serial entrepreneurs are masters at seamlessly flowing from the big picture to the micro-detail and back. This will be referred to as the "Zoom-in, Zoom-out" skill.[1] Zooming in narrows the field of vision and magnifies details. The closer you zoom in, the finer the observable detail. Zooming out is the opposite. Zooming out widens the field of vision which elucidates the big picture. Together, these skills allow you to flow between a macro- and a micro-perspective. While discussing the business discovery section of the Arch we will use this skill to view all four aspects of a business: Motive, owner, activity, and monetization. The four levels of each of these four components are shown in Figure 1.2.

	Motive	Owner	Activity	Monetization
Zoom Out ↑	Macro-driver	Society	Opening	Potential to create value
	General problem	Industry	Capabilities	Create value
	Specific issue	Industry segment	Approach	High value / Capture value
Zoom In ↓	Need/desire	Customer	Offering/actions	Revenue model Margin assessment Investability analysis

FIGURE 1.2 The four necessary aspects of a business

CHAPTER 2   OPPORTUNITY IDENTIFICATION

The first segment of the Entrepreneurial Arch requires you to identify an opportunity to build an organization that can make an impact. This segment of the methodology is described in four steps. These steps will require zooming out and zooming in, divergent and convergent thinking. As will be common throughout this process, you will find yourself iterating within this segment in addition to iterating between sections of the Arch. The four steps that will be detailed in this chapter are summarized below.

Step 1. Zoom out
Zoom out to the macro-driver (or at least the general problem) level by using the 'what–who–what–who' technique in the opportunity space (the fields covered by the Motive and Owner dimensions).

Step 2. Zoom in and identify industry or industries
From the macro-driver level, use brainstorm techniques to identify general problems that are stimulating this macro-driver, and to identify the industries that are struggling with each general problem.

Use convergent techniques to narrow the industry list:
- is there an opening?
- does this industry align with your capabilities?
    If no to either, eliminate this industry.
    Choose an industry:
- initially choose the one that best aligns with your capabilities
- if all industries have been eliminated, return to Step 1.

Step 3. Zoom in to identify a high-value opportunity within this industry
Create a value system for the industry or, if repositioning from Step 4, expand a subsection of the value system created in that step.

Assess to determine high-value issue(s) and industry-segment level owner(s). Choose a high-value issue that has an opening and aligns with your capabilities.

If the high-value issues are exhausted, return to Step 2 to choose
another industry.

Step 4. Business concept convergence

Can you devise an approach that would resolve the high-value issue
identified in Step 3? If no, return to Step 3 and choose another
high-value issue.

Assess value-capture potential by performing a positioning for
value capture (PVC) assessment. Can you capture value with
this approach? If yes, define complete business concept and
move to business design.

If not, alter approach. Reposition firm and return to Step 3 to assess
whether a new approach targets a high-value issue by zooming in
on a segment of the previously crafted value system.

Once all alternative approaches have been exhausted, return to
Step 3, zoom out and choose another high-value issue within
this industry.

The approach taken in this segment is to make large, gross changes
early and continue to refine them as the team progresses across the
Entrepreneurial Arch. The approach is designed to guide you through
these changes as quickly as possible and to make decisions based on
real data, and not your "gut feel." The speed will help to avoid the
kind of attachment to an idea that comes from simply spending a lot
of time focused on it. Once you have worked a year on an idea, for
example, no one is going to be able to convince you it is a bad idea.
Data-based decision making will help you avoid your own biases and
blind spots.

CHAPTER 3   BUSINESS DESIGN

At the end of the opportunity identification segment of the Entrepreneurial
Arch is the identification of a specific, high-value opportunity upon
which your organization has the capabilities to act. This segment
involves a five-step methodology that frames the business. At the
end of this segment, you will have a very specific, albeit qualitative,

description of the business. The five steps that guide you from the opportunity to a qualitative business description are outlined below.

Step 1. Owner/motive: Customer/needs discovery
Zoom in and identify underlying needs that follow from the specific issue. Use elicitation techniques to identify industry segments. Determine the owners of those underlying needs.

> Use elicitation techniques to uncover the customers' root-cause needs. It is very likely that you will discover many customer/ need pairings. Choose a pair that best aligns with your capabilities and with the specific issue (i.e. is a high-value opportunity).
>
> If none (or none left to evaluate) return to opportunity identification.

Step 2. Activity (part 1): Identify an offering that would satisfy that need
Follow logic flow backwards: From need to benefit to effect to offering attribute. Create a story board to articulate the concept. Perform more elicitations to validate hypotheses as needed. Identify offering that would have highest potential adoption rate. Create an offering position statement.

Step 3. Monetization: Identify revenue model for the offering
Is the selected revenue model consistent with customer/needs? Validate with more elicitations as necessary.

> If none discovered, return to Step 2 (determine new offering) or Step 1 (new customer/need) pair.

Step 4. Owner/activity: Develop customer adoption profiles (personas) across the adoption curve for the target segment
What is the minimal viable product that meets the early adopter's needs?

> How do you move from early adopters to later customers? Does the offering change? If so, how?

Step 5. Activity (part 2): Identify specific actions required to create offering and deliver it to the customer

Identify the activities that your organization will perform. Perform PVC (positioning for value capture) to ensure ability to capture value.

If unsatisfactory, repeat previous steps or return to opportunity identification.

Identify collaborators:

- identify their needs via elicitations
- determine value proposition for collaborators
- create collaborator position statement.

Has the "customer" definition changed? If so, return to Step 1.

How will these activities change as you move across the customer adoption curve? Will new capabilities be necessary as you progress? If so, how will you obtain them?

At the end of business design you do not yet have a complete business model; that model will be complete after the business assessment segment. This segment defines the core of the business model, which we call the "business construct."

CHAPTER 4   BUSINESS ASSESSMENT

This segment both completes the business model and assesses the conditions, if any, under which this business can be viable. In performing this assessment, the factors that drive the financial success of the new venture – the critical success factors (CSF) – are identified. In short, this business segment determines whether or not this venture is worth your time and any investor's money. The previous segments viewed your potential new firm from your perspective (alignment with capabilities), the customer's perspective (create value), and the industry's perspective (high-value problem with potential for you to capture value). This segment takes the financier's perspective of your firm.

This segment of the Arch has two purposes. First, it completes the business model for the proposed new venture. This completes the four perspectives of any new venture (customer, entrepreneur, industry, financier), by focusing on the financier's view of your new firm. Second, it performs a feasibility assessment allowing you, if desired, to

write a feasibility study on the proposed new firm. The four steps of
this segment are outlined below.

Step 1. Margin assessment

*Step 2. Determining investment potential (source of capital);
        investment potential framework*

Market sizing. Estimate market adoption rate.

    Earnings projections:

- market value of earnings
- estimate firm exit value.

    Investment amount required and timing.

    Business exit timing.

*Step 3. Financial evaluations (increasingly rigorous financial
        assessments) and externality assessment*

*Step 4. Sensitivity analysis to determine CSFs (are the conditions that
        allow the firm to be financially feasible realistic?)*

For some people, the longer they examine an idea the more holes
they can pick in it. For entrepreneurs it is the opposite: The more time
passes, the more entrepreneurs increase their affinity for their initial
concept. To avoid becoming intransient, one must move through the
first three segments of the Arch quickly. The best way to achieve that
is to go through each segment at a fairly superficial level, then repeat
each segment as the concept morphs. Think of this as spiraling toward
a new business concept rather than going directly at it.

CHAPTER 5   OPERATIONALIZE THE BUSINESS

At the end of the assessment segment is a specifically designed, financially feasible business. You have the "what," now you need the "how."
This segment of the Arch describes how you plan to execute this business
and how you plan to mitigate the risks identified in the previous segment. The business plan has four basic sections: An introduction/sum-
mary, a recapitulation of core elements of the feasibility assessment
(industry, market, and offering), a strategy/operations section and
finally a financial/risk section. These sections are outlined below.

Section 1. Summary/introduction
Executive summary.
   Company description.
Section 2. Industry, market, and offering (i.e. the feasibility overview)
Market; industry and competition; offering.
Section 3. Strategy and operations
Marketing and sales.
   Operations.
   Strategic relationships.
   Ownership and management.
   Action plan.

While your plan is first and foremost a document that describes how you will execute your business, it is also used to "sell" your company to investors and potential employees. You should be able to introduce your plan at various levels, consistent with the zoom-in, zoom-out philosophy. Three pitch levels are described at the end of this chapter. They are:

- *Core concept opener*: One or two sentences that describe the essence of your firm. This ends with an invitation to discuss the business in more detail.
- *Elevator pitch*: One- to three-minute monologue that provides a brief overview of aspects of your firm: The issue the firm is addressing, your solution, the size of the opportunity, etc. Ends in a "happy to tell you more" offer.
- *Investor pitch:* Fifteen- to thirty-minute presentation with visual aids that details the opportunity, the company, and the team. Typically ending in a specific ask, a call to action.

At the end of this segment you have an approach to executing your business. Before you can actually execute that plan, you need to acquire resources. Those resources will come in the form of human and financial capital. Resourcing the business is the next segment of the Entrepreneurial Arch and the subject of the next chapter.

CHAPTER 6   RESOURCE

This segment of the Entrepreneurial Arch layers a detailed resource plan for acquiring both human and financial capital onto the operating plan of the new firm. This phase is about marshaling the resources you need to launch your business. The next segment of the Entrepreneurial Arch, managing growth, will cover the challenges involved in the continued addition of people and resources to the firm as you grow beyond the first five years. This chapter will focus on acquiring the resources you need to survive those critical first five years.

Assembling your initial team is crucial to a successful start. Clearly, you want team members that have complementary skill sets and will drive the success of the business, but you need to consider skills necessary now *and* in the future. Will your team be able to grow with your business? Hire people as you need them. When you are recruiting employees, think about aligning your team's objectives with your own. This chapter covers hiring from how to interpret resumés to candidate evaluation to compensation.

The second critical element to managing the growth of your firm is the firm's financial resourcing. The type of financing that best aligns with the business you are building was identified in the assessment chapter. Your plan outlined the strategy and tactics for funding your business. This segment is about how you will execute that strategy. Beyond the investability analysis you will need to deepen your knowledge of the firm's financing requirements, be they for loans or equity investments.

CHAPTER 7   STRATEGIES FOR MANAGING GROWTH

This segment of the Entrepreneurial Arch covers three aspects of the growth of your business: Corporate, offering, and personal. Corporate growth is examined from both external and internal vantage points.

Growth and renewal are intimately connected to the other five segments of the Entrepreneurial Arch. Growth cannot simply be considered an "add-on" to existing operations, but instead requires the firm to iterate back and through segments across the Arch. Corporate renewal is the most difficult challenge as it completes the arc of the Entrepreneurial Arch, causing the company to re-evaluate its capabilities and start again at opportunity identification. The outline below illustrates the elements of each of the segments of the Arch that impact on growth. The outline also includes the aspects of growth covered in Chapter 7 and illustrates how they reconnect to the other Arch segments.

Step 1. Opportunity identification
Opening (for you; alignment with capabilities).
> Industry selection
> Value system construction: identifying high-value problem.

Step 2. Business design
Elicitation – discovering needs.
> Persona development.
> Adoption profiles across a homogeneous segment (crossing the chasm).
> Developing an offering:
> - connect offering attributes with value proposition
> - minimum viable product.
> Position statement for the segment.

Step 3. Business assessment
Market segmentation: Connection between segments.
> Market quantification.
> Market adoption analysis.
> Pricing: Revenue and sales and profit objectives for each segment.

Step 4. Operationalization
Corporate vision.
> Marketing strategy.
> Marketing mix: 3 of the 4Ps (Product covered in business design);
>   for each segment:
> - Price:
>   - how will the price change over time?
>   - how to get from zero to the long-term profit objectives described in assessment? Is there a pricing path (e.g. systematic reduction of early-adopter discounts)?

- Place (channel)
- Promotion.

Step 5. Resource

Are the right people in place to forward the growth strategy? Is their compensation aligned with this objective? What other resources are necessary?

Step 6. Growth

Corporate:

- market adjacencies (return to business design)
- capability adjacencies (return to opportunity identification with improved capabilities)
- renewal – start from scratch with opportunity identification with broader set of capabilities.

Product growth:

- segment-to-segment (return to assessment)
- growth within a segment (return to business design).

Personal growth.

APPENDICES

The positioning for value capture (PVC) and the investment potential frameworks are referenced in many chapters of this book. To avoid repeating their detailed descriptions multiple times, they are each detailed in separate appendices. Another appendix contains detailed elicitation tactics. Chapter 6 (Resource) provides the financial view of your firm from the financier's perspective. Appendix C takes the oppo-site view, detailing the implications of various financial sources for the founders.

Let the journey begin.

NOTE

1. Hatfield, David (2012). Personal communications. He coined the terms "zoom in" and "zoom out" in the context of evaluating business from various perspectives.

2 Opportunity identification

The purpose of the first segment of the Entrepreneurial Arch is to identify an opportunity to build an organization that can make an impact. Building a business is like building a ladder to climb to a new place. Both the construction and the placement of the ladder are important. How you build it determines the effectiveness of the firm's execution. Where you place the ladder determines where your company can go. Sadly, too many young firms focus entirely on building the ladder and pay little attention to the placement of that ladder. They focus all their energy on developing a product and very little time thinking about the business.

Entrepreneurs are notorious for trying to build successful firms in very unattractive industries. There is a high correlation between the problem an entrepreneur chooses for the business to solve and the attractiveness of the industry in which the business will be launched. That correlation is -0.77 (Shane, 2008). That's a significant correlation, unfortunately in the negative direction! This means that most entrepreneurs are consistently picking unattractive industries in which to start their businesses, thereby creating businesses that are destined to fail. This correlation suggests that our instincts are not very good at choosing high-value opportunities. In fact, the number suggests that we would generally be better off following the opposite of our "gut feel!"

Over the past 25 years or so about 4.2 percent of all startups in the computer and office equipment industry made the Inc. 500 list of the fastest-growing private companies in the USA while only 0.005 percent of startups in the hotel and motel industry and 0.007 percent of startups in the eating and drinking establishments industry made that same list (Shane, 2008). That means your odds of creating a high-growth business that will eventually make the Inc. 500 list of companies is 840 times higher if you start a computer company than if you launch a new hotel. These numbers simply reinforce the fact that the industry you choose to operate within, and the opportunity you choose to apply your business to attain, are critical to your business's success. There is no other correlation that anyone has discovered that influences the potential success or failure of your business more than choosing a high-value problem in an attractive industry. This is why opportunity identification is the first segment in the Entrepreneurial Arch.

The importance of choosing the right opportunity is further reinforced for entrepreneurs by the way venture capitalists choose how to invest in companies. First VCs choose the industry, then they choose the team, i.e. capabilities, then last – some say a long way behind – they choose based on the initial product concepts. Putting it another way, VCs invest first in the tide, then the crew, and finally the ship. A rising tide lifts all boats; you do not need the "best" boat in order to be lifted. A good crew will have the means and capacity to figure out how to navigate uncharted waters and find a way through. The ship is the final basis upon which VCs make their investment, but it is nothing without a capable crew to operate it and make adjustments along the journey.

All this suggests that, while identifying an opportunity may seem trite, your intuition for doing so is extremely poor. In fact, statistics would suggest your instincts are simply wrong! Clearly, in new business development we need to move from a "lottery" mentality toward a methodology that will lead to more consistent and predictable economic growth. To improve the probability of the success of new ventures we will step back and take a different approach to discovering viable opportunities. This chapter will outline one such approach. To be clear, this is not a linear, step-by-step progress to a high-value opportunity, but rather an iterative process of discovery.

Opportunity identification is the fog of new business development. Most are uncomfortable in the fog and seek the fastest way out of it. Indeed, most are much more comfortable with activity than with using their imagination. They simply want to "get moving." While a sense of urgency is important and a consistent trait of entrepreneurs, the ability to be comfortable with ambiguity is one capacity distinguishing successful serial entrepreneurs and successful corporate executives (Gatewood, 2003). I have personally seen too many businesses fail because all of the entrepreneur's time was focused on developing a product and none was spent determining the need for the business or evaluating the ecosystem in which it would operate. This is business development, not product development. While the detailed work must certainly be done for the business to be successful, it is not enough. The longer you can comfortably navigate in the fog, the better your odds of arriving at a viable outcome.

In this chapter we will eventually zoom in to the specific issue level of the four necessary elements for any business. Through the methodology described in this chapter, a high-value problem from which you can capture value will be uncovered. Most entrepreneurs start with a detailed product concept or market need. To avoid myopia and to ensure that you have identified a high-value problem, the first step is to zoom out and broaden your field of vision before zooming in. No matter where your starting point, you should zoom out at least to the general problem level and often the macro-driver level as shown in Figure 2.1.

Once zoomed out, a methodology for zooming in will be described. Note that this is a partial zoom in to the specific issue level, as indicated in Figure 2.2. (A further zoom in, to the narrowest focus, will be done during the business design segment of the Entrepreneurial

	Motive	Owner	Activity	Monetization
Zoom Out	Macro-driver	Society	Opening	Potential to create value
	General problem	Industry	Capabilities	Create value
	Specific issue	Industry segment	Approach	High value / Capture value
Zoom In	Need/desire	Customer	Offering/actions	Revenue model Margin assessment Investability analysis

FIGURE 2.1 Zooming out of the four business components to begin opportunity identification

	Motive	Owner	Activity	Monetization
Zoom Out	Macro-driver	Society	Opening	Potential to create value
↑	General problem	Industry	Capabilities	Create value
↓	Specific issue	Industry segment	Approach	High value / Capture value
Zoom In	Need/desire	Customer	Offering/actions	Revenue model
				Margin assessment
				Investability analysis

FIGURE 2.2 Opportunity identification level of the four business components

Arch.) Depending on how far you zoomed out, you could potentially be moving between three levels during opportunity identification.

At the end of the opportunity identification segment of the Entrepreneurial Arch, you will have focused on a new business, to a significant extent. You may have started with a product concept or a concept for an unmet market need. Regardless, you will end this segment of the Arch with a business concept. At the end of this segment, the questions that you will be able to answer regarding the four business components are listed below. This is a very iterative segment of the Arch. Gross changes in your business concept will and should be made in this segment. These changes could take you into several different industries. The business concept will be significantly refined in the business design segment of the Arch, once you have identified a high-value opportunity in which your new firm can potentially create and capture value. Both this segment and the business design segment to follow will be fraught with dead ends and blind alleys, so iterations within and between these two segments will be necessary. A compete business concept must address all four aspects of a new business and answer these questions:

- *Motive:* What is the specific issue?
- *Owner:* In what segment of what industry is this an issue?
- *Activity:* What is your approach to addressing this issue?
  Which of the five ways to create value in an existing system are you exploiting?
- *Monetization:* How do you know this is a high-value problem?
  Given the above approach to the issue, are you in a position to capture any of the value potentially created?

One of the hallmarks of this overall approach to new business discovery is the identification and mitigation of risks as you move forward. De-risking, therefore, is not a specific segment of the Entrepreneurial Arch, but rather is integrated throughout. You are not searching simply for a business you could launch, but for a business that maximizes the impact of your efforts. As a result, you want not only to discover opportunities that align with your capabilities, but also to select high-value opportunities. High value does not necessarily mean a high-volume opportunity, but rather an important one. The size of the opportunity will be addressed in the business assessment segment of the Entrepreneurial Arch. At this point, we want to determine whether the value-creation opportunity upon which we have the capabilities to act is of high value.

The facilitator's axiom "go slow to go fast" certainly applies here. The investment up-front in identifying a high-value opportunity will pay dividends over the long run. I personally knew two startups, both in the medical device space, that took starkly different approaches to building their respective companies. Both firms started with differentiated technology. The first firm skipped the entire business discovery portion of the Entrepreneurial Arch. This firm wrote a business plan, raised venture capital investments, and immediately went to work developing a specific product. The founders of the second firm spent nine months (part-time, while holding other positions) carefully discovering a high-value opportunity. Once that was discovered, this second firm conceptualized a product based on their differentiated technology, created a business plan and raised venture capital financing. Both firms eventually ended up being acquired for a similar amount of money. The first firm, however, took twice as long to develop (nearly nine years) and consequently required significantly more capital. The consequence of that was a significant lowering of the returns for both the founders and the investors. Time spent up-front pays dividends in the end.

OPPORTUNITY IDENTIFICATION METHODOLOGY OVERVIEW

There are many potential methods to identify new business opportunities. The iterative methodology for business discovery presented in this book takes both an industry and market view. Both views are seen through the lens of your capabilities. The market view determines whether or not you can create value while the industry view aids in assessing your ability to capture any of that created value. In a competitive environment, it is not enough to know the strengths of your organization. You need to understand how those strengths measure up against the competition you will be facing.

The opportunity identification segment of the overall methodology of business discovery is described in four steps. These steps include both zooming in and zooming out in addition to divergent and convergent thinking. The methodology requires both data-driven analysis and creativity. As previously mentioned, it iterates through multiple levels of the four aspects of a business. Once a clear business concept is reached at the end of this segment, further convergent zooming in will continue into the business design segment of the Entrepreneurial Arch. The key to success is to broaden before narrowing. Once you have zoomed out and gained a clear and broad vision then, and only then, should you start focusing on the details. Scope out your trip before packing your bag.

To help you avoid getting lost in the particulars, the entire methodology will be first outlined before being described in detail. This iterative, four-step approach provides you with both a high-level map of the overall method for this segment and specific instructions how to accomplish the tasks required. This is an iterative methodology, not a formulaic recipe for success. There are many decision forks and recycle loops within this method. In addition, some findings will lead you to conclude that there is no business you can conceive that both addresses a high-value problem and allows you to capture a significant share of that value. This should not be surprising; exploration does not guarantee a successful discovery. The methodology described, however, will ensure a thorough search. Before drilling for oil, it is prudent to spend some time scouting for a promising location.

Step 1. Zoom out
Zoom out to the macro-driver level (or at least the general problem
level) by using the "what–who–what–who" technique in the
opportunity space (the area defined by the motive and owner
dimensions).

Step 2. Zoom in and identify industry or industries
From the macro-driver level, use brainstorm techniques to
identify general problems that are stimulating this macro-driver,
and to identify the industries that are struggling with each general
problem.

> Use convergent techniques to narrow the industry list:
> - is there an opening?
> - does this industry align with your capabilities?
>
> If no to either, eliminate this industry.
>
> Choose an industry:
> - initially choose the one that best aligns with your capabilities
> - if all industries have been eliminated, return to Step 1.

*Step 3. Zoom in to identify a high-value opportunity within this
       industry*
Create a value system for the industry or, if repositioning from Step 4,
expand a subsection of the value system created in that step.

> Assess to determine high-value issue(s) and industry-segment level
>   owner(s). Choose a high-value issue that has an opening and
>   aligns with your capabilities.
>
> If the high-value issues are exhausted, return to Step 2 to choose
>   another industry.

Step 4. Business concept convergence
Can you devise an approach that would resolve the high-value issue
identified in Step 3? If no, return to that step and choose another
high-value issue.

> Assess value-capture potential by performing positioning for value
>   capture (PVC) framework assessment. Can you capture value
>   with this approach? If yes, define complete business concept and
>   move to business design.

If not, then alter approach. Reposition firm and return to Step 3 to assess whether a new approach targets a high-value issue by zooming in on a segment of the previously crafted value system. Once all alternative approaches have been exhausted, return to Step 3, zoom out and choose another high-value issue within this industry.

OPPORTUNITY IDENTIFICATION METHODOLOGY DETAILS

The methodology begins by zooming out from your initial idea to discover a wide assortment of potential opportunities. These potential opportunities will eventually be narrowed and reshaped by zooming in and applying convergent thinking, i.e. through a sequential analysis. High-value opportunities can be discovered starting at the world, industry, or personal levels. Where you start is immaterial as we will be using the zoom-in and zoom-out techniques to ensure we cast the net wide enough to allow you to capture a high-value opportunity upon which you can act.

Step 1 Zoom out

The opportunity space connects the "what" in "what problem are you solving?" (motive) with the "who" in "who is struggling with this problem?" (owner). The multiple levels of both the owner and their motives are shown in the Motive and Owner columns of Figure 2.1. Regardless of where your initial idea started, you can use the "what–who–what–who" technique to zoom out and discover the macro-driver underlying the opportunity. As you zoom out, the "who" represents increasingly generalized owners of the issue (customer, industry segment, industry, society), while the "what" represents increasingly generalized issues (customer need, specific issue, general problem, ultimately the macro-driver).

Let's say, for example, that you know that solar energy producers would like more efficient solar cells. If you brainstorm at that zoomed-in level, you may be able to identify a number ways to solve that particular problem. However, you would miss an abundance of other

What/who	Macro-driver/society	Energy independence for the USA
What	General problem	Increase domestic supply of utility-scale and priced energy
Who	Industry	Power generation and distribution
What	Specific issue	Utility-scale electricity from renewables too expensive
Who	Industry segment	Power generation
What	Need/desire	More efficient solar cells
Who	Customer	Solar electrical energy producers

FIGURE 2.3 Who–what–who–what zoom-out technique

opportunities. By alternatively asking "who, more generally, is the owner of that issue" and "what is their motivation to resolve that issue" you can systematically zoom out to the macro-driver/society level as shown in Figure 2.3.

Step 2   Zoom in: Industry identification

Once zoomed all the way out to the macro-driver/society level, it is relatively easy to generate more opportunities. One brainstorming technique that is useful here is to combine divergent thinking with zooming in. This technique will greatly expand the "what" (motive) and "who" (owner) at each level as you zoom in. There are many general problems, for example, that could be associated with our macro-driver of energy independence. These general problems range from energy production to conservation. Each general problem could be addressed by one or more industries. This "zoom-out and diverge while zooming-in" technique expands and challenges your thinking far beyond your initial ideas about solar cell inefficiencies. The key is to fall in love with a high-level problem and not a specific solution. Regardless of where you start, you need to zoom out before zooming in to a specific customer need.

The objective of this divergent zooming-in process is to generate a number of general problem–industry pairs. A specific general problem may be addressed by more than one industry, while another may not. There are several industries, for example, that struggle with the general problem of how to measure small (nano-sized) particles in real time. Folks that measure small things in real time range from pharmaceutical researchers to air quality monitors. As a result, this example would produce a number of industry pairings for the single general problem of how to measure small particles in real time. Many of these initial starting places will lead to dead ends, causing you to cycle back to examine another opportunity. This is an iterative and non-linear process. Beginning the process with a number of ideas will prevent you from grasping any single concept too firmly too early. This is the fog; get comfortable with the ambiguity.

Once you have identified a list of general problem–industry pairs you need to narrow the list down to those where you could build an impactful business. That requires there be a business opening, in general, and an opening for you specifically.

Business opening

The winnowing of the brainstormed opportunities (those general problem–industry pairs) begins by identifying those that have the potential for a new business opening. All businesses are a function of time. This means that there needs to be something that is causing an opening for the new business now. Is a business-environmental discontinuity creating an opening for the opportunity you have identified? Or is new legislation, new awareness, potential for a new solution?

Unmet consumer wants, needs, or desires are not enough to create new business opportunities. From the beginning of time there have been unmet needs. Not every unmet need is the foundation for an exciting new business. While unmet needs are necessary to launch a successful new business or a new product, they are not sufficient in themselves to represent a business opportunity. It is simply not possible to shift from the status quo without some sort of disruption or innovation. Opportunities are time-dependent. Their timing is driven by two meta-drivers – innovation and disruption. The drivers of innovation take two forms. On the supply side, the driver is new capabilities, or new knowledge as Peter Drucker described it (Drucker, 1985). New knowledge begets new technologies and new methods for solving problems. Consumption-side innovation opportunities are driven by

changes in attitudes, laws, and regulations, such as the recent JOBS bill
in the United States that made crowdfunding legal (Pagliery, 2012).

Peter Drucker defined seven sources of innovation that create
new business openings (Drucker, 1985).

1. *Unexpected occurrences*
   The terrorist attacks in the United States that occurred on
   September 11, 2001 have forever changed airport security around
   the world.
2. *Incongruities*
   Traditional healthcare focuses on mitigating or eliminating
   disease, not promoting health. Recognition of this incongruity has
   created the opening that wellness clinics are increasingly
   leveraging.
3. *Process needs*
   There are continual opportunities to make more efficient and
   more effective processes ranging from manufacturing to bank loan
   approval. The 2008 housing meltdown created an opening for more
   robust mortgage loan-approval processes. Additionally, as Henry
   Ford did with the automobile, there are opportunities to develop a
   process for creating something that previously could only be
   produced by a few select craftsmen.
4. *Industry and market changes*
   Industry and market changes range from consolidation of the
   sellers, as occurred with the formation of so-called big-box stores, to
   the aggregation of geographically dispersed markets via online
   retailers.
5. *Demographic changes*
   As the baby boomer generation in the USA ages, its members
   continue to have a significant impact on healthcare and other
   industries as they represent a significant market that desires to
   appear more youthful and active long after retiring.
6. *Changes in perception*
   Changes in perception drive opportunities as they shift what is
   considered valuable. Intel's "Intel Inside" advertising campaign

shifted the public perception of what constitutes a personal computer from the "box" to the CPU (Moon, 2002). This campaign made the CPU more valuable in the minds of the personal computer user allowing Intel to continuously capture value from improving the performance of their chips. Additionally, the green movement is being driven by the perception shift that global per capita resource consumption cannot continue without negatively affecting the Earth and its human inhabitants.

7. *New knowledge*

Drucker's seventh source of innovation expands know-how, and drives the creation of new technologies and methods, both of which allow for new and better solutions.

Drucker stated that creating successful commercial innovations from these sources increased in difficulty as you progress down the list. Hence he felt that new knowledge was the most difficult innovation source to leverage. As part of an organization's capability set, knowledge lies at the widest-focus level of the convergence towards a new business. It therefore covers the broadest number of general problem–industry pairs. This proliferates the number of potential needs and adds an equally large number of potential customers to be addressed. As a result, multiple zooming in and out of the business opportunity space will be needed to discover the optimal initial new business for the new knowledge. In other words, to find a new business differentiated by new knowledge requires that more time be spent in the fog of business discovery than for any other sources of innovation, generally making new knowledge the most challenging discovery for organizations.

Capabilities alignment

Like business opening, capability alignment is an opportunity screening mechanism used at both the general problem and specific issue levels of Figure 2.2 (Steps 2 and 3). While the previous screen determined whether a business opening exists, this screen determines whether there is an opening for you. From this field of vision, this second screen

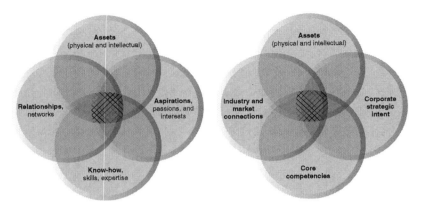

FIGURE 2.4 Team and corporation capability maps

assesses whether your team or organization has the capabilities to act upon this general problem. This is the step in which you determine whether *you* can create value.

Capabilities are defined very specifically in this book. Successful ventures have all four of these elements: Assets, know-how, relationships, and aspirations/passions/interests, and these are in alignment with their offerings. Established organizations are no different; they must also leverage their capability set. Put into corporate vs. individual terms, these capabilities are assets, core competencies, industry/market connections, and corporate strategic intent. While the descriptions change slightly, the implications remain the same. Individual/team and organizational capability maps are shown in Figure 2.4. The vertical bubbles in each of the maps represent "hard" capabilities, while the horizontal bubbles represent "soft" ones. The nexus of the four capability types describes the team's or organization's core capabilities. It is at this nexus that organizations perform optimally.

To get started, choose the general problem–industry pair having the opening that appears to align optimally with your capabilities. This alignment with capabilities will be rigorously assessed in subsequent steps. At this point, the appearance of alignment is adequate.

Step 3   Zoom in: Identify a specific, high-value issue

Not every problem is equally valued by the marketplace. How can you determine whether the opportunity you are attempting to address is highly valued? You can ask the owner of the particular issue directly and they will certainly say "yes." Assuredly, it is valuable to them, but is it valuable to the organization for which they work? No business is an island. It takes an industry to solve a problem. As a result, we need to understand what is considered valuable at the industry level before zooming in to the customer level.

Once an industry is selected, you need to understand how it functions today. The term "industry" is being used in the most general way, as a description for an ecosystem of merchants working together. In order to determine a high-value opportunity, you will need to understand how and why value is currently distributed across the industry. You will eventually need to zoom in further to identify the specific issues with which the industry is struggling, but before doing so you need a better understanding at this industry level. Analyzing the industry is therefore the next step. That analysis will inform you as to which activities and issues the industry values highly and which it does not. That under-standing is crucial if you are to identify a high-value opportunity within the industry that has an opening that aligns with your capabilities.

Value system synthesis

The high-level industry analysis begins with the development of an integrated value system for the industry. A value system, sometimes called a value chain, is a map of the activities that occur within that industry and the connections between the entities that perform those activities. Industry-wide activities transform raw materials into prod-ucts (or services) that are delivered to end users. This system is not the set of activities internal to a single company that Michael Porter suggested in 1985 (Porter, 1985). His description was drafted at a time when companies like Ford Motor Company were completely inte-grated from rubber plantations in South America all the way to dealerships. It is much more common today for these disparate activities to reside in separate companies. As a result the value system, what Porter called the Value Network, is the high-level interconnected map of an industry that we seek to create.

The first step is to determine the boundaries of the industry you are assessing. Defining the value system must begin with a definition of the industry itself. What activities are included within the industry and what are excluded from it? What is its scale and scope: Power generation on the utility scale or on that of a wristwatch? Some research will be required to determine these bounds. Industry and association trade journals are a good source for this high-level information.

Once the boundaries of the industry are defined, the next step is to define high-level blocks of activity that represent the actions that take place within the industry in order to transform raw materials into products and deliver those products to end users. The map you are creating is of the current industry. The activities, therefore, represent the current industry, not what the industry might look like after you launch your new venture. It is best to start at a high-level. Zoom out and get a "satellite view" of the industry. Later, when a specific issue is identified in the industry, you will need to create a more detailed "street view" of the section of the value system that contains that issue. At the beginning, start at a high level that includes eight to twelve activity blocks. The activity blocks represent transformations of material, money, and/ or information. Use verbs to describe these high-level activity blocks.

The connections between the blocks of activity in a value system represent transfers between activity blocks. There are three types of transfer: Material, information, and money. A value system is therefore much more than a material supply chain; there are three flows, not just one. Most industries are dominated by two of these three flows. In the banking industry, for example, money and information flows dominate. There is virtually no significant material flow in this industry. Manufacturing, on the other hand, is dominated by material and information flows. When creating your initial value system it is best to start with a single flow; map out blocks of activity that are related to a single flow and determine how these activity blocks connect. Then layer on the activities and connections for the other flows. In the banking industry, for example, first lay out a flow diagram that follows the money. Create blocks of activity that describe and connect the flow and manipulation of money across the industry. Once this diagram is complete, layer on the information-specific activities. For a manufacturing example, it is easiest to start by creating a material flow diagram across the industry. Once that diagram of activities has been created, the information flow can then be added. The creation of this block diagram for the value system will require research. Start with industry and association trade journals to help you get the big picture and zoom in from there. With that understanding, you then may want to talk to people in the industry. At this level, you are doing secondary and primary research, not customer discovery. Your objective is to discover how the current system works.

The activity-block map provides a high-level view of the operations that take place within an industry. Additionally, it illustrates how those activities are connected. It is not yet a complete value system, however, as you do not yet know how value is distributed across the industry; how the industry values the wide range of activities that occur within it. You need to understand how and why value is distributed across an industry if you hope to alter that distribution through the introduction of your new firm.

Recall that the goal is to separate the magnitude of the problem from the value of the problem. To obtain that value-level measure, we want a transactional view of the value system and not a view of overall profitability. Ideally, we would like to understand the value added by each activity-block in the value chain. Since the value-addition is essentially the sales price of the product or service that leaves the block less the cost of producing and selling it, what we really seek is the EBITDA (earnings before interest, taxes, depreciation or amortization) margins or operational margins for each activity-block in the value system. The best way to estimate this is to find a company, or set of companies, that can represent each activity-block in the system, so finding such a

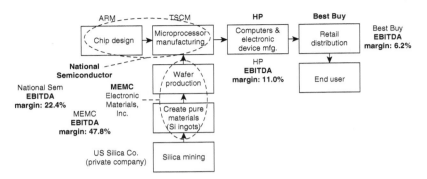

FIGURE 2.5 Complete high-level value system for the integrated circuits industry, March 2011

proxy company (or companies) for each activity-block is the next step. Determining the EBITDA margins of those representative companies will then give you a relative, transaction-level value distribution across the value system.

An example of a high-level value system for the integrated circuits industry, Figure 2.5 shows how specific companies' EBITDA margins have been added to represent each block. Since all financial information changes over time, it is important to date-stamp value systems. That date should indicate the time at which the financial information was reported.

You now have a complete, albeit high-level, value system that gives you an initial indication of how value is distributed across this industry. Even though it is not ideal, in that single companies represent multiple segments of the system and one segment is represented by a privately held company, it is still elucidating. It is, for example, clear to see that in this industry value is not distributed evenly. The margin of MEMC at 47.8 percent is vastly different from the margin of Best Buy, which is 6.2 percent. This does not mean, as previously mentioned, that Best Buy is not a very profitable or "big" company. This simply means that on a transaction-by-transaction basis Best Buy is not capturing as much value as MEMC. Best Buy's corporate profitability is driven by the volume of its transactions.

Understanding industry value distribution

Now that you know how value is distributed, the next step in your industry understanding is to understand why value is distributed the way it is. It is only after knowing "why" that you can determine how to create a business that could shift that value distribution in your new venture's favor. Put another way, your objective is to create a new venture that disrupts the status quo. You need to understand why the status quo is the way it is before you can determine how to shift it. What innovation or disruption will allow you to create value at the industry level?

The value system shows a snapshot of the industry. The current value-distribution equilibrium that the system illustrates is determined by "forces" that are currently affecting the industry. Think of the industry as a large-scale tug-of-war. Each segment of the value system is pulling on its rope (or pulling on multiple ropes) in an attempt to pull more value into its particular segment and thus into firms. In the human version of tug-of-war, adding a big, burly player to your side, or several strong players, can shift the contest in your favor. An industry is similar; shift the forces that drive the value distribution and you will shift the value distribution in the industry.

What are these industry-level forces? In 1979 Michael Porter discussed the five forces that govern an industry's dynamics (Porter, 1979). The general approach is to apply Porter's five forces to each of the activity-block segments of the value system. Understanding the forces behind the equilibrium will provide insights into how to shift those forces and, as a result, shift the value distribution. Make no mistake, this is not the typical, uninspired death march through the list of Porter's forces ... this force is high, this force is low, this one is medium ... rather, it is using Porter's forces to explain an existing value distribution and, as a result, to produce valuable insights that can be leveraged to create a shift in that existing equilibrium.

You have now identified high-value industry issues, know what segment of the industry is dealing with these issues, and have chosen a segment that has a business opening that is aligned with your capabilities. Earlier, at the general problem level, you checked this alignment; we now know more about the specifics of the issue. You now need to repeat that evaluation at the specific issue and specific industry segment level before moving forward. If your capabilities do not align, you have three options:

1. In the industry you are currently evaluating is there an alternative segment that has a reasonably high-value opportunity with issues that align with your capabilities? If so, iterate to that segment.
2. If option 1 is not viable, is another industry dealing with the particular general problem with which your capabilities align? If so, begin an analysis of that alternate industry.
3. If there was no alternate industry (i.e. option 2 is not viable), then you need to zoom all the way out, choose a different general problem, and begin again.

This is the multi-level, iterative nature of opportunity identification.

Step 4   Business concept convergence

Understanding how and why value is distributed across an industry will lead you to a specific, high-value issue, in a specific industry segment. At this point, you still do not know the problems underlying this issue. That you will determine in business design. Before proceeding to that segment of the Arch, there are two more components on this level that need addressing: The approach and the capture-value element of the monetization component (see Figure 2.6). The approach is the tactic you will take to realize that opportunity. It is your strategy

	Motive	Owner	Activity	Monetization
Zoom Out ↑	Macro-driver	Society	Opening	Potential to create value
	General problem	Industry	Capabilities	Create value
	Specific issue	Industry segment	Approach	High value / Capture value
Zoom In ↓	Need/desire	Customer	Offering/actions	Revenue model Margin assessment Investability analysis

FIGURE 2.6 Zooming in from the general problem to the specific issue

for creating value. While creating value is critically important, it is only half the battle. You also need to capture a portion of that created value. As a result, you must also assess your approach's ability to capture a portion of that created value. In other words you, must determine whether you can win the struggle with the other firms in the industry to seize that created value.

Value creation approach
Now that you have determined that your capabilities align with a specific high-value issue within a specific segment of the industry you have been assessing, it is time to think more specifically about your approach to realizing that opportunity. At this level you have not focused closely enough to be able to articulate the business's precise offering, nor should you try. The level illustrated in Figure 2.6 is about developing the concept for a solution, an approach to addressing the issue. Knowing where the high-value problems are in an industry, and understanding why they are currently highly valued, certainly moves you toward that objective, but does not get you quite there. Beyond this understanding of why things are why they are, you need the wisdom of knowing how to change this current industry-level status quo. The question you now need answered is "how can you create value in the ecosystem?" What innovation, what disruption, will allow you to shift the current value distribution in the existing industry ecosystem in the direction of your new venture? If that disruption does not currently exist, is it worth your time and energy to create it? (This should be the question all R&D directors regularly ask themselves.)

You want to understand how to create value at the industry level, before zooming in on a specific customer and creating a specific offering. You will eventually need to understand how value is created both at the customer level and the industry level. Before prematurely zooming in, however, stay focused on the industry-level understanding.

There are only five generic strategies for creating value in an existing value system (Porter, 1980). They are:

1. *New product entry*

   Offer, essentially, a "me too" product (similar to what is currently offered by the industry) but with some inherent advantage. That advantage could be increased convenience, such as when Netflix first introduced DVD delivery to customers by mail. It is the same product that Blockbuster offered, a rented DVD, but the customer did not ever have to leave the house to obtain it. The DVDs could be ordered online, delivered through the mail, and returned through the mail. The process offered a convenience to the customer over driving to a Blockbuster store to obtain and return the DVD. Another advantage a "me too" product might have is some inherent cost advantage: Lower capital requirements, lower raw material costs, and/or some economy of scale. Many "fast followers" use economies of scale as their advantaged differentiation. As a result, the often touted "first mover advantage" gets completely eliminated when a fast follower comes along using economy of scale as their weapon to capture value with a similar product. This tactic is so common that being the first mover is often more of a disadvantage than an advantage.

2. *Substitute product*

   Create a product that performs the same function as the currently available product but in a different way. Like the new product, this offering is often better, cheaper, faster, or more convenient than the incumbent product. However, a substitute is quite different from the incumbent product; it simply performs the same function. An MP3 player performs the same function as a CD player – they play music. The MP3 player is a substitute product because it is very different from a CD player, but has many inherent advantages (smaller, more convenient, etc.). Substitute products can also be better than the incumbent product at addressing an emerging or previously underserved market. Cell phones are a much more convenient way for a mobile society to stay connected than land lines and pay phones, for example.

3. *Aggregation/consolidation of a specific segment of the value system*

Consolidating the number of players in one of the activity blocks reduces competition and can create economies of scale. Retailing is the easiest way to see this in action. Walmart, Best Buy, and other so-called big-box stores simply created an economy of scale that allows them to reduce their costs thus eliminating many smaller competitors in their space. In another approach to the same result, hundreds of small "Mom-and-Pop" pharmacies became CVS stores through acquisition. Beyond economies of scale, segment consolidation increases the buyer power and seller power of those entities.

4. *Collapsing segments across the value chain*

Forward or backward integration of companies across activity blocks of the value system can create efficiencies. When Dell Computer launched, it manufactured personal computers and sold them directly to computer users. HP and other brand-name PC manufacturers created personal computers which, at that time, they sold through retail outlets or resellers. Dell collapsed these two segments of the value system (manufacturing and selling) into one segment, creating more value for itself and sharing a portion of that created value with its customers in the form of lower prices.

5. *Create a new segment to increases efficiencies between the existing segments*

This step creates a new segment of the value system that increases the efficiency and productivity of the entire system. eBay made it easier for buyers and sellers of miscellaneous goods to connect. Before eBay, small sellers typically found buyers through the classified ads in their local newspapers or by having a yard sale. After eBay, the geographic reach of miscellaneous-goods sellers dramatically increased – eventually becoming international. Beyond expanding their reach, eBay drastically reduces the cost to sellers of customer acquisition as well as creating value for buyers by providing the breadth and convenience of their shopping experience. eBay creates value for both buyers and sellers, although it captures value only from the sellers.

Let's examine a specific example to understand how disruptions and innovations over time can cause industry-level value shifts (Evans and Wurster, 1997). You rarely see sets of encyclopedias anymore. These multi-volume sets of books were fairly common in libraries and individual homes in the 1980s. Encyclopedia sets could cost the end user $1,500 to $2,200. Due to the fact that they are printed material, these encyclopedias get outdated and require updating. Generally, encyclopedias were not carried in stores but rather sold door-to-door. The advent of the DVD, as well as the proliferation of personal computers in homes, caused a disruption that eventually impacted the encyclopedia market. To replace that heavy set of books, Microsoft introduced Encarta™ in 1993 (Wikipedia, retrieved 2013). Encarta™ was essentially a set of encyclopedias on a DVD. The cost of Encarta™ to the end user was around $50; significantly less than a set of encyclopedias. More recently, Wikipedia™ is becoming the default "encyclopedia-like" reference; free to anyone with access to the internet. A host of disruptions created this opening for Wikipedia including the drastic reduction in the cost of creating a website, storing data electronically, and the proliferation of high-speed internet access. Examining the value system for encyclopedias will illustrate how value shifted over time through the change from encyclopedias to Encarta™ to Wikipedia™.

A simple value system for the original encyclopedia is shown in Figure 2.7. (Note that this is not a complete value system, as the

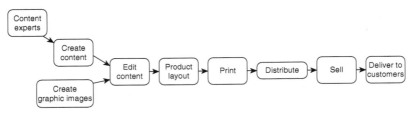

FIGURE 2.7 Original encyclopedia value system

segments have not been assigned EBITDA margins. Nonetheless, it will suffice to illustrate the point.) This high-level value system extends from the content creators, the writers and photographers, through manufacturing, sales, and ultimately to the end user. In addition to the previously mentioned high sales costs resulting from the high customer acquisition costs inherent in a door-to-door sale process, encyclopedias were typically filled with color photographs, making them expensive to print. Their mass also made them expensive to distribute.

When Encarta™ was introduced it was essentially a "me too" product. Despite having some multimedia features, it was still essentially an encyclopedia, simply delivered via a different medium. This new product, however, had two significant advantages over the incumbent. First, Encarta™ was more convenient in many respects than the hard-bound encyclopedias. The DVD was certainly much easier to store and move than a large volume of encyclopedias. It was also easier for the user to search than the original encyclopedias. In addition, it had inherent cost advantages over the hardcopy encyclopedias. Figure 2.8 illustrates the extent to which those cost reductions extended across the value system. The significant cost reductions in creating a DVD version of an encyclopedia drove significant price reductions to the end user. Note that there is no inherent price advantage for "me too" products that do not have underlying cost advantages.

Now let us examine the industry-level shift created by the introduction of Wikipedia™. Wikipedia™ is a substitute product. It

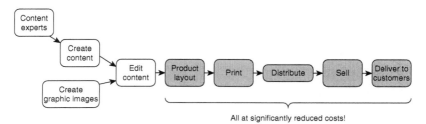

FIGURE 2.8 Encyclopedia value system changes resulting from the introduction of Encarta™

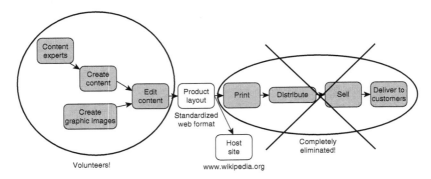

FIGURE 2.9 Impact of Wikipedia™ on the original encyclopedia value system

is not an encyclopedia, but performs the same function as a set of encyclopedias. Being web-based, it is a more convenient and useful form of information, particularly for the generation raised with high-speed internet access. It also has lower production costs. The costs are driven down primarily in two ways. One, the content experts, writers, editors, and photographers of Wikipedia are all volunteers. Second, Wikipedia also creates value by collapsing segments of the value system, as illustrated in Figure 2.9. Printing, distribution, and sales are entirely eliminated. The only cost that has been added to the original value system was the creation and hosting of the Wikipedia™ website itself. This cost was more than offset by the other cost reductions. Wikipedia™ chooses to be a non-profit, but this assessment makes it clear that it had the potential to create value as a for-profit company.

Value capture potential
The next issue to address in the convergence toward a complete business concept is to determine whether your organization can capture a significant portion of the value it creates. Thus far, you have identified a high-value opportunity. In addition, you have determined how to create value for that opportunity. The question now is this: Do you have any chance of capturing a portion of the created

value for your organization, given the industry conditions you will be facing?

The value system provides information regarding the distribution of value in the industry. Zooming in on a specific issue/industry segment and analyzing that portion of the value system will provide insight as to how value could be created by a proposed new firm. But it is not enough. You need to understand whether that new firm can capture any of the value it creates. Successful businesses capture a healthy share of the value their firms create. Clearly you must create value in the marketplace, but though necessary that is an insufficient criterion. What new entrepreneurs often fail to realize is that their business can fail while providing goods for an exceptionally attractive market if the business is not able to capture any of the value created. Once value has been created, there will be a scramble within the industry to capture it. Can your firm win that battle against your industry challengers? Predicting the ability to capture value requires an industry, not a market assessment.

Your organization's ability to capture value is dictated by the relative robustness of your capabilities. In judging the outcome of any competitive sporting event, it is not enough to evaluate the talent of your team; rather, that talent must be evaluated in comparison with that of your opponent. When your business launches, it will become part of the industry, the merchantry, that you have been analyzing. Your firm will leverage that ecosystem. You will need capabilities outside your firm to create and deliver your solution to your customer. Your capabilities, relative to those in the ecosystem that you need to leverage, will determine your organization's share of that created value. David Teece, in his seminal paper (Teece, 1986), discussed the ability of firms to capture value from their intellectual property. The positioning for value capture (PVC) framework, illustrated in Figure 2.10, broadens that work beyond intellectual assets to include the firm's entire set of capabilities as defined in Figure 2.4.

Your organization's ability to capture value is dictated by the combination of how difficult your capabilities are to replicate and how

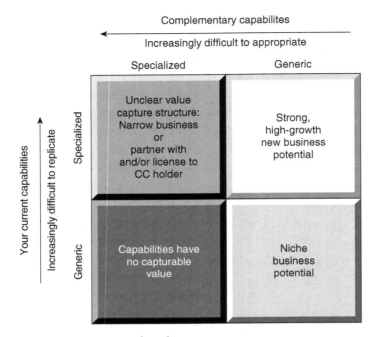

FIGURE 2.10 Positioning for value capture

easy it is to obtain the complementary capabilities you need. In the two-by-two PVC framework, the vertical axis describes your capabilities. Specifically, it defines how easily those capabilities are to imitate or reproduce (i.e. appropriate). Specialized capabilities are difficult to reproduce or appropriate. It is not that they are impossible to reproduce, it is simply that it would take considerable time, effort, and/or money to do so. Generic capabilities, on the other hand, are more common and can be easily acquired or appropriated. Appendix A provides more details on the PVC framework.

The ambition of most new businesses is to be in the high-growth-potential quadrant. If your initial analysis puts you in one of the other quadrants you will need to determine whether you can reposition your firm by taking another approach to addressing the identified high-value issue. A startup should focus on an approach that optimally leverages its capabilities and exploits the ecosystem for the rest. It is an iterative process to arrive at that result. Firms often iterate several times between the value system and the PVC analysis to find an optimal pathway forward. If none is discovered, it will be necessary to return to the previous step in the methodology.

Repositioning from the niche business quadrant
Many firms that begin in the niche business quadrant have grander ambitions. The issue is how do you strategically grow your business to move from the lower right-hand quadrant to the upper right-hand quadrant of Figure 2.10? To move to the upper right-hand quadrant you need to develop some specialized capabilities. While this development usually occurs over time, you must have a vision for your company's future in mind in order to accomplish this shift.

The easiest way to think about this is through a specific example. Consider McDonald's hamburgers in the late 1940s. During that post-war period in the United States there were many hamburger shops in small towns across the country. McDonald's started out as just another, local, "me too" hamburger restaurant. It did not have any particular differentiated or specialized capabilities. So how did it grow and become the global chain that we know today, serving 68 million customers daily in 119 countries around the globe (Wikipedia, retrieved 2013)? McDonald's did this by identifying and focusing on a user need and developing several specialized capabilities. Certainly, today it has one of the most recognized brands in the world. While brand is a specialized asset and building a brand is important, it is usually done along with the development of other capabilities. McDonald's leveraged the disruption of increasing consumer mobility. In the period after World War II in the United States automobiles became more accessible and affordable. People were taking advantage of this new asset to explore their surroundings. The "Sunday joy ride" was becoming commonplace. This disruption created an opening in the fast-food business. While you may know the quality of food in hamburger shops in your own town, you may not have any knowledge of the hamburger shops in surrounding towns. What McDonald's discovered was that people wanted consistent quality food. They did not want to be surprised. When they pulled into a hamburger place, they wanted to know what they were getting. Note that the need was consistency and good quality, not high quality. What McDonald's developed was a process for making hamburgers and french fries that could be easily replicated from restaurant to restaurant. That process produced consistent-quality food. This process is a specialized capability. The second capability that McDonald's developed was in their locations. They became experts at locating their outlets in areas of growth and new road development. The result was that, when you drove into a new town, their outlet was one of the first restaurants you saw. These two specialized capabilities moved the company from the niche business quadrant to the high-potential-growth business quadrant.

Repositioning from the specialized–specialized quadrant

Most concepts for new firms start in this quadrant – see Figure 2.10. This is often because the initial firm concept is beyond the reach of the limited capabilities of the new firm. Additionally, new technology-based firms, particularly those with intellectual assets, typically find themselves in the upper left-hand quadrant of the PVC framework. Typically, these technology-based firms also need specialized, complementary capabilities, which could include background technology beyond the firm's control, but necessary to ensure their right to employ their intellectual property (IP). Alternatively, the proposed product or service may only be sold bundled with other related offerings to which the startup does not have access. There are a number of reasons why you need specialized, complementary capabilities (CC). The fundamental issue is how to capture the most value from your capabilities.

New firms finding themselves in this quadrant have three options: To license their specialized assets to the CC holder, to partner with the CC holder, or to reposition the firm. Established firms seeking to expand into a new line of business have a fourth option: To acquire the CC holder. Of the three options for new firms, licensing is likely the option that captures the lowest value. All three options require a redefinition of the customer and potentially of collaborators, which means rediscovering their needs. If licensing, for example, you need to understand why the licensee would license the technology and how developed the technology must be before they are likely to license it. If partnering, you may need to shore up your capabilities in order to obtain a better partnership deal.

Repositioning a firm in this quadrant typically involves narrowing its scope. That repositioning may move the firm directly to the high-growth-potential quadrant, or initially to the niche business quadrant – see Figure 2.10. If repositioning moves the firm to the niche business quadrant, then the comments apply that I previously made relative to repositioning from that quadrant. A new firm with tire technology that allows automobiles to have superior handling may initially fancy itself as a sports car manufacturer. This firm would find itself in the upper-left-hand quadrant as it would not have nor be able to easily appropriate the design or manufacturing capabilities (among others) necessary to become an automobile manufacturer. What often occurs next is that teams finding themselves in this position throw up their hands and say they will simply license their technology to the automobile companies that hold the specialized CCs. But hold on, there are other options. What if this firm narrowed its scope from an automobile manufacturer to a tire manufacturer? Could it obtain the CCs to make that transition? If not, it could further narrow the scope of its business to be a tire design firm. Perhaps a specialized design firm at first, putting it in the niche quadrant, but one that could potentially grow to a more expansive firm if it could develop other specialized capabilities over time (such as industry contacts, contracts, and a reputation for excellent designs).

Product development companies
Another reason you may land in the specialized–specialized quadrant is that your firm is a product development company. You may be developing a product that you either do not have the capability to finish or

cannot deliver to the market. In other words, you may not have a direct means of monetizing the product you are creating. Pharmaceutical discovery and development is the classic example of a product development company. Your firm likely has very significant and difficult-to-replicate skills and know-how in developing new pharmaceuticals. It may also have a patent on a new drug formulation. What your firm does not have is the means to get the drug all the way through the approval process of the United States Food and Drug Administration (US FDA), nor the ability to manufacture or distribute the drug. You therefore have no means by which to monetize the drug you are developing. Product development companies are eventually sold to the CC holder. In pharmaceutical development, this sale typically takes place after completion of the Phase II (efficacy studies) under the US FDA's approval process. This is because the cost of the remaining studies is prohibitively expensive for a startup, but the drug has been sufficiently de-risked to justify the acquisition cost for the larger organization. In fact, it is estimated to cost over \$1 billion to bring a new drug to market in the USA; well beyond the reach of most biotech startups (Keating, 2002). Developing a product and selling it to the CC holder can be lucrative. It is not, however, business development. You typically have few or no monetization options should the CC holder choose not to purchase your product. YouTube and Instagram, purchased by Google and Facebook respectively, are high-profile examples of non-pharmaceutical product development companies. These firms had little or no possibility of directly monetizing their products owing to their lack of complementary capabilities. This lack of capacity to monetize makes such firms very risky endeavors. The ones that are acquired, however, as the YouTube and Instagram acquisitions certainly illustrate, do make their founders' firms very wealthy – both were acquired for over a billion dollars (Arrington, 2006; Constine and Cutler, 2012). The press loves these kinds of deal, but when developing a product development company you must be aware you are buying a lottery ticket. Most of those tickets end up in the trash.

Iterating between steps 3 and 4

The process that converges on a complete business concept involves a natural iteration between the value system you have created and the PVC assessment. You will alternate back and forth between the two frameworks several times in order to identify a high-value issue that has an opening that aligns with your capabilities for which you can create and capture value. This creates a logical loop between step 4 (business concept convergence) and step 3 (high-value-opportunity identification). Each subsequent iteration will likely require you to refine your value system, as described next.

Refining your value system

Narrowing the scope of the firm typically requires you to zoom in and expand the appropriate section of the value system in order to get a clearer view of the system. This expansion takes your initial "satellite view" of a whole industry closer to a "street-level" view of a specific section of the value system. Figure 2.11 shows an expansion of a section of a high-level value system for the mobile education industry. In order to fully understand how you can create and capture value in a sub-segment of an industry, you will need to repeat the techniques used in the creation of the original value system every time you zoom in and expand a section of it. Those techniques for building a value

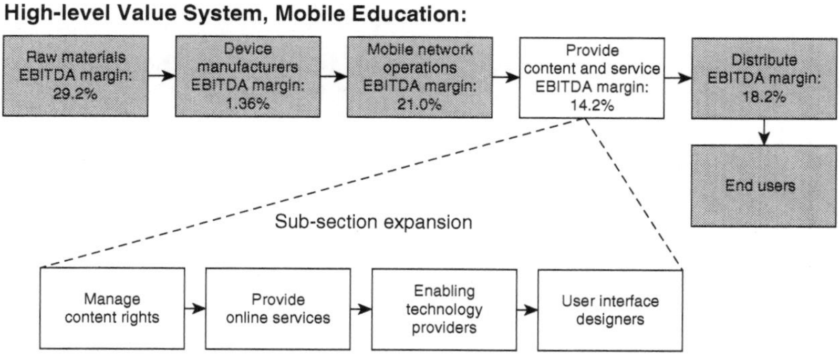

High-level Value System, Mobile Education:

FIGURE 2.11 Expanding a section of the high-level value system, May 2012

system include the identification of proxy companies with EBITDA margins for each new segment and the performance of Porter's Five Forces analysis to understand why the value is distributed the way it is in this sub-segment.

COMMON MISTAKES

There are two mistakes that are often made when attempting to discover a new business opportunity. The first common mistake is that entrepreneurs think too soon about a specific customer or a specific product as opposed to an industry. All the analysis remains at the customer level and never raises to the industry view. Without an industry analysis, there is no way to determine whether the entrepreneur is solving a high-value industry problem (despite the fact that it may be important to the customer). Without this perspective, the entrepreneur could be attempting to solve a penny-problem, not a million-dollar-problem. Instead, the entrepreneurs making this mistake get locked in on a specific customer and simply develop different products for that customer. What typically ensues is that product development activities dominate before understanding whether or not this is even a high-value problem worth solving in the first place. No industry analysis also means that the entrepreneur does not understand how he or she is creating value in the industry, specifically which combination of the five ways to create value within an existing value system is being employed. Without this understanding, it is difficult to align the business's activities with any coherent strategy. To avoid this trap, first zoom out from the customer to (at least) the general problem level of the opportunity space. Once there, the entrepreneur will have a broader field of focus from which (s)he can create a firm that will create and capture value.

The second common mistake that entrepreneurs often make at this stage is to get "stuck" in a specific industry. This segment is an iterative discovery process that takes place primarily between two levels – general problem and specific issue – of the four business aspects (Figures 2.1, 2.2). Once zoomed in to the specific issue level, if viable high-value opportunity is not identified, then the next step is to zoom back out to the general problem level and start again. Identification of the general problem will point to an industry or industries struggling with that problem. The next step is to perform an analysis of the industry. If the industry analysis shows that there is no high-value opportunity, or that there is currently no disruption that can create a shift in the current value distribution in that industry, or that your capabilities do not align well with the industry's specific issue, then the process iterates back to the general problem level and subsequently to a different industry. If there is no other industry struggling with that particular general problem, then you must iterate to another general problem. This, in turn, leads you to another industry and the industry analysis then begins again. Getting stuck in an industry seems particularly problematic for entrepreneurs that start with a specific customer concept. The initial customer seems to bias them toward the specific industry that is currently serving that initial customer. One method for getting unstuck, as previously discussed, involves zooming all the way out to the macro-driver/society level of the opportunity space, then applying divergent thinking techniques as you zoom back in to the general problem level to identify a diverse set of general problems and industries that are struggling with these problems (Figure 2.2).

SUMMARY

At the end of the opportunity identification segment of the Entrepreneurial Arch you will have a concept for a product that your organization is capable of producing, given its capabilities, that addresses a specific issue, owned by a specific segment of the value system, and one from which you can capture a portion of the value created. All these elements, taken together, as shown in Figure 2.2 and repeated below, produce a complete business concept. This is more than the product development most entrepreneurs engage in at this stage. The "more" is that we also examine your firm's ability to capture value by creating the product concept, not simply determine whether the product will create value for the user. This combination of value creation and capture is arrived at through the integration of a market needs analysis and an industry analysis; all viewed through the lens of your capabilities.

An iterative, four-step method was outlined to identify each of the business elements at this intermediate level (see Figure 2.1). The first step is to zoom out. Regardless of the point from which your initial idea starts, you can use the "what–who–what–who" technique to zoom out of the opportunity space and discover the macro-driver creating the opportunity (see Figure 2.3). As you zoom out, the "who" represents increasingly generalized owners of the issue (customer, industry segment, industry, society), while the "what" represents increasingly generalized issues (customer need, specific issue, general problem, ultimately the macro-driver). The next step involves zooming in. The first part of the zooming process uses divergent thinking to broaden the definition of the potential problems. This combination of zooming out, followed by zooming in with divergent thinking, greatly helps the entrepreneur to avoid getting fixated on the original idea. The second half of this step narrows the diverse list and associates it with specific industries that have potential business openings that align with the organization's capabilities. In the third step you further narrow to a specific, high-value issue within the industry. This industry analysis, produced via a combination of primary and secondary research, helps to eliminate the bias towards the original idea. The fourth step converges to a final business concept that addresses the questions below, by assessing the proposed new firm's ability to capture value from the creation of a solution that could address the specific issue. This final step requires both creativity and analysis; ensuring both halves of your brain are fully engaged!

- *Motive:* What is the specific issue?
- *Owner:* In what segment of what industry is this an issue?
- *Activity:* What is your approach to addressing this issue?
    Which of the five ways to create value in an existing system are
        you exploiting?

- *Monetization:* How do you know this is a high-value problem? Given the above approach to the issue, are you in a position to capture any of the value potentially created?

The approach taken in this segment is to make large, gross changes early and continue to refine them as the team progresses across the Entrepreneurial Arch. The approach is designed to guide you through these changes as quickly as possible and to make decisions based on real data, rather than your "gut feel." The speed will help to avoid the attachment to an idea that comes from simply spending a lot of time focused on it. Once you have worked a year on an idea, for example, no one is going to be able to convince you it is a bad idea. The data-based decision making will help you avoid your own biases and blind spots.

3   Business design

Now that a high-value business opportunity has been identified by working through the opportunity identification segment of the Entrepreneurial Arch, it is time to enter the design phase. The business design segment of the Entrepreneurial Arch, Figure 3.1 below, is the segment in which your business will be framed (designed). The axiom for product development is "design–build–test." This approach creates a natural feedback loop in which designs are built, tested, and then redesigned based on testing results. Products that are complex and expensive to build are generally tested, via computer simulations, before construction begins. The designs are updated after the testing portion. This is not to say that, after the product is eventually built, there are not re-adjustments to the design; there are. The approach does succeed in accelerating learning and translates to faster product development.

The purpose of the Entrepreneurial Arch is to accelerate learning and thereby accelerate the development of viable new firms or new lines of business within large firms. To do this, companies should follow a mantra slightly modified from that of product development: Design–test–build. The goal is to "get to plan B" before ever launching a flawed "Plan A." That certainly does not mean that there will not be adjustments to the plan once the company is launched; of course there will be. As German military strategist Helmuth von Moltke (1800–1891) is paraphrased as saying, "No battle plan survives contact with the enemy." It is not a question, therefore, of whether your business will change as you progress across the Arch – it will – the only question relates to the degree of that change. The goal is to make substantial changes during the design stage and smaller refinements once you have launched.

As product developers know, designs must be precise. It is not enough to say that you have a "microprocessor chip," you need to be

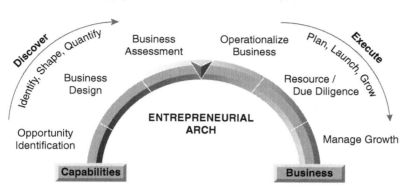

FIGURE 3.1 The Entrepreneurial Arch

specific and precise. However, to fully describe the design of the micro-processor chip, you do *not* need to also describe the manufacturing process that will produce it. Those questions of execution are not part of the design, although they are a critical part of the evaluation of the product. Similarly, at this stage we need not focus on how this business will be executed. We will address those issues as part of a later segment of the Arch, primarily in the operationalization segment.

The design itself must be complete. A product design, for example, must fully describe the product. You do not have a complete design if you only describe a portion of the product. A design for an automatically reclining chair is not complete if it meticulously describes the shape of the chair, the chair's fabric, the materials and configuration of its frame, only to say that it will have "some mechanism allowing the chair to recline." Similarly, it is not enough to define a business by only defining the product or the customer or both. You need to understand all four foundational aspects of a business: Motive, owner, activity, and monetization.

In this chapter we will define all the elements of a complete business design that together produce the business construct. Consistent with the overall hypothesis-directed discovery process, that construct is a hypothesis that will need to be tested in the business assessment

phase of the Entrepreneurial Arch. The hypothesis will be built upon
what was learned as part of each previous segment of the Arch and
refined in the current segment. So, by the end of the opportunity identification segment, you had zoomed in far enough to identify a specific,
high-value issue that is currently being addressed in a specific sector of
an identified industry. You had also identified an approach to solving
this issue (one of five ways to create value in an existing industry) that
aligns with your capabilities and indicates that your capabilities should
be sufficient to capture the value that you will create from this solution.
This intermediate, zoomed-in level is illustrated in Figure 3.2, below.

In the business design segment of the Entrepreneurial Arch, the
objective is to zoom in one more level as illustrated in Figure 3.3, below.

Note that at the end of business design you still will not have a
complete business model. The purpose of the business design segment is
to generate a conceptual framework for your business. This framework
will not be quantified until the next segment of the Entrepreneurial
Arch, the business assessment segment. While the revenue model will
be identified at the business design stage, where components of the
business model need quantification – assessment of the offering's margin and analysis of the firm's investability – that will not be done until
the business assessment phase. The business design segment is

	Motive	Owner	Activity	Monetization
Zoom Out	Macro-driver	Society	Opening	Potential to create value
↑	General problem	Industry	Capabilities	Create value
↓	Specific issue	Industry segment	Approach	High value / Capture value
Zoom In	Need/desire	Customer	Offering/actions	Revenue model Margin assessment Investability analysis

FIGURE 3.2 Zooming in on the four business components at the conclusion of opportunity identification

	Motive	Owner	Activity	Monetization
Zoom Out	Macro-driver	Society	Opening	Potential to create value
↑	General problem	Industry	Capabilities	Create value
↓	Specific issue	Industry segment	Approach	High value / Capture value
Zoom In	Need/desire	Customer	Offering/actions	Revenue model Margin assessment Investability analysis

FIGURE 3.3 Business design level of the four business components

conceptual and qualitative. The business assessment segment that follows is quantitative. Attempting to do both qualitative and quantitative analyses simultaneously often leads to two incomplete descriptions of the business. Define the business first, and then quantify it. If there is no rational business frame, then there is no reason to move forward with detailed quantification. This intermediate point, slightly short of a complete business model, is the "business construct." A complete business construct must address all four aspects of the business and answer these questions:

1. *Activity:*

   Offering: What precisely is your product/service?

   Actions: What precisely does the company do?

   How does this leverage your capabilities?

   What activities do you leverage from the existing ecosystem?

2. *Owner:*

   Who are your customers? Describe your target persona (need-based market segment).

   Who are your collaborators?

3. *Motive:*

   Why do your customers/collaborators buy your offering/collaborate with you?

   What value do you create/problem do you solve for your customer and collaborator?

   How does your offering compare to existing solutions?

4. *Monetization:*

   How does your company make money – revenue model – (i.e. what is your value capture mechanism)?

On your way to developing a complete business construct, you will be defining your customers and collaborators and the value your business creates for them through your offering. Forcing yourself to write clear and concise customer and collaborator position statements will test the clarity and precision of your understanding of each. Frameworks and examples for each of those position statements are shown below:

Customer position statement

Clearly articulated customer positioning statement

For ... (target segment/persona)
The ... (product/service)
Satisfies ... (most important user need)
By delivering ... (key benefit or feature)
Through/via/created by our ... (underlying capability)

Example

For small or home-based business owners.
Symantec Endpoint Protection, Small Business Edition *prevents*
cybercriminals from accessing and destroying your vital business
information, *by* protecting your computers and servers *through*
seamless, user-transparent updating of your machines with the most
current antivirus, antimalware technology updates.

Collaborator position statement

Clearly articulated collaborator positioning statement

For ... (collaborator)
Our ... (product/service)
Effect ... (what does it do for them?)
Benefit/value ... (what is the benefit or value to them?)
By ... (means of achieving benefit/value)

Example

Ultrasound manufacturer.
Our image-enhancing software *provides* a differentiated scanner in a
crowded marketplace *that* will allow them to increase market share *by*
helping hospitals reduce patient length-of-stay through improved
diagnoses.

BUSINESS DESIGN METHODOLOGY OVERVIEW

Business design is an iterative methodology within a larger iterative system, described as the Entrepreneurial Arch. Business design is built upon opportunity identification, which, in turn, is built upon your capabilities. The overall result is a nested, iterative methodology. Deconstructing this complexity into manageable segments is the key to making it teachable and learnable.

As with the previous chapter, to avoid getting lost in particulars the entire methodology that will be detailed in this chapter is first outlined below. This outline provides you with a high-level map of the overall method for this segment. It is shown as a five-step process, but the methodology is by no means linear. Neither is it a formula for success. There are many decision forks and recycle loops within this method. In addition, some findings will lead you to conclude that there is no business you can design that can satisfactorily address the specific issue identified in the opportunity identification segment of the Arch. This should not be surprising, as not every problem can be solved by a business or, as Peter Drucker said long ago (1985), the sober realization is that most concepts do not hold up to the rigor of business. Such a conclusion will cause you to return to the opportunity identification segment of the Entrepreneurial Arch and begin your search for a new business again.

In addition, the summary shown below is but one possible direction of focus in zooming in to the next level. The goal is to zoom in on all four dimensions of the business structure: Owner, motive, activity, and monetization. In a way, you will be determining all four simultaneously. Doing this, however, can be quite intimidating and perplexing. As a result, the methodology described through the remainder of this chapter is broken down into parts or steps. There are multiple ways of achieving the desired outcome and this chapter describes one rational path toward that end. It is not the only path. You can drive the major highways or the back roads and still get to your destination.

With experience, you will find the approach that works best for you and the business you are attempting to discover.

Step 1. *Owner/Motive: Customer/needs discovery*
Zoom in and identify underlying needs that follow from the specific issue. Perform industry segment elicitations.

> Determine owners of those underlying needs. Perform customer elicitations to uncover their root-cause needs.
>
> It is likely that you will discover many customer/need pairings. Choose a pair that best aligns with your capabilities and with the specific issue (i.e. is a high-value opportunity).
>
> If none (or none left to evaluate) return to opportunity identification.

Step 2. *Activity (part 1): Identify an offering that would meet that need*
Follow the logic flow backwards, from need to benefit to effect to offering attribute. Create a story board to articulate the concept. Perform more elicitations to validate hypotheses as needed.

> Identify the offering that would have the highest potential adoption rate. Create an offering position statement.

Step 3. *Monetization: Identify revenue model for the offering*
Revenue model consistent with customer/needs? Validate with more elicitations as necessary.

> If none discovered, return to step 2 (determine new offering) or step 1 (new customer/need pair).

Step 4. *Owner/Activity: Develop customer adoption profiles (personas) across the adoption curve for target segment*
What is the minimal viable product that meets the early adopter's needs?

> How do you move from early adopters to later customers? Does the offering change? If so, how?

Step 5. *Activity (part 2): Identify the firm's specific actions to create offering and deliver it to the customer*

Identify which activities your organization will perform. Perform PVC (Positioning for Value Capture) analysis to ensure ability to capture value. If unsatisfactory, return to previous steps or to opportunity identification.

Identify collaborators. Identify their needs via elicitations. Determine value proposition for collaborators. Create collaborator position statement.

Has the definition of "customer" changed? If so, return to step 1.

How will these activities change as you move across the customer adoption curve?

Will new capabilities be necessary as you progress? If so, how will you obtain them?

BUSINESS DESIGN METHODOLOGY DETAILS

The following provides detailed descriptions for the methodology outlined above. As previously mentioned, the order is but one possible way to move forward. No matter what path you take, however, the goal is to adopt a systematic methodology that allows you to zoom in one level on all four elements of the business (motive, owner, activity, and monetization).

Step 1   Owner/motive: Customer/need

One way to begin is to zoom in on the owner and motive dimensions. In this segment of the Entrepreneurial Arch, you are in search of the root-cause need of a specific potential customer. The customer discovery you will be doing in this segment of the Arch is directed customer discovery. You already know, from the opportunity identification segment, what the specific issue is and what segment of the industry is addressing this issue. As a result, you will not be talking to random people, but drilling down from that specific starting point to find a root-cause issue and its owner. Too many entrepreneurs skip the opportunity identification segment and start at this step. As a result, they have no idea whether they are addressing a high-value problem or whether they can capture any of the value they create. As we saw in the previous chapter, ignoring the opportunity segment markedly increases the odds against you being successful.

By far the biggest challenge of this step is that people cannot typically tell you their needs. What is worse is that they are often more willing to suggest solutions than to describe their underlying circumstance. Unfortunately, those proposed solutions may or may not actually address their root-cause needs; typically such proposals only address a symptom caused by the root-issue. You must keep in mind that the people you talk to are not the innovator. You are. You need to get beneath what they are saying to understand the underlying needs. Of the five most usual primary market research methods only personal interviews and observations allow you to drive down to these root-cause issues. While surveys are great to quantify an understanding, they are a poor tool for getting at that fundamental understanding because neither do you know what questions to ask nor does your surveyee likely even know the answer. Focus groups can be misleading in that they can be driven by the loudest voice in the room. Field trials are not possible, as you do not yet have anything to trial. Observation, while very useful, can be quite time-consuming. This is why "virtual observation" – putting your interviewee in a situation and observing them virtually – should be part of your interviewing method. The elicitation techniques described in Appendix B of this book will be very useful as you proceed.

Be aware of your own biases during this discovery process. You may have a particular problem in mind that you think is the root-cause issue. You may even have a particular solution in mind. It is fine to have hypotheses. But that is all that they are. Many an entrepreneur has been misled by disregarding the data that is inconsistent with their hypotheses. Doing so is cognitive dissonance. Be aware of that trap. Write down your hypothesis and, if you discover information that is inconsistent with it, change the hypothesis. That is the scientific method. The scientific method will lead you toward a potential business; cognitive dissonance will lead you to a mirage.

Needs discovery process

Identifying your customer is a process of discovery. You will be spiraling in toward your customer by zooming in on the motive/owner. We will be using a variation of the who–what–who–what technique discussed in Chapter 2. In opportunity identification, we used this technique to zoom out; now we will be using a slightly modified version of this technique to zoom in.

The zoom-in process will look like this: What→Who→ Elicitation→What→Who→Elicitation. You will continue this process until you reach a root-cause need with an associated owner. This discovery process will likely uncover many different branches as you zoom in and, as a result, will likely end up looking something like Figure 3.4 below. Some of the branches may have common underlying issues and therefore rejoin as you zoom in (as illustrated in Figure 3.4) and some will not. It is impossible to predict in advance how many branches you will uncover or how many layers you may discover before hitting on the root-cause needs. There is no pre-determined pathway; it is a discovery process. Begin by engaging with someone at your current level of understanding. What are the underlying issues? Why do these issues arise? Who is dealing with them now? Engage with the people that are the owners of issues at this new level. Repeat the process until you uncover the root-cause issues and their owners. If you

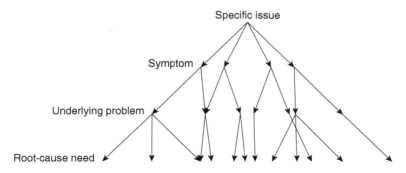

FIGURE 3.4 Needs discovery process

do this correctly, you will end up with multiple pairs of root needs and owners.

For example, you discover in your industry analysis that there is a shortage of a particular raw material. The first step is to discover the underlying causes of this shortage. Let's say you discover three issues: Production yields are low, it is expensive to build new facilities, and current plants have frequent breakdowns that cause them to go off-line. The next step is to zoom in closer to each issue to try to find a root-cause need. Let's pick just one of these three issues and see where that could lead. Why do the existing facilities have frequent breakdowns? Discussions with facility managers may uncover several symptoms, including the fact that the facility's pumps often fail unexpectedly. Why is this happening? Discussions with plant maintenance personnel may lead to several revelations; such as that there are no scheduled, regular maintenance programs for the pumps or that the pump bearings often fail, causing the pumps to seize. Pushing on the bearing issue may uncover the fact that many replacement bearings do not meet specifications. Why not? Discussions with the purchasing department may lead you to uncover the fact that counterfeit parts are slipping into the supply chain. Why? The purchaser cannot tell upon ordering or upon delivery whether the parts are genuine. The root-cause issue for the raw material shortage could be counterfeiting of parts. Like any detective, you must set aside your presumptions and biases and follow the evidence as you gather it in order to avoid the trap of cognitive dissonance. This is much easier said than done.

After you have found a root-cause issue, you still need a clear description of your customer. Through the elicitation process you have zoomed in all the way to individuals. You need to zoom out slightly to aggregate these individuals into groups. People have many needs. When it comes right down to it, however, upon which need do they base their final decision? This regrouping joins the divergent branches in Figure 3.4 back into groups sharing the same root-cause decision-making need. Each end point at the bottom of Figure 3.4 represents a need/customer pairing. You may find it helpful to personify those arch-type customers as detailed in Appendix B.

If done correctly, as you drill down to the root-cause need level illustrated in Figure 3.4, you will more than likely end up with a number of customer/need pairings. To screen these pairings, you will use the convergent-thinking methods discussed in Chapter 2.

1. *Is there a business opening?*
   Do one or more of Drucker's seven sources of innovation apply?
2. *Is there an opening for you?*
   Do the needs align with your capabilities?
3. *Is this a high-value problem?*
   It likely is, given that you started with a high-level high-value problem, but if in the process of zooming in you ended up in another industry, you will have to re-do the industry analysis to make this determination.
4. *Is this a problem where you can capture value?*
   Perform PVC analysis to determine.

You may have to zoom in closer to a section of the value system you created in the opportunity identification segment to determine the answers to questions 3 and 4. If your discovery took you to another industry, you will need to construct an all-new value system. Regardless, you need to be able to answer "yes" to all four questions before moving on to the next step. If you cannot, you must return to the opportunity identification segment of the Entrepreneurial Arch and begin again.

Even after the screening process, you may be left with more than one customer/need pairing that you could pursue. You must choose one pairing to take to the next step. If in subsequent steps you hit a dead end with that pairing, you can return to this step and select another one. If there is no pairing left to select, you will need to return to the opportunity identification segment.

A number of entrepreneurs make the mistake of stopping as soon as they find a "customer" with a "problem" and do not drive down to the root cause. Regardless of the starting point for your initial idea, you can use the "who–what–who–what" technique to zoom out and discover the macro-driver underlying the opportunity. Then use the "what–who–elicitation" technique to zoom back in and uncover root causes. A second mistake is believing that because you now know the customer and the need you now have defined the business. You have not. You have four more steps to complete before you can state with any level of confidence that you have defined the business.

Step 2   Activity (part 1): Offering identification

The activity component (see Figure 1.2) has two parts at this most narrowly focused level. Those parts are the offering, the product or service that your firm will deliver to a customer, and the activities that the firm performs in order to create and deliver this offering to the customer. It is simpler to consider these two parts separately. In this second step, you will focus on the offering and consider the actions your firm will perform in the creation of this offering in step 5.

The objective of this step is to determine an offering that meets the need of a specific customer. In the previous step, you identified the root-cause need. It is helpful to work backwards from that need to your capabilities in order to expand your thinking about possible offerings. As Figure 3.5 illustrates below, the offering does not satisfy the need directly. Working backward from the need (left to right in Figure 3.5) is the benefit to the customer, the value proposition. The offering creates an effect that generates that benefit. Attribute(s) of the offering drive

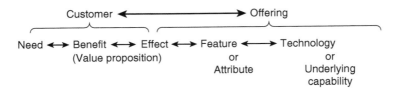

FIGURE 3.5 Customer/offering connections

this effect and those differentiated attributes will be enabled by your underlying capabilities.

When you are shopping for a new automobile you may be looking for a vehicle that obtains high miles per gallon. High MPG is a feature of the vehicle. This feature reduces the quantity of fuel consumed by the vehicle. The benefit to you as the purchaser of the vehicle is reduced cost of operating the vehicle. When comparing one gasoline-powered vehicle to another gasoline-powered vehicle, the MPG feature makes a good proxy for the benefit you desire, reduced vehicle operating cost. This is why features and benefits are often confused. One is often a good proxy for the other. However, when comparing two vehicles with different power-trains, say an electric vehicle and a high-efficiency diesel-powered engine, the MPG feature no longer is a meaningful proxy for the desired benefit. As a result, a new basis for comparison must be created. Understanding this difference is important as the objective is not to optimize the feature, but to maximize the customer's benefit (value proposition). Focusing on optimizing features creates a myopia that will cause you to miss new opportunities and chase phantom ones.

You will know when you have reached a clearly defined offering that has a clearly defined value proposition for a clearly described customer when you can write a clear and concise offering position statement like the one shown below.

Offering position statement

Clearly articulated positioning statement

For ... (target segment/persona)
The ... (product/service)
Satisfies ... (most important user need)
By delivering ... (key benefit or feature)
Through/via/created by our ... (underlying capability)

Example

For automobile manufacturers in the low-fuel consumption vehicle market, *our* gas-sipping engine *will* provide you product differentiation in a competitive marketplace *by* producing the highest miles-per-gallon of any gasoline-fueled engine, *which* is possible via our unique and patented gasoline-atomization injector system.

You will and should generate many ideas for potential offerings that apply to a given customer and need. How do you choose which to pursue first? All new businesses need to generate revenue sooner than later. You therefore want to create an offering that is within your ability to produce and will have the quickest adoption. We will discuss the potential evolution of your offering over time, as your capabilities evolve, in step 4. For now, we will focus on adoption. For the majority of new products, as noted by Everett Rogers in *Diffusion of Innovation*, adoption is driven by the perceived attributes of the innovation (Rogers, 1995). These attributes consist of the relative advantage of the offering, compatibility with previous products, complexity, scope to try them out, and observability. It is no accident that Apple Stores let you play with their products (try them out) in an open environment where others can watch (observability). The other drivers of adoption include the number of people that need to be included in the purchase decision. Is it an individual decision, or is it a group collective decision? The more people involved in the process, the slower adoption will be. Other attributes that affect adoption include the communication channels (mass media or interpersonal) necessary to spread awareness of the product, the nature of the social system (norms, standards, network connectedness, etc.) that need to be in place, and how far agents' promotion efforts will need to change. An easy check for this last item is to determine whether there is a distinct market pull (the customers know they have this problem), or push (where you first need to convince the customer they have a problem, then that you have a solution to it). Overcoming market push is often referred to as "missionary sales."

Such sales have long customer acquisition times, which is the antithesis of what a startup company is seeking. Given that, for the majority of new products, adoption is driven by the five perceived attributes of the innovation (Rogers, 1995 – see above), entrepreneurs should focus on these issues. The mistake they tend to make is thinking that advantage is related to features as opposed to need. The fact that your product is 50 percent stronger does not matter unless that strength translates into a distinct value proposition for the customer, as shown in Figure 3.5.

Another way of thinking about what Rogers referred to as "relative advantage" (Rogers, 1995) is to consider the intensity of the pain or desire of the customer. How far away are the current offerings from satisfying the real need? The more intense the pain, in other words, the greater the relative advantage over the current solution, and the faster the adoption rate. If I have a new pharmaceutical that could eliminate your headache 50 percent faster than the current products on the market, but came with some potentially nasty side effects (nausea, potential toe fungus, etc.) you would likely not take a chance on the new drug. Your problem is just not that intense. However, if my drug could extend the life expectancy of terminal cancer sufferers by 50 percent, they would likely overlook the side effects and readily adopt the product. Advantage is relative to the intensity of the customer's pain.

Once an offering concept has been determined, perform more elicitations to ensure your assumptions about the customer and their adoption of your proposed offering are correct; in other words, that you have developed a working hypothesis about the customer, their needs, the value proposition of the offering, and the rate at which your offering will be adopted. More elicitations, with more specific questions, will be helpful at this point to ensure your assumptions are correct.

Features and products

No discussion of an offering would be complete without a discussion of the difference between a product and a feature. Far too many proposed offerings are simply features of competitor's products. Features are the qualities, characteristics, and elements of the product. They describe size, shape, materials and construction, the product's functionalities, and its capabilities. A product is something you can build and sell directly or indirectly.

A feature can be a differentiating element of the product. In some cases you cannot transform this feature into a product because you do not have the complementary capabilities necessary for this transformation. As an example, let's say that in your offering discovery process, you discovered a compelling unmet need for red Saran™ wrap. Let us further say that you have the capabilities necessary to create red Saran™ wrap. However, SC Johnson holds the patents, trade name, and other know-how related to the production of Saran™. Therefore you cannot manufacture red Saran™ wrap because you do not have access to the associated assets that would be necessary to transform this feature (color red) into a product (red Saran™). Alternatively, even if you could manufacture and sell the product, the feature would be a minor element of an existing product that the original product manufacturer could easily replicate. Say you could produce a red generic plastic wrap. Once you demonstrated that there was truly a market for red plastic wrap, SC Johnson could easily create red Saran™ wrap. If you had no other differentiating attribute, you were not less expensive to produce, functioned no better, etc., your product and your company would soon disappear owing to the superior brand recognition and marketing of Saran™. Recall from the previous discussion on how to create value in an existing value system that, to create value with a "me too" product/service offering, one must have sustainable advantages over the incumbent's products.

For physical products the distinction between the feature and the product is fairly straightforward. In software, it is a little more challenging to differentiate between features and products. Many software products masquerade as products when they are really features. Mark Cuban, serial entrepreneur and owner of the Dallas Mavericks basketball team, illustrates the product vs. feature conundrum this way (Cuban, 2010):

Xmarks is a really good service that I have used since it first came out. What it does is synchronize your browser bookmarks. Add a bookmark on your laptop and boom, it will be added to your desktop browser. Great feature.

Which is the problem.

Many companies start out with what they think is a great product because it adds a valuable feature to an existing product. Or it is a standalone product that differentiates itself from a competitor by a couple unique features. Xmarks was conceived as both.

The problem for Xmarks and for any product that merely adds a few features to an incumbent product is that the incumbent product, in this case every browser on the market usually isn't deaf, dumb and blind. They see the value in the features of the competitive product and they realize they have to add the feature to their own product. And they do.

In this case, all of the browsers have added bookmark synchronization to their newest versions.

Today (September 30, 2010), Xmarks announced they were closing their doors after 4 years in business.

Before you ever release any product or service and try to build a business around it, you always have to ask yourself: "Is this a real, stand-alone product, or can the competition add my differentiated features to their own product and put me out business?"

The difference between a feature and a differentiated product attribute lies in your ability to maintain that differentiation and your ability to monetize it. Is the speed of Intel's microprocessors a feature or a differentiating attribute? That speed is grounded in Intel's design and manufacturing abilities which they protect with patents and trade secrets. As a result, this feature is sustainably differentiated (at least for a while). Intel can also monetize that speed because it creates value for their customers (saves time). Speed is therefore a differentiating attribute of their microprocessors. The monetization issue leads us to the next step in the discovery methodology used in the business design segment: determining the monetization scheme.

Step 3   Monetization: Revenue model

The third step in the business design methodology is to identify a revenue model for the offering. A revenue model is a key characteristic that separates a product from a business. A business, enterprise, or venture is an organization engaged in the generation and trading of goods, services, or both to customers (Sullivan and Sheffrin, 2003). It can be for-profit or non-profit, large or small. In each case, the business supersedes the product. Products may come and go, but the business should remain. Investors understand the importance of a business. Yes, a product is extremely important, especially to a new venture, but it is not sufficient to create a great business. As Roelof Botha, a leading VC with Sequoia, said, "founders should think of their business as a product and build it and shape it with the same passion and care that they use in the development of their product" (Tenner, 2011). A product is something you can build and sell directly or indirectly. The business is an organization, tools, and processes that enable the creation and delivery of a product or set of products to customers. A sustainable business – even a non-profit business – must perform these activities in a manner that keeps it financially sustainable over time. That financial sustainability requires a revenue model.

Revenue models

Every firm, for-profit or non-profit, needs a revenue stream in order to be a financially sustainable, ongoing concern. One of the first issues that needs to be determined is the complexity of the revenue model. There are a number of business and revenue models that could be considered. To simplify this complex landscape, we will initially consider revenue streams in terms of single- or multi-platform businesses. Single platform businesses are the most straightforward. In these businesses, the firm sells its product or service to its customer. That product or service creates value for that customer and the firm captures a portion of that value directly back from that customer in terms of some form of revenue flow. While the revenue flows can be very complicated, the money path is straightforward.

Multi-platform businesses are another matter altogether. Multi-platform businesses must create value for representatives of each platform. Google's Adwords business illustrates a classic two-platform business. In this type of model, the firm needs to create value for both parties. All non-profit businesses are examples of two-platform businesses. The non-profit typically offers a service to its clients at reduced or no charge. These firms must raise operating revenue from a second party, for whom they must also create value. The value proposition for each platform will be different, but it must exist. Google, for example, creates value for searchers of information by making it easy and simple to search World Wide Web for information. Those searchers, however, pay nothing for the service. The presence of all of these visitors searching for specific items creates value for advertisers interested in selling those items. It is the advertisers that generate the revenue that flows to Google.

In multi-platform models, it is the synergy among the platforms that creates value. In other words, the value is created in bringing the two groups together. It is because there are now hundreds of people searching for tractor parts that it is valuable for tractor-part firms to advertise with Google. In non-profits, generally the service provided is not paid for, at least not in full, by those that receive the service. The foundations, however, value the providing of that service and therefore fund the non-profit organization. By their nature multi-platform models are more difficult because you must create value for two separate parties simultaneously. Many entrepreneurs, particularly in the IT space, focus on creating value with their product for the non-paying platform. They then wave their hands, saying they will generate revenue from advertisers. That makes them an advertising company. Accordingly, they must understand where they fit within the advertising value system and how they will create value for those advertisers in order for this multi-business platform to work. Having vast numbers of users that do not pay for the service may be necessary to create value across platforms, but it is not sufficient. It is only part of the puzzle of creating a viable business.

Once the source of revenue has been identified and the value proposition for that source determined, it is time to think more specifically about how your firm will collect revenue. The simplest revenue model is the retail sales one. In this model, you sell your product or service to your customer and they pay you directly for it. For example, you walk into a store and purchase some ice cream, or go online and order a computer from Dell. In both cases, you pay directly for the product. The same applies for business-to-business sales. If you are supply components to Dell, you sell your product to Dell and it will pay you for that product. There are, however, many, many other methods by which to attain revenue. You could get paid for advertising, licensing your technology, etc. The list below, although by no means complete, lists the variety of revenue models in use in 2013:

- *product retail sales:* using a value chain, such as Hewlett-Packard PCs
- *product internet sales:* direct to customer, such as Dell PCs
- *business-to-business:* commercial purchase on terms, such as Xerox or BASF
- *advertising:* provide advertising space, such as Yahoo! or ABC
- *licensing:* revenue payable per unit, such as IBM and large universities
- *consulting:* fee for service or impact, such as McKinsey
- *services:* charges per unit, such as H&R Block
- *transaction fees:* per activity, such as eBay
- *subscription:* content over time, such as Consumer Reports
- *affiliate:* referrals and partnerships, such as Amazon
- *rent:* such as a housing landlord and
- *asset leasing (equipment):* such as server farms or hardware stores renting tools.

Alignment is the key. Your revenue methodology must be aligned with your customer's needs and desires. If you are licensing technology you must consider how your customer will create value with that technology. Will they use it to create and sell products? If so, then you will want to capture value through a royalty, as that method of payment aligns with your customer's success; they sell more product, you receive more revenue. However if your licensee is using your technology to build a business which they plan to sell, then you need to create a revenue stream that aligns with that measure of success. Since success in this case is defined by selling the firm at a high valuation, then you would want to take equity in the firm in exchange for your technology. Creating alignment is the only way to create win–win value propositions.

Step 4 Owner: Adoption profiles across the homogeneous segment

In Step 1 of the business design methodology you defined a customer. You were careful to keep your definition specific. In doing so you considered only groups that are making choices based on the same decision-making needs. You wrote a clear position statement for this customer. The result is that you defined a precise, target, market segment. In the seminal work, *Crossing the Chasm*, Geoffrey Moore explains that there are varied adoption preferences even in homogeneous market segments (Moore, 1991). One of the challenges that new product developers face is crossing the chasm that exists between early adopters and innovators, who may only make up 15 percent of the segment, and the remaining segment as shown below:

- innovators, technology enthusiasts
- early adopters, visionaries

– The chasm –

- early majority
- late majority and
- laggards.

This phenomenon can be observed with the launch of most new products today. The first adopters of smart phones are what Moore called Innovators. They are willing to work with complex and underdeveloped ideas because they want to be on the leading edge. The second group, Early Adopters, often have the highest degree of opinion leadership. These visionaries are more likely to propagate information about your product. The Early Majority are more deliberate. These pragmatists have longer decision-making processes. The Late Majority are more conservative. They are driven by economic necessity and peer pressure. The Laggards are strong skeptics and the last to adopt. They will not likely adopt until they have no other choice. Think of when your grandparents finally gave up their rotary-dial phone. It was likely when they could no longer buy an equivalent replacement or the phone company forced them to have a touch-tone phone!

You have a description of your target market. You may have even created a persona for this segment, as described in Appendix B. However, to understand how your product will be adopted within a segment you need to zoom in one level closer. You need to develop profiles for the customers adopting your offering across Moore's members of the target segment. Who will be the early adopters? The laggards? When you first thought about your offering in Step 1, you likely envisioned the early or late majority customer. While these represent the bulk of the market for your target segment, they will not be your offering's first adopters. The question your team needs to consider, therefore, is whether there exists an offering that you can produce immediately: It may not have all the characteristics necessary to attract later adopters, but be one that you can produce very soon and start generating revenue. This this would be the minimum viable product or MVP.

MVP

The development of your initial offering must extend beyond thinking about the adoption of a single product, but rather to the adoption of a series of products based on your current and future capabilities. The first product a new firm releases will not always be the ultimate product they imagined, but it will be the one they can produce the quickest that someone is willing to buy. Blank and Reis have recently referred to this as the minimal viable product (MVP), although companies have been following this course of action for decades (Blank, 2006; Ries, 2011). A new firm's initial product should put it on a path to future products. In the late 1990s Rain-X, maker of a line of consumer automotive and surface care products, introduced their original windshield "wax" that forces water to bead and roll off the windshield, often without the need for wipers. While the product worked great, it took some effort to apply. That meant that the segment willing to purchase the product would be relatively small – auto enthusiasts. Some years later the company released a combination 2-in-1 glass cleaner and window protectant. Easier to use, broader customer appeal, but much more difficult to create and manufacture. By the time Rain-X launched the 2-in-1 glass cleaner, the innovators and early adopters had already sung the praises of the product. Now that the product is in a form the majority could easily use, the new product was quickly adopted.

Offerings and customers can and often must change as the firm grows. Rather than thinking of a startup's offering in the singular, it may be more helpful to think of the company's initial growth path. The firm's first product, as was the case with Rain-X, was targeted toward a relatively niche market. On the PVC framework (Figure 3.6 below, and detailed in Appendix A), they were a specialty niche business. This product, however, was on the development path of future products. The company did not have the capabilities necessary to launch the 2-in-1 cleaner at the onset. It took time to develop these capabilities. During that development time, they could produce and sell a product. Not the ideal product they likely envisioned, but something that could generate revenue and create brand awareness. That brand awareness, when combine with other specialized capabilities the company developed in the creation of the 2-in-1 glass cleaner, would propel them

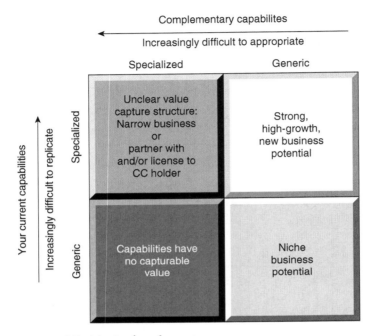

FIGURE 3.6 Positioning for value capture

into the upper right-hand quadrant of the PVC. Success, as they say, is a journey.

Step 5.   Activity (part 2): Specific actions that create the offering

The activity portion of the four business components has two parts at this most close-up focus. The first part, the offering, was originally discussed in Step 2. In the previous step, we discussed how it might be more beneficial to think of the offering as a series of items rather than a singular item. In this final step, we will discuss the actions the firm undertakes in the creation and delivery of that offering to the customer. These are the activities that take place within the fence line of your firm, so to speak, rather than the ones you leverage the ecosystem to perform. As in the Rain-X example, these activities will evolve with your firm's growing capabilities.

Firm activities

A common mistake is to believe that your business's activities are to "produce the offering." While generally true, it is not specific enough to describe the design of your business. What activities will your firm actually perform and what activities are you leveraging outside firms to perform in the creation and distribution of your offering to your customer?

Let's take the very simple widget manufacturing example illustrated in Figure 3.7. In order to create the widget and have it reach the customer, it needs to be designed, manufactured, marketed, sold, and distributed to your customers. That does not mean the firm will perform all of these activities. You could choose, for example, to perform only the activities indicated in shaded area in Figure 3.7. You could design the product, outsource the manufacturing, market and sell the product yourself, and use an external service provider to do the physical distribution of the product to the customer. You could, alternatively, do the opposite; choose only to do those activities indicated by the white arrows, for example. In this scenario, you would outsource the product design, do the manufacturing yourself, outsource the marketing and sales, and have your firm distribute a product.

What this example illustrates is that every new business has choices to make when it comes to the activities the firm will carry out itself. To make those choices the firm must understand how the

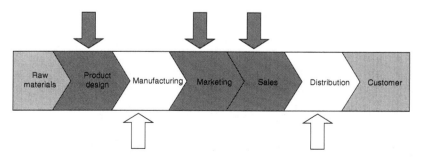

FIGURE 3.7 Simplified widget manufacturing activities

larger, existing ecosystem works now; you must know how business is currently done. That knowledge, combined with an understanding of your own capabilities, will guide you in the decision as to which activities will be performed by your business and which the collaborators in the ecosystem will perform.

The goal of any new venture should be to partake in as few activities as possible in order to maximize the firm's capturable value in the creation and delivery of its product to its customer. The activities the company does choose to perform should differentiate it, be grounded in its differentiated capabilities, and allow the firm to capture the maximum value possible. Differentiated businesses focus on leveraging the organization's differentiated capabilities. Minimize re-invention of the wheel. Minimize the number of moving parts that your firm initially has to create and manage internally. A startup should focus on those activities that best leverage its core capabilities, and exploit the ecosystem for the rest. This is a problem of optimizing value-capture, and the firm must solve it, as every collaborator must have a value proposition to guarantee their collaboration; that value proposition typically results in sharing a portion of the created value. The result is a natural iteration between the business design and the opportunity identification segments of the Arch as the business is formulated.

Finally, your firm should have a path for growth. As mentioned in the previous step, where you start may not at all be where you want to end up. What is your strategy for your initial adoption, for longer-term growth, for the development and/or acquisition of additional capabilities that will further differentiate your firm in the ecosystem in which it plays? That longer-term growth will be addressed in Chapter 7, "Strategies for managing growth."

Core vs. context

To better understand which activities you will want to perform inside your business and which you will want to leverage from the existing ecosystem, you will need to think in terms of core and context. Core activities are those that are vital to your business. They differentiate your business. Performing core activities at a higher level increases the value of the business. If you are Wal-Mart, for example, logistics are central to your low-cost advantage in the marketplace. The lower the transportation costs, the lower your costs of goods (COG). Having COG lower than your competition is critical to your market position as a low-cost seller of goods. Logistics is a core activity of Wal-Mart's business.

Activities that are labeled "context" are those that need to be carried out in order to stay in business, but doing them exceptionally well neither differentiates nor increases the value of the firm. Wal-Mart, as all firms do, has an accounts-payable department that ensures their suppliers get paid. You can imagine how long Wal-Mart would stay in business if they stopped paying suppliers for their goods: Not long. Accounts payable is therefore a necessary function of the business. However, what would Wal-Mart gain from having the world's best accounts-payable department? Nothing. Certainly, their accounts-payable department needs to be good, but being great does not add to Wal-Mart's differentiation. In fact, having the world's greatest account-payable department would likely be a detriment to their business; particularly if they had to pay a differentiated price to have the best department. Without an additional business benefit, that additional cost would increase their COG and reduce the advantage of the low-cost position they have adopted. It would simply make no strategic sense for them to have the world's greatest account-payable department.

Core and context are firm-specific. One company's context is another venture's core and vice versa. While accounting is not core to Wal-Mart, it certainly is to PricewaterhouseCoopers (PwC), an international accounting and advisory services company. PwC differentiates itself in the marketplace by its accounting services.[1] As a result, differentiated accounting capabilities yield a differentiated business. Differentiated logistics, on the other hand, add no value to PwC and as a result they outsource what little of that they do to firms specialized in that business (Federal Express, UPS, DHL, and probably others).

As organizations grow, the scale of those non-core activities often makes it more cost-effective to bring them in-house rather than continuing to outsource. Startup firms typically do not have this luxury. New ventures need to determine the company development path that requires the least resources, in terms both of people and of money. As a result, it is critical that you understand your core and your context, as well as how each fits into your long-term growth.

Collaborators
You will have identified two different kinds of collaborator. The most common one will be those firms you will directly leverage in the creation and distribution of your offering. You will be outsourcing to these firms. You will need to understand and articulate how their collaboration with you creates value for them. For the most part, this is straightforward. If their business is contract manufacturing or logistics, then performing those tasks for you increases their revenue. Other times it is not so obvious. Why, for example, will the manufacturer of a medical imager collaborate with you on the development of your advanced imaging software? It may be that they are need a differentiating element for their machine in a crowded and commoditized market. The value proposition to them, in this case, is increased market share, or a product that can demand a differentiated margin, or both.

If your value proposition is to create value for an end user several links in the value chain away from your firm, then there is a second group of collaborators you will need to think about. This group will contain all those firms that lie between your company and the ultimate end user for whom you are creating value. Let's say that my firm is developing software that will improve the data-handling characteristics of smart-phone operating systems. This improvement will require less computational power, consume less energy, and thereby extend the battery life for the phone user. That is a clear value proposition to the end user. Unfortunately, my firm does not sell directly to them. Instead, my firm plans to license software to smart-phone operating system developers, such as Google's Android. Those operating system developers are my customers. Clearly I need to articulate the value I create for my direct customer. However, I also need to articulate the value proposition for every other firm in the chain between my customer and the end user for whom I will ultimately be creating value. If everyone in that chain does not capture value from the adoption of my new software, it will not be adopted. It is not enough to generate value for the end user, value must be generated all along the chain. Unless every player in the value system between you and the ultimate purchaser captures value, the activity will not occur. These links in the chain are also collaborators, for without them there is no value creation for the end user. In short, your potential collaborators simply will not collaborate with you as there is no financial win for them.

All collaborators must have a value proposition. The value proposition for collaborators generally falls into one of three categories: increasing their sales volumes at the same margins, increasing their margins, or some combination of the first two. For example, our business could help increase their margins by either lowering their costs, or adding valuable features to their product or service that could allow them to raise their price. We can also help them increase market share by creating a differentiated product or allow them to move into markets that they were unable to penetrate before this because their current price structure is too high or their product is insufficiently differentiated. You should be able to write a very specific position statement for every collaborator in the form developed earlier in this chapter (see above).

Redefining your firm's activities may have caused you to redefine your offering, or your customer, or both. Perhaps you started originally thinking you were creating widgets, only to discover that your core strength was in their design. Now you are a design firm. That redefinition will cause you to loop back to step 1 (customer/needs) and may cause you to bounce all the way back to the opportunity identification segment of the Entrepreneurial Arch, as shown in Figure 3.1, if your PVC positioning does not appear compelling. The challenge with the first two segments of the Entrepreneurial Arch is that there are iteration steps within each segment as well as iterations back and forth between segments. This is the challenge of new business discovery. There is simply no shortcut to excellence.

COMMON MISTAKES

There are a number of common mistakes made in the business design segment of the Entrepreneurial Arch. A number of those mistakes are rooted in confusing customers with end users, as discussed in Chapter 2. This is particularly true with multi-platform businesses. Your customers pay you, your users may not. While you may need these end users to create value for your customers, it is extremely important to explicitly understand your customers' needs and the value you create for them. Too many doomed businesses have been built around serving the needs of users and giving short shrift to the needs of the customers, who will actually support the firm financially.

Another significant oversight is that collaborators are often undervalued or ignored. One of the core tenets of capitalism is that activities that are not financially rewarded are extinguished. If there is an activity that you want your collaborators to perform repeatedly, then they must be rewarded for that effort. This is particularly true in the case where there are many activity blocks in the value system between your firm and the end user. You need to understand how your end user's needs flow through the system to your customer and to you. You also must know how the benefits of your offering flow through the system to your end user. The end user needs and benefits usually change somehow as they flow through your customer. These needs and benefits can be enhanced, minimized, emphasized, de-emphasized, or deleted altogether. In addition, your customer will have additional needs and require additional benefits that your end user may not share at all. While it is important to understand how you create value for the end user, it is critical that you can articulate how you create value for your customer.

Another common mistake made by new ventures is the assumption that the new firm will do everything related to creating, developing, manufacturing, delivering, and maintaining the offering for the customer. The firm is simply defined too broadly. Just how big is your firm when it starts out? Most ventures are pretty small in people and financial terms. They must therefore focus on the activities that leverage their core competencies and maximize their ability to capture value.

The other mistake new firms often make is in the initial product offering. New businesses will often try at first to create the "ultimate" product that "laggard" customers would want to purchase. These firms instead need to determine the minimal product and the pathway from that initial offering and customer to more expansive markets. Related to this mistake, the firm's MVP tends to be a watered-down version of the ultimate product, rather than a different, narrower offering. Firms miss the half-steps that often must be taken along the product development path. One does not start by creating enterprise software, or creating enterprise software with a minimum number of features, but by creating a specific, stand-alone program that can be sold immediately, yet grows over time to become a portion of an integrated enterprise software offering.

SUMMARY

The goal of this segment of the Entrepreneurial Arch has been to define a business in precise enough terms, starting with a high-value opportunity, to be able to quantify and assess it in the next segment of the Arch, the business assessment segment. It started to feel like a business at the conclusion of the opportunity identification segment of the Arch. You identified a product concept that you know solves a high-value problem. You know this offering creates value and you understand that you can capture some of this value. You even have a pretty good idea where you fit into the value system. You know a lot, but at the end of opportunity identification you do not yet have a defined business. Before we can call your entity a specifically designed business there are several additional items you need to know. To attain that understanding, the business design segment zoomed in one level closer (see Figure 3.3).

A five-step method was outlined to identify the detailed elements of the most closely focused components of a business: Motive, owner, activity, and monetization. The tightest zoom of the monetization component focuses on three elements: Revenue model, margin assessment, and an investability analysis. The first two ensure that the organization's offering can be sold for more than it costs to produce. The third element ensures that the business has the potential to attract the investors it needs to be successful. Being qualitative, this segment does not address the quantitative elements of the monetization component of the business. At the end of this segment of the Entrepreneurial Arch, the revenue model portion of the monetization scheme, and only the revenue model, was determined. This segment of the Arch also narrowed the field of vision, from the product concept to the business's offering. As that offering became more clearly defined, the activities that lead to the creation and delivery of that offering to the customer also became equally defined. Some of the activities necessary to create the company's offering and deliver it to the customer will be performed by the firm while others are performed by collaborators in the ecosystem. Accordingly, the firm's collaborators and a value proposition for those collaborators were also articulated. The entire process culminated in a business construct that addresses all of the following:

1. *Activity:*

    Offering: What precisely is your product/service?

    Actions: What precisely does the company do?

    How does this leverage your capabilities?

    What activities do you leverage from the existing ecosystem?

2. *Owner:*

    Who are your customers? Describe your target persona (need-based market segment).

    Who are your collaborators?

3. *Motive:*

    Why do your customers/collaborators buy your offering/ collaborate with you?

What value do you create/problem do you solve for your
customer and collaborator?

How does your offering compare to existing solutions?

4. *Monetization:*

How does your company make money – revenue model –
(i.e. what is your value capture mechanism)?

NOTE

1. Statement taken from PricewaterhouseCoopers' website. Retrieved June 8,
2012 from www.pwc.com.

4 Business assessment

The business assessment segment is the final segment of the business discovery side of the Entrepreneurial Arch, as shown in Figure 4.1. This left-hand side of the Arch started with the determination of an opening for a new business. This opening, which was typically driven – from a macro-perspective – by one or more of Drucker's seven sources of innovation (Drucker, 1985; see Chapter 2), indicated an opportunity to create value. The next step was to determine whether there was potential for you to create value. This was determined by testing the alignment of the opening with your capabilities. This was followed by determining the high-value potential of the problem, in other words, whether the problem was worthy of your time and effort. That insight was acquired via industry analysis that began with the creation of an industry value system and ended using Porter's five forces analysis to explain the current EBITDA (earnings before interest, taxes, depreciation and amortization) margin distribution across the industry (Porter, 1979; see Chapter 2). An approach was then envisioned from which you could capture value. The business design segment zoomed closer one more level to qualitatively define a business through which you could create and capture value. The final step, which will be completed in the business assessment segment, is to determine whether this qualitative business description stands up to a quantitative examination. In short, is this business segment worth your time and any investor's money? The previous segments viewed your potential new firm from your perspective (alignment with capabilities), the customer's perspective (create value), and the industry's perspective (high-value problem with potential for you to capture value). This segment will view your firm from a financier's perspective.

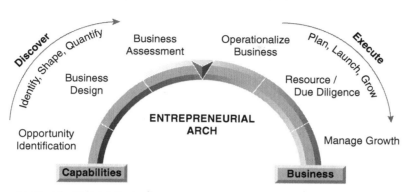

FIGURE 4.1 The Entrepreneurial Arch

This segment of the Arch has two objectives. First, it completes the business model of the proposed new venture. This adds the last of the four perspectives of any new venture (customer, entrepreneur, industry, financier), by focusing on the financier's view of your new firm. Second, it performs a feasibility assessment allowing you, if desired, to write a feasibility study on the proposed new firm. Through both objectives this segment determines a business model that is both economically viable and investable. Most importantly, a sensitivity analysis of the business model will reveal the conditions under which the new venture is viable and investable. The next segment of the Entrepreneurial Arch will focus on operationalizing the business model: First the model, then the plan.

Nearly all entrepreneurs will determine whether or not their proposed offering will be worth more than it costs to create. However, most neglect this question as it applies to their business. No one would argue with the proposition that it would be economically futile to produce a product that one could sell for $2, but would cost $10 to produce. However, many entrepreneurs fail to determine whether the investment required to build their new enterprise is justified. As a result they spend time, sometimes years, developing a business that may not be fundable. Knowing that the value of the business you are creating will be worth more than the investment required to build it is *the* question that equity investors want answered. It is therefore imperative that the entrepreneur know the answer to this question and know which business variables have the biggest impact on that answer. Knowing both will allow entrepreneurs to focus on the aspects of their business that will ensure it is worth their own time and the resources of their investors.

The paradox is, of course, that you would like to know the potential value of a business before you invest the time in determining how to operationalize it, but it seems that you need to operationalize the business to understand the timing and magnitude of the resources required to launch and grow it. Yet we know that the more time you spend holding onto an idea, the more affinity you develop for it. It is our nature as humans. This means, unfortunately, that if you spend a couple of years developing a business concept, no one is going to be able to dissuade you that it was worth your time: Not even your proposed customers! I once consulted for a company that performed three years of research to determine whether a project was worthy of research. Although it sounds absurd, there were rational reasons for this. Since it was a capital-intensive industry the project economics were primarily driven by the capital requirements. The capital was, in turn, determined by the process by which the product could be created. The process, however, could not be articulated with any degree of specificity without performing three years of research! Of course, being humans, after three years of effort on these projects it was very, very rare for them to be assessed as not worthy of further research. We love what we hold dear to us. What the company needed was a methodology for a "good enough" capital estimate that required much, much less than three years of effort to attain.

The same paradox holds for building a new company. We tend to spend excessive time operationalizing businesses in order to determine their viability. However, once we spend the time and energy operationalizing them we will not stop for, as the time passes, we fall deeper and deeper in love with the business concept. What we should be doing instead is spending a minimum amount of time finding an economically viable business model before operationalizing the business. To do that we need to determine the potential future value of the business before we have the operational details necessary to do so, or so it seems. What is needed to resolve this paradox is an estimation method that is "good enough" to support a decision to move forward. Ideally, the methodology would be market-based, yet could be performed without investing an enormous amount of time. This is the only way to "fail fast" and reposition the proposed firm as something more viable.

The aim of the business assessment segment of the Arch is to gather as much information as necessary to make a decision as to whether or not you wish to spend more time pursuing this business. The objective here is not deep due diligence. That will be performed in the resources segment of the Arch. The objective here is to determine whether the proposed business is viable and under what conditions it can be so. This is step-wise de-risking. The entire business discovery section of the Entrepreneurial Arch works together in this way. The objective is to obtain enough information to make a determination and move on. This will not be a complete set of information, but enough to decide whether it is worth spending additional time to dig deeper. As a result, entrepreneurs will likely cycle through the first three segments of the Arch many times as they spiral in toward a detailed, viable business. The first time through, the information gathered will be fairly high-level. This may be deep enough to eliminate most ideas from further consideration. Those that look promising will need further refinement by going through the processes again in a more detailed manner.

The business assessment phase will be approached in the same layered-analysis manner. The first layer of assessment can be high-level and quick. If that produces a promising result, then the next layer will take more time and require more data. Even this level of assessment, however, will take less time than it would take to fully operationalize the business. Ultimately, the objective is to find the conditions under which the proposed business is financially viable. Few businesses are obviously viable or not viable; most are viable under certain conditions. This segment of the Arch will determine those conditions. The business elements that drive those conditions are the business's critical success factors (CSFs) (Mullins, 2003).

BUSINESS ASSESSMENT METHODOLOGY OVERVIEW

The business design segment, described in the previous chapter, led to the business construct, a qualitative description of your business. That starting point for this segment of the Arch is the most closely zoomed level of the four business components shown in Figure 4.2. This chapter will outline a methodology for quantifying that business. The final elements of the monetization component of the business will be defined and quantified, as illustrated in Figure 4.3. Completing the monetization component requires moving beyond the revenue model to determine the product margins and determining whether or not the firm is capable of attracting the type of capital it may need to launch. Quantifying the business and completing the monetization component will complete the business model. That complete business model will address all four aspects of the business: Activity, owner, motive, and monetization. It will also view your business from all four perspectives: Entrepreneur, customer, industry, and financier.

Quantify

Completing the business model is only one of the two objectives of this segment of the Entrepreneurial Arch. Determining the conditions, if

	Motive	Owner	Activity	Monetization
Zoom Out	Macro-driver	Society	Opening	Potential to create value
↑	General problem	Industry	Capabilities	Create value
↕	Specific issue	Industry segment	Approach	High value/Capture value
Zoom In	Need/desire	Customer	Offering/actions	Revenue model
				Margin assessment
				Investability analysis

QUANTIFY

FIGURE 4.2 Business design level of the four business components; components of the business model added in assessment

any, under which the proposed new venture is feasible is the second objective. Feasibility is typically not a yes-or-no, black-and-white evaluation. Instead, a feasibility assessment is performed to understand the elements of the proposed new venture that most significantly affect its financial viability. This feasibility assessment is accomplished by completing a financial analysis and examining other conditions beyond the control of the new venture that could seriously impact on its success (externalities). The final step of the business assessment phase is to perform sensitivity analyses around these identified success-conditions to elucidate the key business elements that will drive the business's success. These drivers are the new venture's CSFs.

A complete feasibility assessment of your business will allow you to answer all the questions listed below. Note that in addition to the financial assessment and the externality assessment, more forward-looking questions have been added to the business description elements. These additional questions generally relate to the sustainability of your market differentiation. All entrepreneurs need to answer three elemental questions: Is this business worth your time? Is it worth your customer's attention? Is it worth your investor's money?

1. *Activity:*
   Offering: What precisely is your product/service?
   How much will it cost to produce?
   How will you maintain differentiation and/or keep others out over time?
   What stage of development has the offering reached?
Actions: What precisely does the company do?
   How does this leverage your capabilities?
   What activities do you leverage from the existing ecosystem?
2. *Owner:* Who are your customers?
   What is your target persona (need-based market segment)?
   What size is the market (number of buyers, units sold, currency value of sales)? Estimate the total addressable market, target market, and initial target segment (target persona).
   Who are your collaborators?

3. *Motive:* Why do your customers/collaborators buy your product/ collaborate with you? What value do you create/problem do you solve for your customer and collaborator? How does your offering compare to existing solutions? Quantify your customer's willingness to pay for your offering. What is your customer's current solution?

   How do you believe the industry will react to your launch?

4. *Monetization:* How does your company make money (revenue model)? In other words, what is the value capture mechanism?

   What are the offering's expected margins (margin assessment)?

   Is the company investable (what is the investment model)? What are the size and type of investment? Returns congruent with investment source?

5. *Financial assessment:*

   Revenue potential: Estimated price, EBITDA margin; estimated adoption rate.

   Business-building cost estimates: How much will it take to develop this business? Over what period of time?

   Financing the business: Based on the investment potential framework what type of financing best fits this business?

   Equity financing: Potential value at exit. Can equity investors meet return expectations? Under what conditions?

   Non-equity financing: Cash flow and break-even models. How easily will you obtain debt? How do you financially manage pre-debt? Under what conditions does this venture make financial sense?

   Success conditions: Identify three to five CSFs. Under what conditions is this venture feasible? Are those conditions realistic?

6. *Externalities:* Government/regulatory.

   Industry reaction.

In addition to the completed business model and feasibility assessment elements, you will also have the clear customer and collaborator position statements you crafted in the business design segment (see Chapter 3). Together, the position statements and the feasibility assessment questions provide a complete outline for the desired output of this segment of the Arch (see Figure 4.2 above). As with the previous chapter, to avoid getting lost in the details, the entire methodology that will lead to this output will first be outlined. The method involves a number of estimates and calculations, making it far too easy to get overwhelmed by detail. To avoid this, the objective is to proceed through steps 1 through 3 at a high level the first time around. If the viability of the business remains positive after this high-level assessment, then a deeper analysis is warranted before proceeding to step 4.

Step 1. *Margin assessment.*

Step 2. *Investment potential determination (source of capital);*
   investment potential framework:
 Estimate market size.
 Estimate market adoption rate.
 Earnings projections: market value of earnings, and estimate of
  firm's exit value.
 Investment amount required and timing.
 Business exit timing.

Step 3. *Financial evaluations (increasingly rigorous financial*
   assessments) and externality assessment.

Step 4. *Sensitivity analysis to determine CSFs:* (are the conditions
   that allow the firm to be financially feasible realistic?)

The first three steps are also all potential "stop" points in the method which, if reached, will send you back to the business design segment for repositioning. For example, if the margin assessment in step 1 shows unacceptably low (or negative) margins, there is no need to proceed. Similarly, if you calculate that the firm will not be equity-investable in step 2 and it is your desire to build a VC-backable firm, you should stop there and return to the business design segment. This further illustrates the iterative nature of the business discovery half of the Entrepreneurial Arch, depicted in Figure 4.1. It is very common to iterate among all three of the business discovery segments during this exploratory phase. Business assessment is built upon business design, which is, in turn, built upon opportunity identification. The overall result is a nested, iterative methodology. Deconstructing this complexity into manageable segments is the key to making it work.

BUSINESS ASSESSMENT METHODOLOGY DETAILS

The following provides detailed descriptions of the methodology outlined in the previous section of this chapter. The order of the steps is not crucial. The proposed order is suggested only as a means of minimizing your effort since the vast majority of business concepts will need to be repositioned before they are ready to be operationalized. The key to the success of the business discovery side is to proceed as quickly as possible. This speed will help you avoid getting locked in on a single business concept. However, like learning any new skill, your first time through this methodology will not be particularly fast. But subsequent evaluations will become increasingly brisk. The focus should be on obtaining enough information to make a decision (but no more), make that decision, and proceed as warranted. Proceeding could mean moving to the next step of this segment, returning to a previous segment of the Arch, or it could mean returning to a previous step of this segment to obtain more detailed information.

The overarching philosophy is to determine as quickly as possible the conditions, if any, within which the proposed new venture can be financially viable. The starting point is a qualitative description of the business as determined in the business design segment of the Entrepreneurial Arch. To avoid performing three years of research to determine whether the project is worthy of research, it will be essential to estimate the required elements accurately. The initial estimations will be based on comparable products and companies. As the ultimate value of both the offering and the business will be determined by the market, we will want market-driven estimations. The overall methodology uses both public-company proxies and private-company proxies. The place to start, however, is the margin assessment. If the margins are not attractive, there is no reason to proceed further.

Step 1   Margin assessment

The financial assessment for any new venture starts with an assessment of the margins of its proposed offering. Since we desire a quick estimate of the margins without either building the product or the company, we will be using public companies as proxies for estimating our new venture's EBITDA margins. EBITDA margins are simply the EBITDA values divided by the revenues. Cost of goods (COG), sales, general, and administrative costs (SG&A), ongoing research and development costs (R&D), if any, as well as the price of your offering vs. that of the proxy can then be adjusted based on the information you obtained in the elicitations performed in the business design segment. The relationships are shown in Figure 4.3.

Entrepreneurs often balk at this point, arguing that it is impossible to estimate an EBITDA margin for a completely new-to-the-world product. The fact is, it is not. In the opportunity identification section you determined an approach to creating value. There were only five. Most likely your new-to-the-world offering is a "new product" or a "substitute product." For example, if your offering is "new," then it

```
Revenue (sales, $)
 − Raw materials ($) ⎤ Cost of goods
 − Labor ($)         ⎦     (Raw material + Labor costs)
Gross profit ($)        Gross profit % = Gross profit ($) / Revenue ($)
 − SG&A                 (sales, general, & administrative; i.e. indirect costs)
 − R&D                  (ongoing R&D costs)
EBITDA                  (earnings before interest, taxes, depreciation, amortization)
 − Depreciation
 − Amortization
EBIT                    (earnings before interest, taxes)
 − Taxes
Net operating profit after tax
 − Interest payments   (or add interest earnings)
Net earnings            (or Net income)
```

FIGURE 4.3 Relationship of EBITDA to the income statement

is essentially a "me too" product relative to that which is currently offered by the industry, but with some inherent advantage. You can alter the EBITDA margins of the existing product to reflect your advantage, to estimate your new product. On the other hand, if your offering is a "substitute product," it performs the same function as an existing product, but in a better, cheaper, faster, or more convenient way. Understanding that way, and understanding how your potential customers perceived the value of that way through the elicitations you performed in the business design segment, you can adjust the EBITDA margins of the constituent product accordingly. You may have to get creative in mashing components of existing product EBITDA margins. For example, if you are creating mobile phones for the first time, you may want to combine the COGs of transistor radios with the revenues of land-line telephones, appropriately adjusted for the added convenience your interviewees stated the mobile device provided. You must, however, keep in mind, from your opportunity identification analysis, that you may not be capturing all, or even the lion's share, of the value you are creating.

Start with the public proxy companies identified in the opportunity identification segment. These comparators often make good starting points for estimates of SG&A, R&D, and gross margin. You may also want to look at companies in other segments. For example, if you are looking at replacing textbooks in classrooms with electronic tablets, you may want look at the margins of electronic devices for that portion of your EBITDA margin estimate.

Product designers and engineers often get very nervous at this approach to estimating margins for the new venture's offering. Part of this anxiety is that they think of cost-based pricing vs. value-based pricing (Nagel and Holden, 1987). Since the product has not yet been designed and therefore the cost has not yet been determined, then how can you possibly base the price (revenue) on cost? Unless they are producing commodities, which is highly unlikely, new firms will use value-based pricing, where the price is proportional to the value as perceived by the customer. Since your elicitations in business design indicated to you how your proposed offering would be valued relative to existing offerings in the minds of the customer, you can adjust the price of your product relative to those offerings. Is this the ultimate price the buyer will pay or the final price for which you will sell the offering? Probably neither, but it is a very good estimate. Like all the variables you will be estimating, if it is later determined that this value is a key driver of the economic viability of the company, it will need to be assessed further. Despite this anxiety, however, the margin estimates are typically the best of all those that you will be making in this segment. It is the magnitude of revenue numbers of which you need to be most wary.

Cost-based pricing

Product → Cost → Price → Value → Customers

Value-based pricing

Customers → Value → Price → Cost → Product

FIGURE 4.4 Cost-based vs. value-based pricing

A word of caution about choosing your comparators. Since EBITDA is calculated from elements in a company's income statement, it represents only a snapshot in time of the company. If the company is in steady-state, i.e. has consistent financials over time, then the numbers will be representative. Fast-growth companies typically must increase SG&A costs and/or R&D costs ahead of sales. This skews their EBITDA numbers, which makes them poor firms to use in comparisons. The optimal proxy is a publicly traded company with a very narrow offering focus. "Wicker Basket Company" is a better proxy for a basket company than the "Consolidated Container Company" that might make everything from baskets to oil storage tanks. Rarely do you find the perfect proxy. The guidelines suggested when you created your value system in the opportunity identification chapter also apply here. That is, find smaller public companies with narrow offerings, rather than highly integrated, Fortune 100 firms. Search for firms using key words in Google Finance, for example, not in Google. The top searches in Google will tend to be large firms and private ones;

neither of which will be the best choice for comparators. Alternatively, searching in Google Finance or Yahoo! Finance, for example, will bring up more obscure firms that, once you check their description, may be just what you need to base your EBITDA margin estimate upon.

Step 2   Investment potential determination

The financial evaluation methods used to evaluate an equity investment are different from those for a non-equity investment. In addition, some entrepreneurs are only interested in creating firms that depend on certain investment types. Determining the investment type that the firm can potentially attract is therefore an important next step. While this chapter assesses the firm from the perspective of the financier, the implications for the firm, and subsequently the entrepreneurs, vary with investment type. This later perspective is detailed in Appendix C.

The investment potential framework shown in Figure 4.5 and detailed in Appendix D takes an investor's perspective of the new venture.[1] It segments new businesses into four quadrants based on their size and return potential. Successful businesses capture a healthy share of the value their firms create. Clearly a new firm must create value in the marketplace, but that is a necessary but insufficient criterion. The PVC framework, discussed at length in Chapter 2, suggests the probability of a firm being able to capture the lion's share of the value it creates in the market. The vertical axis of the investment potential diagram below (Figure 4.6) is a measure of the relative magnitude of the value the firm can capture. A large market in which the firm can capture large EBITDA margins represents the top of this axis. Identifying a large market is not enough by itself. The vertical axis on the investment potential diagram is the size of the *capturable* value. It is not the size of the market (value creation potential), but the size of the share that you can capture that counts. It does not matter if your firm is in the large-market smart phone industry, for example, if you are a small supplier to a major player. Your firm will just not capture much of the value of the phone from that position in the value system. This is the essence of the PVC framework. If your firm ends up on the

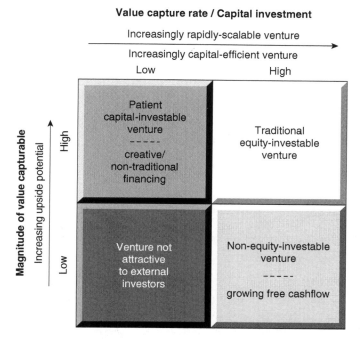

Value capture rate / Capital investment

FIGURE 4.5 Investment potential framework

left-hand side of the PVC framework, it will likely not be suitable to be in the top half of the investment potential framework diagram. The lower portion of the vertical axis of Figure 4.5 can either represent a small market in which your firm can capture a significant share of the value created, or a large market in which your firm can only capture a small fraction of the value created.

There is a natural tension that exists between the PVC and the investment potential frameworks. As we saw in the business design segment, narrowing your firm will increase your ability to capture value. Doing so will also narrow the market your firm addresses. While increasing your ability to capture value will push you up in the investment potential framework, decreasing the size of the market will drive you down. The vertical axis of the investment potential framework represents a product of those two elements, causing you to strike a delicate balance in the creation of your firm.

While the vertical axis of the investment potential framework diagram (Figure 4.5) represents the magnitude of the value the new firm could potentially capture, the horizontal axis of the framework represents the relative rate at which this value could be captured per unit of capital investment. This axis speaks to how rapidly scalable the firm is and as well as how capital-efficient it is. A firm on the far right-hand side of the horizontal axis would be quickly scalable and very capital-efficient. A software company that is producing a product for which the market demand is such that the company could grow very quickly would meet both the scalability and capital-efficiency criteria, assuming that the software could be easily distributed electronically over the internet. That is attributable to the fact that once the product is developed it takes relatively little additional capital to increase production and distribution capacities. This is very different from, say, a chemical manufacturer that, even if it could grow rapidly, would take significant capital investment for each block of new volume it would need to produce. This is because costly new production plants would need to be built for each significant quantity of new market volume the firm would need to satisfy. Restaurants are similar. A restaurant can increase its volume somewhat by increasing its table-turns, but if the company wants to continue to grow its revenue and market share, at some point it will have to construct a new restaurant, which is a significant capital expenditure. A firm's fixed assets ratio is an indication of how much revenue a firm produces per dollar of PP&E (property, plant, and equipment). That ratio, combined with the expected EBITDA margin, provides a good indication of the capital efficiency of the firm's ability to capture value.

Firms targeting large markets, that have the ability to capture a significant portion of the created value (upper half of Figure 4.5) and that also have relatively high rates at which value could be captured per unit of capital investment, find themselves in the upper right-hand quadrant of the investment potential diagram. These firms have the potential to grow quite large and are capital-efficient in their growth. This is the traditional quadrant of venture capital investments.

Venture capitalists typically target companies having growth that can be rapidly accelerated through an infusion of capital, but that do not need continued additions of significant capital to sustain that growth. High-margin software firms or electronic hardware firms where the manufacturing can be readily scaled or outsourced are two traditional targets.

As the capital-efficiency wanes or the business scaling is less dramatic, the firm will slip into the upper left-hand, "patient capital" quadrant of Figure 4.5. These firms still target large markets, like clean energy, but are unable to produce rocket-growth rates (because customer acquisition times are prolonged, for example) and/or need continued, additional capital to grow (project financing of wind farms, for example). The increased time or investment (or both) will reduce the return rate for investors as well as the timeframe for that return; hence the label "patient." Traditional equity financing with its relatively short investment-to-return targets (three to five years) typically will not operate here. Government economic developers, with longer time horizons, are attracted to this quadrant, but must be creative in financing firms here, such as through the creation of Public–Private Partnerships (PPPs) (DeWulf, Blanken, and Bult-Spiering, 2012). Entrepreneurs finding their firms in this quadrant must address the challenge of raising large amounts of capital with long pay-back horizons.

Firms in the lower right-hand quadrant will scale quickly and will be capital-efficient, but not much capital will be required to launch them. Firms in this quadrant do not have the potential to grow nearly as large as the firms in the upper right-hand quadrant, but because they do not need nearly as much capital (perhaps as much as 1,000-fold less) their growth potential per invested dollar will be similar. Entrepreneurs with these types of high-ROI-potential firms are often befuddled by the fact that they are "too small" to attract venture capital. Since these firms have the potential to generate a significant amount of cash flow, their long-term growth can easily be supported by debt financing: Hence the "non-equity investable" label for this quadrant. The firms in this quadrant will increase their equity value along with their rapidly increasing cash flow. Hence the founders may one day find a buyer for their firm at a valuation significantly greater than the capital it took to start the business. The challenge these firms face is in finding the initial capital they need to get started. These firms often need to scale back from their initial vision to a model that they can start with self-financing or monies from friends and families. These firms need a clear strategic path to continue expanding to the firm they dream of creating or they will be in danger of slipping into the lower left-hand quadrant of Figure 4.5.

Unlike firms in the lower right-hand quadrant of Figure 4.5, firms in the lower left-hand quadrant do not have the potential for rapid growth. These firms may not have the potential for much growth at all without significant, additional, capital infusions. Once up and running, these firms can often produce enough cash flow to provide a nice financial life for their founders. This type of firm, as a result, is often labeled a "lifestyle" company, as it is not attractive to outside investors but may provide a very healthy lifestyle for the founders provided they can find the patient debt financing required to get the firm started. When exited, these firms often sell for just slightly more than their PP&E (property, plant and equipment) values. The quintessential example of this type of firm is a singular convenience store. It requires significant capital to launch (purchase the building, stock the shelves), will generate a decent cash flow (depending on the location), but will likely sell for the PP&E value when the owner eventually decides to exit. The value of the business is not in its escalating equity value, but in the cash it generates for the owners. Hence the quadrant label "not attractive to outside investors."

It is important to note that the investment potential framework is not a judgment on the quality of the business. It is simply a question of the alignment of the potential of the business with the type of investment that the entrepreneurs could reasonably expect to obtain. Recall that this is a view from the investor's perspective, not the entrepreneur's.

For an initial high-level assessment, you want a quick way to position your firm in the appropriate quadrant of the investment potential diagram. You may initially chose to place your firm on the vertical axis of the framework based on your sense for the market size combined with your position on the PVC analysis from your business design segment. Your position on the horizontal axis could be calculated using your sense of the growth potential and capital-efficiency of your firm. If this initial placement is inconsistent with the entrepreneur's desires, then the entrepreneur can circle back to a previous Arch segment and reposition the firm. If the initial assessment appears desirable, a more rigorous assessment can then be performed or, alternately, you could proceed directly to step 3 to perform the financial analyses consistent with that placement on Figure 4.5. However, you will eventually need to come back and perform a more detailed analysis of the positioning and the elements that support that positioning. Without that, you are subject to the "garbage in, garbage out" concept familiar to anyone with a computer background. Any model with questionable or nonsensical input data will produce nonsensical or variously interpretable output; the investment potential framework is no different.

To perform a more rigorous investability analysis will require the quantification of the five components of the proposed new venture listed below, in addition to the margin assessment completed in step 1:

- market size
- market adoption rate estimates
- market value of earnings
- investment amount/timing required to build the business and
- business exit timing.

The remaining components needed for the investability analysis can be derived from these six as shown in Figure 4.6. Once determined, the potential of the proposed firm can be properly placed on the 2×2 grid of Figure 4.5.

If it is known *a priori* that the proposed business will not be equity investable or that the founders are not interested in seeking equity investment, then two of the six components ('market value of

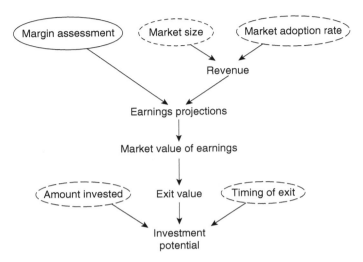

FIGURE 4.6 Components of an investment potential analysis

earnings' and the 'timing of exit') can be eliminated as these will not be material in evaluating the economic viability of a non-equity invest-able firm. However, if the founder is hoping to build a bootstrappable firm with the goal of a relatively short time-to-exit, it would be greatly beneficial to include these two components in the assessment.

The offering margin was addressed in step 1. The order for determining the remaining five components is not critical. It is rec-ommended, however, that the components be determined following the flow-chart in Figure 4.6 from left to right, then top to bottom. The philosophy here is to estimate reasonable values for the remaining components relatively quickly. All of these will be estimates. Clearly, to ascertain the true margins, for example, you would have to build a complete beta unit, test it with customers, etc. By the time you com-mitted that much time to developing the offering you would think it was the greatest product ever offered! The key with all the components is to determine an estimate that is accurate enough. The analysis will likely need to be performed in multiple passes. Quickly estimating all six components, perform the financial evaluations and subsequent sensitivity analyses of steps 3 and 4. After the completion of step 4, spend time obtaining better estimates of the components that signifi-cantly impact the economic viability of the proposed venture. Then repeat the analyses of steps 3 and 4. This method will be unnerving for the analytical types who will want "accurate" values for all the elements of step 2 before moving forward. The philosophy, however, is to spend time focusing on the things worthy of this attention.

Market size

Given that you already have a margin estimate from step 1, the next element to tackle in Figure 4.6 is the size of the market. When estimat-ing anything, it is preferable to take multiple perspectives. Your esti-mate will never be "right," but if several approaches to estimating the values lead you to a similar value, you can assure yourself that the estimate is at least reasonable. While taking multiple approaches for estimation values is important in all cases, it is particularly important for sizing the market as there are no comparators to fall back on.

There are three descriptors for sizing a market. It is important that you know all three. These descriptors are the number of units sold, the number of customers, and the total monetary value spent. It is a mistake to concentrate solely on the monetary value of the market as this disguises a highly disaggregated market that may be difficult to penetrate. Looking solely at the monetary value also makes it too easy to get seduced into thinking you "only have to attain 2 percent of the market" to be successful. Who are those 2 percent? Where do they live? How can you access them? The 2 percent solution is the death sen-tence for many startups.

Size the market from both a top-down and a bottom-up perspec-tive. From a bottom-up perspective you can start with the customer described in your position statement (see Chapter 3). How many of these are there? Leverage both primary and secondary research. Surveys and other primary research methods are one way to address the volume question. While surveys were highly discouraged during the business design segment when you were trying to understand the "why" underlying customer needs and choices, they are great tools for establishing "how many." If you know how many people are at a job site and you survey them, you can determine how many are likely to eat their lunch off-site, for example. Secondary research, however, is usually the best place to start your size-estimating. If your target was urban hospitals in the United States with a minimum of 500 beds, you would likely uncover that number through researching existing documents and reports. The combination of both primary and secondary research will readily get you to a defendable value.

Beyond your initial target segment, you will need to add the volume of additional segments. You likely already thought through the sequencing of this segment during business design. Your initial segment might have been urban hospitals in the USA with more than 500 beds, followed by urban hospitals with more than 200 beds, followed by rural hospitals with more than 300 beds, etc. You will not need to identify and quantify every segment, however, as you are interested in revenue estimates for the first five to ten years, not forever.

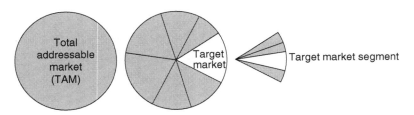

FIGURE 4.7 Relationship of marketing terms

The alternative to building up the market size from the bottom up is to take the more commonly used top-down approach. This is also the most erroneously used approach, owing to the fact that market research reports tend to report market sizes as aggregates of end users, for example describing the mobile-phone handset market as a $245 billion market (ITCandor.com, 2012). Entrepreneurs often mistake this number for their TAM (totally addressable market). Your TAM is the total size of the market if everyone that could purchase your product did so. This value is very dependent on where in the value system your firm is located. Since your firm will not represent the entire value system, as a result the total market value of the industry will not be your firm's TAM. Your firm's TAM therefore needs to be parsed from that of the entire industry. Subsequently, your target market will be a segment of your TAM, and your target market segment will be a segment within this target market, as shown in Figure 4.7, above. That homogeneous target segment, as discussed in Chapter 3, will have an adoption profile as discussed in that chapter.

Let us look at a simple example to illustrate how market sizes are often erroneously overestimated. Let us say that your team is creating software that would augment a smart phone's operating system. This augmentation would allow the operating system to handle memory more efficiently thereby speeding up the operation of the phone, particularly in photo and GPS-related applications. In addition to the increased speed, the processing efficiency would reduce the power consumption and therefore extend the phone's battery life. What is your firm's TAM?

With a bit of searching on the internet, you uncover the handset market data shown in Figure 4.8 below (ITCandor.com, 2012).

A common mistake is to say that the TAM for your proposed firm is 267.8 million units (20.6 percent of 1.3 billion units) and $117.1 billion (47.8 percent of $245 billion). This is not correct. A look at the very over-simplified value system (see Figure 4.9) will illustrate why this is the case.

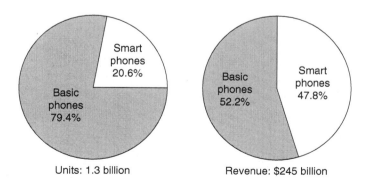

FIGURE 4.8 Mobile phone handset data for year ending March 2012

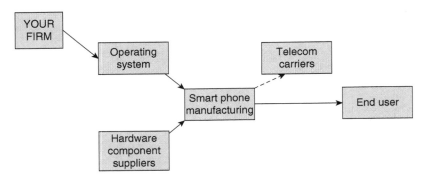

FIGURE 4.9 Simple mobile phone handset value system

The original market data is usually presented from an end-user perspective. Your hypothetical firm is not selling to the end user, but to the provider of the operating systems of the smart phones. For each smart phone unit purchased by an end user, you could potentially sell one unit of your software. The unit TAM previously calculated, 267.8 million units (20.6 percent of 1.3 billion units), is indeed correct. What is not correct is the revenue generated from those sales. The previously calculated $117.1 billion value (47.8 percent of $245 billion) is for the sales of the units to the end users. Certainly, that is not your firm's potential revenue. Your firm's revenue TAM is significantly lower than this number. One way to get at your firm's revenue TAM is to determine the value of the operating system to the phone, and then the value of your augmented software to the operating system. For the sake of this example, let's say that the operating system represents 10 percent of the value of the phone and that your improvement represents 3 percent of the value of the operating system for a smart phone. The value of your firm's TAM would then be ($117.1 billion) × 10 percent × 3 percent or $351.3 million dollars. That's a far cry from $117.1 billion. From this TAM, you would then have to further segment the market, say, by operating system. Your target market could, in turn, be Android-operated smart phones, which comprise 43.7 percent of the market (Reisinger, 2011), making the value of your initial target market $153.5 million.

Market adoption

The third and final component of the top row of Figure 4.6 is the market adoption. The market adoption is the most difficult component to estimate in approximating the rate at which your new firm's revenue will grow. Revenue growth, in turn, is nearly always a significant factor in estimating the economic viability of a new firm. Adoption and sales cycle (time between product introduction and purchase) are driven by perceived attributes of the innovation and the type of purchasing decision, as shown below (Rogers, 1995: Chapter 6).

Perceived attributes of innovation:

Relative advantage
Compatibility
Complexity
Scope to try before buying
Observability

Type of purchasing decision:

Individual
Collective
Authoritative

How fast will your customers adopt? Here too, insights have been gained during the business design segment. Did you discover a big pain? Ineffective current solutions? Potential customers aching for an alternate solution? Alternatively, at the other end of the adoption spectrum, do your potential customers not even recognize or admit that they have a problem? This latter condition is often an early indicator of a missionary sales condition. Such a condition represents two sequential sales challenges: Selling the problem and subsequently selling your offering as a solution to that problem. That's two sequential adoptions to achieve!

Private companies are the best comparators when estimating adoption. Unlike the EBITDA margin estimate, you are not seeking companies in steady state, but ones in transition; ones displaying accelerated growth. You therefore do not want public companies, but private ones as proxies. The ideal private proxy is in your industry and serving your customer. They are, for example, offering hospital labs different kinds of testing equipment than what you are offering, but are selling to your customers. Like the public proxy, the ideal private proxy has a narrow offering, as will be typical for a new firm. Finding private proxies with publicly available data is the challenge. Search entrepreneurial economy news sites such as xconomy.com, or specific industry-tracking sites such as the Cleantech Group. Another good option is searching through public databases such as CrunchBase.com or s10 filings of companies that recently went public or are preparing to go public.

No matter what technique you use to find publicly available adoption data for private companies, this search will be difficult. There is, however, an alternative to quickly getting an estimate. This method is rough – think of it as a zero-order estimate – but it can be performed quickly and is a reasonable place to start while searching for more specific data. It is the s-curve revenue estimator. Adoption tends to advance along an s-curve, definitely not the revenue hockey-stick you will find in most business plans. It starts with understanding the size of the market that you hope to attain one day; that you estimated in the previous section. The question is how long will this adoption take? It is always longer than you think. It took nearly forty years for the mass adoption of the radio, thirty years for the microwave oven, fifteen years for the personal computer, twelve years for the cell phone, and even seven years for the iPod (Catlett, 2009). Which adoption timeframe is closest to your new offering? You can create a map of revenue over time, by fitting the ultimate market size onto an s-curve extended over the estimated years of adoption. Make no mistake, this is not a great estimate of adoption, but it is much better, and often shows much slower growth rates, than the notorious hockey-stick many entrepreneurs tend to use. Given you will be performing a sensitivity analysis on this later to see how this variable impacts the overall viability of your firm, it is a reasonable place to start. Of course, any real data, even adoption rates of products only quasi-related to your offering, will a better and preferred approach.

One advantage of evaluating margin, market size, and adoption rates separately is that you may be able to combine different comparisons in order to get a reasonable estimate. Large companies A, B, and C, may be suitable comparators for estimating the sub-components of your margins. Public company D, in turn, may be useful in estimating your market size, while private company E may provide insights into your adoption rate. Again, the numbers will not be right, but reasonable, rational, and defensible.

Having now determined the margin, the size, and the adoption of your offering you can calculate your revenue and earnings projection. To convert that into a company valuation you will need to know how the market values earnings. This will be the focus of the next section. If you know that your firm will not be equity investable, then you can skip the valuation section, evaluate the size of investment necessary to start the new business, and go straight to the non-equity assessment steps. However, if unsure what investment type is appropriate for your firm, you will need to make a valuation. To do that you first need to determine the value of your earnings.

Value of earnings

Just as it is inconceivable to believe you can be successful selling a product that costs more to create than it will sell for, it is equally odd not to consider whether your business will be worth more than it costs to build. The resistance to this question often stems from the early determination of the future value of the business. Of course, it is impossible to determine a precise value for a business before it is operationalized and launched, just as it is impossible to determine the precise market value of a home without knowing that home's detailed features and amenities. However, just like home prices, business values are not random. A flat in a prime district in London may go for $350–450 per square foot, while a home in rural mid-west United States may only sell for $100–150 per square foot. Similarly, a dollar of EBITDA may convert to $10–15 of enterprise value in the medical device industry and less than $1 in the toy industry. The market sets these valuations based on the anticipated growth rates, among other factors, of the industry as a whole. The entrepreneur must keep in mind that the methodology is similar to trying to get an initial understanding of the value of your home; the goal is to find something "in the neighborhood" rather than finding an exact replicate of your house. If houses are selling between $250,000 and $350,000 in your neighborhood, then there is a high probability that your home will sell for somewhere in that range. The fact that your house has a slightly different floor plan from any other house in the neighborhood, has granite countertops, etc., will certainly impact on the ultimate selling price of the home, but at this point the objective is to get "in the neighborhood" with a reasonable estimate of that selling price.

Your new venture will be in a given industry. Even though your business is new and unique to the world, some market analyst will eventually lump it, at a very high level, into an existing industry. The question for you, therefore, is what industry segment accurately represents your business. The answer lies in the value system you created in the opportunity identification segment. Once an industry is identified, as in the work you did in creating the value system, you can identify a public company, or companies, as a proxy to determine how your industry values earnings. The advantage of using public companies as proxies for the value of your startup is that these public company values are determined by the market. Such a comparison therefore gives you a market-based value.

Comparing a nascent startup company to a fully operational, publicly traded company may seem absurd. The advantage of using market-valued companies is, of course, that the information on the values of publicly traded companies is constantly being update by the financial markets. The weakness in using public companies as a proxy to value a startup is that one is comparing a fully operational company to an entity that typically has no product, no buyers, and an incomplete management team at best. Keep in mind that we are trying to determine the potential future value of the business; the value sometime in the future when it does have team, staff, customers, and sales, not the value of the firm in its current state.

There are two main issues to consider in comparing the value of your privately held startup company to a public company. The first is that public companies generate value in a number of different ways. Startup companies are like the power trains of automobiles: Engines, transmissions, axles, and wheels. They can move, but these companies definitely have "no frills." When comparing the potential future value of a startup to a large going concern, we want to compare that startup to the drive train of the large company. We want to ignore the navigation screens, stereos, etc. of the publicly traded company. We want a drive train to drive train comparison. In other words, we want to parse the value of the public firm created by operating-related activities from its overall market value, since a startup has none of these "non-operating" contributors to value.

The total value of a public firm is its market capitalization, or market cap. A company's market cap is simply the number of outstanding shares times the share price. The enterprise value (EnV) of a company is a subset of the market capitalization value of that company and represents the value of its core operations. The enterprise value excludes non-core, value-generating activities, investments not related to the business, and sundry other items. As a result, conceptually we want to distill the readily available market cap value of the public firm to extract an enterprise value that reflects the contributions that the core operations make to that total value. Doing so, fortunately, is mathematically straightforward. The market cap is equal to the enterprise value of the firm plus the net cash. The net cash, as we shall see from the example in the next section of this chapter, is cash less debt, where "cash" is typically taken as the "total current assets" from the public proxy's balance sheet and debt is typically taken as the sum of "total current liabilities" and "long-term debt" from the proxy's balance sheet. Now that the enterprise value of the public proxy is known, as well as its EBITDA, the ratio of the public proxy's enterprise value to its EBTIDA can be determined (EnV:EBITDA). Like the house value per square foot value, this ratio is a ball-park estimate for the value of a public company in this industry per dollar of EBITDA.

Our startup, however, is not a public company, so we will have to adjust for that, which is the second significant issue in relating the value of a public company proxy to a privately held enterprise. Liquid assets, those that can easily be converted into cash, are worth more than illiquid assets. To convince yourself that this is true, ask yourself, would you rather have a bar of gold now or a certificate that you may, someday, be able to exchange for a bar of gold? No doubt you would take the gold now. That means that the certificate is discounted, in your mind, against the actual gold. How large that discount is depends on how easily convertible that certificate may be. In comparing the future value of privately held companies with that of public companies, the rule-of-thumb discount rate is 30 percent, meaning that, once you estimate the future EBITDA value for your firm and determine the EnV:EBITDA ratio for a proxy company in your space, then you need to discount that by 30 per cent. Succinctly put it is:

$$\left(\frac{EnV}{EBITDA}\right)_{Private\ New\ Co} = \left(\frac{EnV}{EBITDA}\right)_{Public\ Co} \times (1-30\%)$$

making:

$$EnV_{Private\ New\ Co} = EBITDA_{Private\ New\ Co} \times \left(\frac{EnV}{EBITDA}\right)_{Public\ Co} \times (1-30\%)$$

Warning: All valuations are time-dependent. Whenever you estimate the value of a firm, this valuation should be date-stamped, noting the date and source of the financial data used in the estimate.

One caution about choosing public financial proxies: As with the public proxies you identified while creating your value system you need these firms to be stable over time. Rapid growth means that firms are investing a great deal on PP&E (property, plant, and equipment) and expanding working capital. These are items that show up on the firm's balance sheet, not their income statement. High-growth public firms typically do not make good financial proxy companies because the market values of these public companies will account for their accelerated future growth based on today's investments, but the income statement (EBITDA values) will not contain those future sales. In such cases the two values in the EnV:EBITDA ratio are not congruent, resulting in a misleading ratio. Companies with accelerating growth rate, operations not in a steady state, are not good candidates for public financial comparators, therefore. A good public financial proxy company is one that has steady growth and investments over a period of time.

Startup exit value example

This section pulls all the concepts from the previous sections of step 2 together into a simple example. Entrepreneur Mary Jane believes that she could develop and copyright a software program and create a company that sells the software and associated services. Given the track record of another, similar firm in which she was involved, she believes that this company could be sold once the company reaches $400 million in annual sales. Based on other proxy companies, she believes her gross profit margins at that point will be 85 percent with SG&A estimated to be around 50 percent of sales and on-going R&D estimated at 25 percent of sales. She wants to know the potential value of the company at acquisition. Mary Jane believes the company AutoDesk is a good proxy for the kind of software and services that her company will develop and sell.

Searching Google Finance shows the market cap for AutoDesk on April 26, 2013 to be $8.35 billion. Income statement data from the year ending January 31, 2013 shows:

Revenue:	$2,312.2 million
Cost of revenue:	– $238.5 million
Gross profit:	$2,073.7 million
Total SG&A:	– $1,123.9 million
R&D:	– $600.0 million
EBITDA:	$349.8 million

Since EBITDA is before depreciation and amortization (Figure 4.3) you need to make sure that these values are not included in the reported cost of goods. In this example, the D/A value is listed separately and shown as zero. However, in many financial reports it is included in the cost of goods. When that is the case, you can find the D/A values on the Statement of Cash Flows and then add them back to obtain the true EBITDA value.

The balance sheet data for AutoDesk, reported for the three months ending January 31, 2013:

Total current assets:	$2,552.4 million
Total current liabilities:	– $1,043.7 million
Total long-term debt:	– $745.6 million
Net cash:	$763.1 million
Market cap:	$8,350.0 million
Net cash:	– $763.1 million
EnV:	$7,586.9 million

making the EnV:EBITDA ratio: 21.69 (for a public company).

Mary Jane's projected EBITDA:

Revenue:	$400 million
COG:	– $ 60 million
Gross profit:	$340 million (85% of revenue)
SG&A:	– $200 million (50% of revenue)
R&D:	– $100 million (25% of revenue)
EBITDA:	$40 million

Mary Jane's projected company value at the time of aquisition:

$EnV_{NewCo} = EBITDA_{NewCo} \times (EnV{:}EBITDA_{PublicProxy}) \times (1{-}30\%)$

$\$607.3 \text{ million} = \$40 \text{ million } (21.69) \times (1{-}30\%)$

or approximately $600 million. Since these are approximate valuations, you definitely need to round off the numbers. Note that the time value of money is also being ignored. Since we are comparing present values of public companies with future values, one might think some accounting for the time value of money was in order. However, the accuracy of the estimate does not justify this refinement. We are not trying to anticipate the exact value on sale of Mary Jane's company, but simply get a sense of how much it could be worth at some time in the future (which is usually the time of the anticipated exit).

Investment and timing

The final pieces necessary to perform subsequent financial analyses are the amount and timing of the investment required to build your new firm. As with the market adoption rate, private proxies are the best proxies for estimating these values. The same recommendations apply to finding data for investment timing as for market adoption rates: Searching through databases such as CrunchBase.com, industry tracking sites such as xconomy.com, or s10 filings of companies that recently went public. The private proxy companies used for the investment need not be the same as those previously used. Searching for acquisitions in the same space as your firm, you can determine at what point (revenue, age, etc.) other firms in your area were acquired or had initial public offerings (IPO).

Summary for step 2

You now have all the components necessary to place your firm in the investment potential analysis two-by-two framework shown as Figure 4.5. Figure 4.10, below, summarizes the sources of information for the components of the investability analysis.

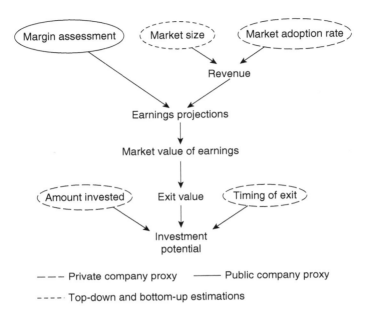

FIGURE 4.10 Proxy sources for components of an investment potential analysis

The investment potential analysis is a very powerful tool when used in combination with the PVC framework. However, the PVC analysis must be performed first. Companies that require repositioning based on their PVC assessment should be repositioned before performing the investment potential analysis to avoid nonsensical results from the latter. These are two sequential assessments: The PVC comes first and the investment potential analysis second. The PVC framework – repositioning – PVC framework sequence must be performed to the satisfaction of the entrepreneur before the investment potential analysis is carried out. Failing to do that is tantamount to asking "What is the optimal way to invest in a non-viable business?"

Step 3   Financial evaluation

Once the proposed new venture has been placed in one of the quadrants of the investment potential framework (Figure 4.5), the next phase of the investability analysis is to drill deeper into its economic viability.

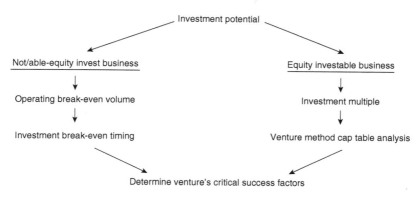

FIGURE 4.11 Investability assessment flowchart

Consistent with the overall fail-fast approach, this further assessment is performed as a series of increasingly rigorous assessments as shown in Figure 4.11. If the business fails the first assessment, there is no reason to continue, but instead you should return to the business design segment. If the first screen produces an encouraging result, the second, more rigorous assessment will be performed. As Figure 4.11 illustrates, the assessment methodologies bifurcate depending on investment type. While many financial assessment methodologies are possible, this section will illustrate two sequential approaches for both equity and non-equity investments. The first pass through this method, you may want to do a high-level placement of your firm in the investment potential framework in step 2, followed by the high-level financial evaluation of the appropriate type. If this high-level assessment looks positive, you could then cycle back and perform a more rigorous step 2 analysis before proceeding to the more rigorous analysis in this step. The point is there are many ways to get through the process quickly. The goal is a quick first assessment before the cement hardens – at least in your own mind – on your business concept.

Non-equity investments

The two sequential financial analyses that we will use for a non-equity business are break-even volume and break-even investment timing.

Both are business assessments and not product assessments. The operating break-even determines how many units you will need to sell in order to break even. This view can be assessed on any time basis, weekly, monthly, or yearly, for example. The basis is whatever makes sense for the business. This method breaks down the expenses of the business into variable and fixed costs. Fixed costs include such things as rent, insurance, and perhaps salaries. Variable costs include product material costs, taxes, and salaries if paid on a commission or piece-work basis. The break-even volume is the volume at which the fixed plus variable costs match the total revenue.

As an example, my wife Kelley has a small, art-based business through which she sells hand-made items that are based on her original art. She knows the cost of goods for each item, based on the materials and the amount of her labor that goes into its production. This portion of her labor is variable. She then sells these items at local art fairs. These fairs charge a booth fee (fixed cost) and often she will hire an assistant at a fixed price per show (another fixed cost). She can then determine how many items she will need to sell at any given art fair in order for that fair to create value for her. If that is a reasonable number, significantly less than her target market, for example, then the fair becomes a worthy endeavor. Otherwise she should re-evaluate her pricing strategy or the business itself. Let's say her gross margin (sales price less the cost of materials sold and the variable labor costs) is $5 per item. For a specific art fair the booth fee may be $300 and the fixed labor another $100. Her total fixed costs for this art fair are then $400. She must sell eighty items [$400/($5/item)] in order to pay off her fixed costs. This is her break-even sales volume. If she deems this a reasonable number then she can move on to the next assessment level. If not, then the business needs to be altered. Perhaps the prices of her items need to increase or she needs to figure out a way to decrease the manufacturing costs. Alternatively, she may want to share a booth with another artist in order to defer some of the fixed costs. There are many repositioning options if the assessment is done prior to the businesses being immovable in the mind of the entrepreneur.

Given the business seems reasonable based on the operating break-even analysis, the next level of assessment is to determine the time it would take to return the investment necessary to create the business. This is a cash-flow, project-financing type of assessment. It is one that many small-business owners neglect. In this assessment, you eliminate depreciation from the cost of goods as that is a non-cash cost that you will be accounting for in the up-front investment of the firm. Let's say Kelley believes she can earn a net operating profit after tax of $100 per art show. She has a small investment in this business: Computer, printer, tent, and a few items to aid in the display of her products. We will say that these items represent a $7,000 up-front investment in her business. Even though we determined that she is profitable at each fair, it would then take her seventy art fairs to achieve cash-flow break-even. If she averages seven shows a year, that would take ten years. And this is before discounting the future revenue streams, which would further lengthen the pay-back time! She may want to consider repositioning this business.

Equity investments

Similar to the non-equity approach, the assessment for equity investable businesses progresses over two different screens, with the second screen building upon the first. While non-equity businesses are cash flow-driven, equity investments can only be justified by reference to the escalating equity value of the firm. There must also be an exit for the investors in order for them to transform their illiquid private equity investment into cash or its equivalent. The first assessment approach for equity investable firms is to assess their cash-on-cash multiple potential. In other words, what is the ratio of the value of the investor's share of the firm at exit to the amount of the investment? If this multiple is not at least five, then the timing from investment-to-exit will need to be fairly short, or the business should be repositioned.

The second level of assessment drills deeper into the investor's potential returns. Equity investors hedge their investments by investing in tranches. Each tranche of funding is aimed at the successful completion of a critical objective, or milestone, that lies along the path to the creation of a successful company. Assuming success, the next funding will be at a higher company valuation, as the company has been slightly de-risked by the successful attainment of the prior milestone. If success is not achieved, there will likely be no further investment and the company will cease operations.

The list below shows typical internal rate of return (IRR) expectations by investment stage. The list also articulates the activities that typically take place at that stage. Most venture capital firms focus both on an investment area (such as medical devices) and an investment stage. Early-stage investors – seed and startup stages – will usually also invest in the later rounds, but they tend not to be the significant investors (in terms of total capital) for those rounds. This means that a venture firm's IRR for a given investment in a portfolio company will be a blended rate of those given in the below (Brophy, 2000).

Pre-seed investment stage

This investment stage seeks answers to questions such as:

- Is the science repeatable?
- Have you created a working prototype of the idealized product?
- Is there substantial intellectual property (IP) to protect the proposed product?
- Does the company have the freedom to practice this IP?

This milestone is targeted at mitigating the technology risk. IRR target 100 percent and up for venture capitalists.

Seed investment stage

Beta-product development.

- Can a quasi-commercial product be created?
- What is the market's reaction to this product?

This milestone is targeted at mitigating the product risk and obtains the first market feedback.
IRR target 80 percent and up.

Startup investment stage

Create commercial product.
Obtain first sales.
Compare product costs and margins to those projected.
This stage targets more of the market risks.
IRR target of 50–70 percent.

First-stage investment

At this stage the aim is to accelerate growth.

- Can the product manufacturing and sales be scaled?
- What are the cost and speed of customer acquisition?
- Are there limits to growth on the supply side (availability of product) or demand side (product adoption rates by customers)?

More market risk mitigation is sought.
IRR target of 40–60 percent.

Second-stage investment

This stage focuses on profitability:

- making the company profitable
- accelerating profitable growth and
- mitigating market/execution risk.

IRR target of 30–50 percent.

Mezzanine or bridge investment

The firm seeks capital to extend/expand operations to IPO or sale:

- grow the company to make it a good acquisition target or IPO candidate
- can require acquisition of smaller competitors and
- many companies can complete this phase only with the use of company profits.

For companies that need further investments, the IRR targets are 20–35 percent.

Year →	1	3	5	7	9
30%	1.30	2.20	3.71	6.27	10.60
50%	1.50	3.38	7.59	17.09	38.44
70%	1.70	4.91	14.20	41.03	118.59
90%	1.90	6.86	24.76	89.39	322.69

FIGURE 4.12 Investment multiples required to achieve IRRs

If investors made only a single investment in the development of a startup company you could use the target IRR numbers, in combination with the previously calculated exit value-to-investment ratio and the table below, to determine the maximum time from investment to exit that would achieve that IRR. For example, using Figure 4.12, a startup-stage investor seeking a 70 percent IRR for a firm that could achieve a exit value-to-investment ratio of 5 would need the time from their investment to the company's eventual exit to be less than three years (as Figure 4.12 shows a 70 percent IRR in three years would produce a 4.91 multiple.)

But alas, investors do not typically make single investments so the calculations are not that straightforward. Equity investors mitigate their investment risk by investing in tranches. This means that, in order to check the equity investability of your firm, you will need to see whether it is likely for multiple investors to attain their investment-stage-specific IRR goals at multiple times. Take heart, it is not as difficult as it sounds. Capital tables, more commonly called cap tables, are used to track investments, company ownership, and ultimately investment returns over time. The venture method is essentially a cap table calculated in reverse, assuming the returns and calculating the ownership.

A simplified version of the venture method is all that is required to assess the equity investability of the firm and subsequently perform some sensitivity analysis. The methodology is best illustrated with an example.

The figure below shows the inputs for the hypothetical startup company that will be used to illustrate the equity assessment methodology. This example shows the investment will have three rounds of funding. The first round is a seed-stage investment, the second a startup

Investment round	Investment year	Investment amount ($m)	Investment IRR target (%)	Exit valuation ($m)
1	0	$1	100%	
2	1	$7	70%	
3	3	$20	40%	
	4			$100

FIGURE 4.13 Venture method example model inputs

stage and the third a first-stage-of-growth investment as shown in Figure 4.12. The exit value, which was presumably determined by the method described previously, is shown to be $100 million.

From this limited input can be determined how much of the company was sold at each round and how much each round of investors retained at the exit, assuming all investors will hit their IRR targets. The following details the calculations that are made given the inputs shown in Figure 4.13.

Final equity percentage = (required return × investment) / (exit value)

Round 1 = $((1 + 1.00)^4 \times \$1m)/(\$100m) = 16.0\%$

Round 2 = $((1+0.70)^3 \times \$7m)/(\$100m) = 34.4\%$

Round 3 = $((1+0.40)^1 \times \$20m)/(\$100m) = 28.0\%$

Retention percentage per round

Retention percentage = 100% – future expected dilution

Retention percentage = (final round percentage ownership)/(round percentage ownership)

Round 1 retention = 100% – 34.4% (from round 2) – 28% (from round 3) = 37.6%

Round 2 retention = 100% – 28% (from round 3) = 72.0%

Round 3 retention = 100%

Percentage of company purchased per round

Percent purchased per round = final equity percentage/round retention percentage

Round 1 = 16.0%/37.6% = 42.5%

Round 2 = 34.4%/72% = 47.8%

Round 3 = 28.0%/100% = 28.0%

These calculations show that the round 1 investors originally purchased 42.5% of the equity of the startup with their $1 million invest-
ment and ended up owning 16% of the firm at the end of all of the
investments. Of course these calculations force the investors to reach
the set IRR targets. The calculations, as a result, can return nonsensical results indicating ownership of more than 100 percent of the
company. When this occurs, it means the investors could not attain
their target IRRs given the other assumptions. That would indicate
the firm would not be equity investable under those conditions. If, for
example, everything in the above example stayed the same except that
the exit timing changed from four to five years, the investors would no
longer be able to meet their target IRRs. This means that if this firm
takes five years to exit, rather than the predicted four, then this is not
an attractive investment for the equity investors. Clearly the investability in this case is quite sensitive to the exit timing. This leads us to
the next step: Determining the critical factors in the financial success
of the firm.

Step 4   Sensitivity analyses

The preceding portion of this chapter described how the type and
amount of capital that may be available to various types of nascent
firms can be determined. In short, we know that the proposed firm is
investable and the type of capital the firm can attract. We further know,
as discussed in Appendix C, the implications of that type of capital
for the entrepreneur. We have further assessed the firm to determine
whether it is investable by assessing it by two increasingly rigorous
methods. The next issue is to determine the drivers of that investability.
What are the most critical elements in determining the success of our
business model? Of all the things there are to be concerned about in
the creation and launch of this new business, which are the half-dozen
that you should particularly focus on? In other words, which are your
Critical Success Factors (CSFs)? Determining the CSFs is the purpose
of this final step in the business assessment segment.

We will again be taking an investor perspective on the proposed new firm. The step will build upon the financial model created for the second financial assessment in step 3. Working through a series of "what-if" variations on the previous financial assessment model, by changing the model's inputs we can readily determine the conditions that allow the firm to be an attractive investment for equity investors. We can simultaneously determine the conditions that make it unattractive for investors. In the last example, we illustrated the impact of lengthening the time to exit by a year. We could also create scenarios that altered the investment amount required, or the value of the firm. Since the exit value of the firm is based on many inputs (such as estimated revenue at exit), we could subsequently assess the impact of each of these variables on the ultimate investability of the firm.

A systematic analysis that determines which elements create the largest variance in the outcome will reveal the venture's CSFs; its primary economic drivers. These CSFs will allow the entrepreneur to know which aspect of the business to focus on as the company develops. Figure 4.14 sets out a tornado diagram for a hypothetical firm

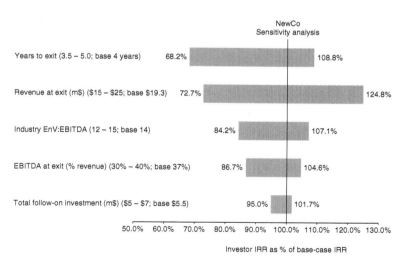

FIGURE 4.14 Tornado diagram for hypothetical startup company

showing how a number of variables impact on the investor's IRR. Tornado diagrams provide a visual way to show decreasing sensitivity. Figure 4.14 illustrates, for example, that a change in the follow-on investment has little impact on the ultimate return to the investors, while the time to exit is significant. Knowing that, the entrepreneur can loop back and focus on obtaining better data on the assumptions that impact years-to-exit, such as customer adoption rates, and concern him- or herself less about the assumptions that relate to follow-on investment.

As with the macro approach outlined by the Entrepreneurial Arch itself, the method for assessing a business is iterative. With the objective of moving quickly, the method illustrates ways to expeditiously estimate the proposed firm's value and its investability. The sensitivity analysis then highlights which components of that valuation are most crucial to the investor's success. Those elements are subsequently re-assessed in more detail.

COMMON MISTAKES

The single biggest mistake entrepreneurs make is not doing any kind of business financial assessment. They perform a product-level analysis of income statements, conclude that the margins are positive, and proceed to operationalize their business. Completely ignoring the investability of the business is to proceed in blissful ignorance. I often tell my engineering classes that I'm working on a writing instrument that will someday replace the pen. I tell them that I'm estimating the cost of this new device to be $10,000 per unit. They laugh. But asking for $10 million in equity financing and having no idea what potential business value it will create is equally laughable.

The next common mistake that entrepreneurs make is to do a five-year cash-flow projection as their only financial analysis. This is the correct analysis for the operationalize segment of the Entrepreneurial Arch, because it conveys the timing of the capital consumption in the development of your business. However, it provides absolutely no insight into the financial feasibility of the business or its investability.

This is particularly absurd for those seeking equity capital. The only way to determine whether an equity investment will potentially generate a positive rate of return for its investors is to project the future value of the firm. As uncomfortable as it may be, there is simply no way of getting around this fact. Investors do this analysis, even if solely based on their experiences. Entrepreneurs need to do likewise.

Those with equity investable business are not the only ones that make financial assessment errors. Cash-flow startups have the bad habit of providing only income statement projections, not a complete cash-flow analysis. Again, the perspective they need is that of the financier, not the entrepreneur. The question that needs to be answered is can this business create a return for the investors?

Other common mistakes have been highlighted throughout this chapter. Revenue is assumed to grow far too quickly, and costs are assumed to be too low. It is usually the SG&A and ongoing R&D costs that are undervalued or ignored altogether. Using comparators will force you to confront reality. And do not forget about the customer acquisition time. I once worked with a startup that had a five-year lag between first customer contact and first sale. While highly unusual, this highlights the need to account for the lag. As previously noted, exaggerated revenue numbers can stem from erroneous TAM values. Knowing where the firm sits in the value system, who the firm sells to, and the value of the offering to your customer eliminates this mistake. Lastly, there are many options available to finance new ventures. It is a mistake to assume that venture capital is the only option.

SUMMARY

The left-hand side of the Entrepreneurial Arch, illustrated in Figure 4.1, is a systematic method for business discovery. It moves from value creation to value capture to the focus of this segment, feasibility. The approach is designed to gather enough market-based information to decide whether the concept is worth further investigation. This approach helps you avoid becoming intransigent with respect to your initial concept. It also means that not only will you iterate within this segment of the Arch as you spiral in towards a viable business, but you will also iterate freely among the first three segments.

The assessment methodologies articulated in this chapter take an investor perspective of the new venture, although some time was spent in Appendix C addressing the impact on the entrepreneur of the various financial options. Financing a startup is one of the most important decisions an entrepreneur will make for the company. Venture capital is only one, albeit a very important, option to be considered. The tools and methodologies that have been discussed are meant to provide the entrepreneur with the ability to screen the financial viability of business concepts and to determine the sensitivity of various scenarios for the financial outcome of the company. It is not meant to provide a substitute for the experience needed to negotiate a company's financing.

The methodologies described in this book are aimed at guiding the entrepreneur to making better decisions. The entrepreneur's time is the most precious resource. More ideas can be hatched. More money can be found. But entrepreneurs never get back their time. The entrepreneur should therefore spend it wisely, spending it on those ventures that have the greatest opportunity of making an impact on the world through their success.

At the end of the business design segment a complete business construct could be articulated. At the end of business assessment that construct has been transformed into a complete business model. Determining that business model was the first of the two objectives of this segment of the Arch. The second was to perform a feasibility assessment of the firm. The elements of the feasibility assessment, shown at the beginning of this chapter and repeated below, could be assembled into a feasibility study of the proposed venture, if desired.

1. *Activity:*

   Offering: What precisely is your product/service?

   How much will it cost to produce?

   How will you maintain differentiation and/or keep others out over time?

   What stage of development has the offering reached?

Actions: What precisely does the company do?

How does this leverage your capabilities?

What activities do you leverage from the existing ecosystem?

2. *Owner:* Who are your customers?

What is your target persona (need-based market segment)?

What size is the market (number of buyers, units sold, currency value of sales)? Estimate the total addressable market, target market, and initial target segment (target persona).

Who are your collaborators?

3. *Motive:* Why do your customers/collaborators buy your product/ collaborate with you? What value do you create/problem do you solve for your customer and collaborator? How does your offering compare to existing solutions? Quantify your customer's willingness to pay for your offering. What is your customer's current solution?

How do you believe the industry will react to your launch?

4. *Monetization:* How does your company make money (revenue model)? In other words, what is the value capture mechanism?

What are the offering's expected margins (margin assessment)?

Is the company investable (what is the investment model)?

What are the size and type of investment? Returns congruent with investment source?

5. *Financial assessment:*

Revenue potential: Estimated price, EBITDA margin; estimated adoption rate.

Business-building cost estimates: How much will it take to develop this business? Over what period of time?

Financing the business: Based on the investment potential framework what type of financing best fits this business?

Equity financing: Potential value at exit. Can equity investors meet return expectations? Under what conditions?

Non-equity financing: Cash flow and break-even models.

How easily will you obtain debt? How do you financially

manage pre-debt? Under what conditions does this venture make financial sense?

Success conditions: Identify three to five CSFs. Under what conditions is this venture feasible? Are those conditions realistic?

6. *Externalities:* Government/regulatory.

Industry reaction.

NOTE

1. This framework was co-developed during my collaboration with Peter Adriaens at the University of Michigan (2008–13).

5   Operationalize the business

This chapter marks the passage from the left-hand section of the Arch, the section in which you discovered a potentially viable business, to the right-hand section, in which you execute that business (Figure 5.1). A plan describing how this business will be executed is the first step toward its realization.

At the end of the business assessment segment of the Entrepreneurial Arch, you now have a business model. It is specific. It articulates the offering, the firm's actions that create the offering, and the specific customer that will purchase the offering. It also articulates the key collaborators in the creation and distribution of the offering to these customers. You also have a complete monetization model, which includes a value proposition for both your customers and your collaborators, in addition to a complete financial feasibility analysis. Despite its detail, a business model remains an architectural-level view of the business (Leung, 2007). It tells you *what* the business intends to do; it does not tell you *how* this will be done. The operational plan is the *how*. It is the building construction plan of attack. The business model plus the business's strategy plus the business's proposed tactics provide the operating plan for your business. The first step in operationalizing that business is to create an executable plan.

This executable plan for your business is commonly called a business plan. Business plans have been the target of a lot of disparaging remarks recently. They certainly are not everything; this stage represents only one segment of the Entrepreneurial Arch. Past business people have attempted to use a business plan to cover most of the discovery portion of the Entrepreneurial Arch. That is nonsensical; the business plan is an execution document and that is all. But that, in and of itself, is important. The other dirt being tossed on business

132

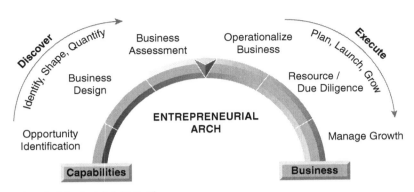

FIGURE 5.1 Progressing across the Entrepreneurial Arch from discovery to execution

plans is that they often do not get realized exactly as written. Seriously? Your life has gone completely according to the way you planned it? Mine has not; often it has been better! As German military strategist Helmuth von Moltke (1800–1891) is paraphrased as saying, "No battle plan survives contact with the enemy;" and as Dwight D. Eisenhower, Supreme Commander, Allied Forces in World War II, said, "Plans are worthless, but planning is everything." Both men were earnest strategist/planners. In today's vernacular, people like to talk about "pivoting." Clearly you have to adjust as you move forward. That's exactly what von Moltke and Eisenhower were saying. However, if you do not have a well-articulated plan to start with, in other words a definitive pivot point, how are you going to incorporate the new information and adjust your plan? Pivot implies a stable point around which you are moving. Without that your "pivot" becomes a random walk. Random walks rarely get you to a desired destination.

Even entrepreneurs that "never had a business plan," had business plans. They had a plan for operationalizing their business. They simply did not write that plan down. When experienced carpenters are asked to put up the frame of a house, they do not have to have a written plan telling them how to proceed. They are experienced and the outcome is predictable. New entrepreneurs are not experienced and the outcome of their plan is not predictable. If you are a sole proprietor, having a plan in your head could be adequate. But what if this is not the case? Even if this is your third enterprise software company launch and you feel comfortable knowing how to operationalize the business model, what about the rest of your team? Are they equally experienced? Can they stay on the same page as you when things change? You have designed the business and tested your business (assessed it); now plan the operations of your business to keep everyone on the same page during the launch and through the inevitable adjustments that will come as new information is discovered.

Many entrepreneurs approach the creation of a business plan as an item that must be checked off a to-do list before meetings with banks, angel investors, or venture capitalists can be scheduled. This is in part the drive behind the current push to launch your business after you have discovered the business model. Yes, communicating your business is important and no, you do not actually need to have an operational plan to make a three-minute elevator pitch on your business. However, without a plan, you have no systematic way to execute the business. Yes, there are many investors that will ask for a business plan they will never read. Why? They want to know that *you* have thought through the operations of this business. They want to know that you have analyzed the firm and have a strategy for mitigating its risks. There are investors that skip the plan requirement, but those investors are often investing in product development firms; firms that are solely developing a product or app that will hopefully be acquired by a larger firm (Facebook, Google, Apple, etc.). These types of venture have little in the way of operations to be concerned with, beyond the development of the product, so creating a "business plan" in these cases is overkill. But for businesses that will be operating as businesses, an executable plan is essential.

Beyond creating a plan to construct, resource, and grow your business, the other key element of your operating plan is to determine how you will manage the crucial drivers of your business's economic success that you uncovered in the feasibility portion of Chapter 4. The business plan will articulate how you will mitigate these risk factors. As previously implied, another fundamental aspect of the plan is to get and keep everyone involved with your firm – investors, advisors, partners, and employees – on the same page. It helps create a shared vision for the current team and one for future team members to understand before they join. The plan ties all the elements of your business together into one complete description. It allows you to connect the vision of the company with the activities that make it happen. Mostly, as Eisenhower stated, it is the planning process that is the most important aspect.

The plan is also used to "sell" your company to investors and potential employees. You should be able to introduce your plan at various levels, consistent with the zoom-in, zoom-out philosophy. Each level will be detailed in the "pitching" review at the end of this chapter, but essentially they fall into three categories:

- *Core concept opener.* One or two sentences that describe the essence of your firm. This ends with an invitation to discuss the new venture in more detail.
- *Elevator pitch.* One- to three-minute monologue that provides a brief overview of the aspects of your firm: The issue the firm is addressing, your solution, the size of the opportunity, etc. Ends in a "happy to tell you more" offer.
- *Investor pitch.* Fifteen- to thirty-minute presentation with visual aids that details the opportunity, the company, and the team. Typically ends in a specific ask, a specific call to action.

The terms "pitch" and "plan" are used so synonymously that some are starting to think they are the same. They are not. The plan is an operational document. It articulates the actions that will be taken in the company's path forward. The pitch is a sales proposal, often a high-level one. You do not need a plan to create a pitch. But you do need a plan to execute a business once it is successfully pitched, which is why the preferred order is to create the plan, then the pitch. The next section will outline the creation of the business plan.

THE DOCUMENT

As so much has already been written on the mechanics of the actual creation of the business plan document itself, this section will focus on an overview of the content that should be considered for inclusion in the plan. The other challenge in providing any further detailed instruction for the creation of your plan is that the content is very context-specific. It is for these reasons that this chapter will provide a detailed outline of the elements of your plan. The goal of this chapter is to challenge you to think about topics to include in your plan that may otherwise have escaped your attention.

Ernst & Young's "Guide to Producing a Business Plan" is a good, concise document to help you get started (Ernst & Young, 2001). Much of what Guy Kawasaki has written and the documents supplied on his business's website, Garage.com, are good supplemental readings. My colleague for over a decade at the University of Michigan, Paul Kirsch, calls the step in which the business plan is created the "integration" phase, as it integrates an operations view of your firm with the information generated from the previous segments of the Entrepreneurial Arch into a single document. The remainder of this section will break the plan down to into specific elements. The plan, however, is the story of *your* business. The goal is not to include every detail that could be included, but to choose those elements that are most germane to *your* business. Every business plan will be different.

The business plan has four basic sections: an introduction/summary, a recap of core elements of the feasibility assessment (industry, market, and offering), a strategy/operations section, and finally a financial/risk section. Those sections are outlined below (Faley and Kirsch, 2005b). The plan should have numbered pages and a font size (at least 11-point) and typeface that make it easy to read. It should also include a table of contents to help navigation. Major topics included in the four major sections are shown below.

The remainder of the chapter will outline each of the plan elements in more detail.

Summary/introduction

Executive summary

Company description

Industry, market, and offering (i.e. the feasibility overview)
Market
Industry and competition
Offering

Strategy and operations

Marketing and sales
Operations
Strategic relationships
Ownership and management
Action plan

Financials and risks

Risk assessment (from feasibility) and their mitigation strategies
Detailed financial discussion (note this is different from the feasibility financials)

Scope of the document

A business plan should not be a tome containing everything you know on the topic your business is addressing. It should be relatively succinct. What Albert Einstein once said about theories applies to the plan: It "should be as simple as possible, but not simpler." It should tell your story, but not in a way that would put your most enthusiastic supporter to sleep. The business plan should be around twenty pages total, including a maximum of ten pages in the appendix. Thirty pages, perhaps, if you have the full ten pages in the appendix, but it is certainly not the hundred-page document many have written. In addition, your plan is not a mystery bestseller. Most people you give the plan to will never read it in its entirety. Start with your conclusions and provide further detail as you proceed; do not leave the reader hanging until the end to determine how this business will fare! Finally, the plan is a playbook by which you will keep your extended team on point. Many investors are now looking for a ten-page plan, but that is more of an extended executive summary than an operating document. This may work for the investors, but it will not help you keep your team aligned. This is the challenge of a business plan; it is written for many audiences: Investors (Friends and Family, VCs, banks, grantors), business partners (beta customers, suppliers, distributors), and employees (management team, new recruits, etc.). First and foremost it is the operating document for your firm. It is how you are going to execute the business model that you developed in the previous segment. Included in those operational details are your strategy and tactics for mitigating the risks of the business. Investors may not want to see all that detail, at least not at their first screen, but that does not mean you do not need it.

The remainder of this section, as previously stated, will outline the content that *could* be included in each section of your business plan. Remember that each plan is unique to the context of the company that is being created. Therefore do not consider this summary prescriptive, but rather thought-stimulating. As you tell your story, you will be zooming in and out of the four elements of your business (motive, owner, activity, and monetization). Most sections of the document will include combinations of these four elements.

Introduction/summary

This first section of your business plan is intended to introduce your firm to the reader. It will provide the broadest perspective of any of the sections of your plan. It will also generate your audience's first impression of your firm. As it will be the section most read by those outside of your firm, it would be wise to make it the last item you write. It is also worth the extra time you should take in the creation of this section of your plan.

Executive summary

This is without question the most important section of your plan. It will be by far the most-read section. It is therefore essential that it accurately summarizes as well as sells your business. Given its capstone nature, it is highly recommended that this be the last part you write since it is based on the details you have provided in the rest of the business plan. This summary provides a condensed overview of your company and where you would like to take it. While I have personally seen executive summaries that range from 250 words (half a page) to 10 pages long, the true "executive" summary is short, in the order of 250 words. A "summary" of your business may be from one to three pages in length and may substitute for the executive summary. Many venture capital firms are asking for an "extended executive summary" of your plan; which is typically a five- to ten-page summary of the business. This is a condensed summary of the plan, and, as a result, excludes the operational details important to your execution of this business. That is not to say that these details are not important; they are simply not as important to investment screeners as they are to those charged with operating the firm (you). The mixed messaging here can be taken back to the need to communicate the plan to multiple audiences, as was mentioned previously.

Make no mistake, the summary, in any form, is a sales document for your firm. Like any document, it must be written from the perspective of the reader. Summaries intended to be viewed by investors must speak to how they will benefit; the fabulous returns that are possible through investing in your company. Yes, they want to help you build a great company, but they are in the business of making a return on other people's money. If you do not address the financial return potential of your business, they simply will not be that interested.

You must sell your firm. If you cannot get people excited about your firm and its potential in this section, you will not get a chance to extol its fine intricacies. This section needs to be written in an upbeat, present-tense, action-word-oriented manner. Start with a big issue that people can get passionate about. One way to insert passion is to use reductionism to connect your particular offering to a larger issue. So, for example:

> Every year 7.6 million people die from cancer. More people die from cancer than from AIDS, malaria, and tuberculosis combined. The World Health Organization projects that, without immediate action, by 2030 the global number of deaths from cancer will increase by nearly 80 percent (CDC website). Where are the cures? Hidden among a plethora of potential drug candidates, like needles in the preverbal haystack. We have developed a unique device that will allow researchers to quickly, accurately, and inexpensively locate those precious needles in those enormous haystacks: A device that will have personal and global impact.

Not this:

> Combining laser technology with the latest microfluidics research breakthroughs has led us to a patented new device for counting nano-sized particles in a moving fluid in real time. This device has a broad range of research applications in the biology and chemistry fields. Our system is equipped with a blue and a red laser, two light-scatter detectors, and four fluorescence detectors with optical filters optimized for the detection of fluorochromes such as FITC, PE, PerCP, and APC. A compact optical design, fixed alignment, and pre-optimized detector settings make the system straightforward to use. Optional filters and the Selectable Laser Module expand the available fluorochrome combinations. Pre-settings ensure the users do not need to adjust detector voltages.[1]

You do not need to say everything in this summary. Sometimes less is more. What you want is the next meeting. The point of a resumé is to get an interview; the point of an interview is to get a job offer; and the point of a job offer is to have a choice to make regarding your future employment. No one has ever handed their resumé to an employer and been offered a job without any further interaction. The executive summary is your company's resumé. It is the path to a longer conversation, or to no conversation.

Company description

This section must provide an overview of how the elements of your company fit together. The challenge here is that it must accomplish those objectives without providing a great deal of detail. You will have the opportunity to discuss each item more completely in other sections of the plan. The company description is a chance to get into more specific elements of your firm, its offering, the market, the team, and its competencies. It is also a chance to speak to the activities the firm will undertake in the creation and delivery of the offering to your customer. This section is still summary level and not meant to be explicitly detailed. This should tie the other, more detailed, sections of your plan together. Hence, this should be the second-to-last section you write – the last being the executive summary. This section ties all the pieces of the plan together. It offers a clear link between the firm's vision and the company that will realize this vision. This is a more closely focused description than the executive summary. In some business plan descriptions, this section will be a part of the executive summary.

This is also your opportunity to articulate the strategic intentions of the firm (Prahalad and Hamel, 1989). What are your corporate-level aspirations? In short, "what kind of company do you want to be?' In their 1995 book *The Discipline of Market Leaders*, Treacy and Wiersema argued that a clear strategic intent will help keep everyone in your organization aligned with the corporate vision. Do you aspire to be a "best product" firm, always having the leading-edge product: Apple, for example? Are you the low-cost producer, always looking for ways to improve on your company's efficiencies (WalMart), or are you focused on service, trying to deliver the best service to your customers (Zappos). Your growth path needs to be congruent with that vision, as do the capabilities you invest in as a corporation. Do you invest in product development, efficiency innovations, or customer service training? Startups know this truism and many corporations have also determined that being 'muddled in the middle' of the triangle Treacy and Wiersema used to explain their analysis is a formula for disaster. Again, you cannot be all things to all people. Trying to be this is a sure-fire formula for disaster.

The high-level vision for your firm should be followed with a equally high-level strategy for arriving at that destination. Professor Allan Afuah introduced three overarching corporate strategies – run, block, and team-up – to assist companies in their drive to stay sustainably differentiated (Afuah, 1999). The "run" strategy is to continually innovate to stay ahead of your competition. Intel during the early development of personal computer processor chips is a great example of that strategy. Staying on the curve of Moore's Law was a clever way to keep the entire company running. The "block" strategy is typically based on patents or other barriers to entry designed to keep others out of your space. Clearly Intel also used this strategy in the development of their microprocessors, but they knew this would only slow competitors down, not keep them totally at bay. They therefore used this strategy in combination with the "run" strategy. The "team-up" strategy appears the opposite of the "block" strategy, but the objective remains to limit your potential competition. This strategy is used in promoting your product as the industry standard, or otherwise limiting your competition by creating a limited number of strategic alliances. Many technology cross-licensing agreements, while appearing collaborative, actually succeed in limiting the firms that can compete in developing certain products.

The strategic intent and the strategy for achieving it provide a broad perspective of your firm. While this shows the big picture, this section of your plan also needs to include some specific details as well. The following outlines specific items to consider in the summary.

1. *Nature of your business:*
     Brief offering description and the customer needs being satisfied.
     Major activities conducted by your business (e.g. product design,
        manufacturing, marketing, customer service, etc.).
     Form of company (i.e. corporation, partnership, or proprietorship),
        and its origin (i.e. new, leveraged buyout, or spin-out).
     Geographic location.
2. *Your sustainable advantage and differentiated capabilities:*
     Unique assets (intellectual or physical): Differentiated know-
     how, relationships.
3. *Remaining business construct elements:*
     Primary business activities and collaborators. State what key
     activities your company will execute (e.g. R&D, product design,
     manufacturing, marketing, sales, distribution, customer service,
     etc.). State what other key activities will be done by collaborators.
     What is the collaborator's motivation to collaborate?
     Revenue model: How will the firm capture value?

Market/industry/offering

The good news is that you already have this information. The data for
this section comes straight from the feasibility assessment that you
performed in the business assessment segment of the Entrepreneurial
Arch. It is primarily a zooming in on the owner and activity elements
of the business.

Market (your customers)

This section is the articulation of your market. It sizes, segments, and
identifies your initial target market. It also discusses the directional
indicators of your market; is it growing, maturing, or declining? This is
also an opportunity to introduce the source of future firm growth
beyond this initial product and market. This is also where you describe
the persona of the target market, if you chose to discuss your market in
this way. This section is not your go-to-market strategy. That is
described later. As discussed in the business assessment segment,

there are three descriptors for sizing a market. It is important that you describe all three in this section of your plan: Number of units sold, number of customers, and the total monetary value spent. You should be able to lift this section of the plan from your feasibility assessment, including a summary of the methodology you used to segment the market and your rationale in choosing the initial target market.

This section, as in the business assessment phase, also identifies where in the value chain your firm resides. It differentiates between your customer (who you sell to) and the end user (for whom you may create additional value). This section is aimed at segmenting and quantifying the market. The plan generally covers the first five years of the firm's operations, although it may allude to potential beyond that timeframe. Chapter 7 on managing growth will discuss how to continue to grow the firm beyond that time period. Elements to consider for this section of your plan include:

1. *Overall market* (this description should come straight out of your assessment research):

    Qualitative description and distinguishing characteristics of your total addressable market and key market segments.

    Who are your customers? What is the need/desire that motivates your customer to purchase your offering? How did you segment the market (demographic, geographic, psychographic, behavioristic)?

    How are your customers' needs currently being met? Seasonal/cyclical trends.

    Quantitative description of your total addressable market.

    Size the market: Number of prospective customers, number of units purchased annually, dollar amount of annual purchases.

    Anticipated market changes: Key trends and growth trends: growing, declining, or flat.

2. *Primary/target market size:* Narrow your target markets to a manageable size. Efforts to penetrate target markets that are too broad are often ineffective. Be sure to cite sources.

Quantitative description of your primary target market. (persona description).

Size the market: Number of prospective customers, number of units purchased annually, dollar amount of annual purchases.

Anticipated market growth, decline, or steady-state situation.

Geographic location.

Market penetration: Indicate the extent to which you anticipate penetrating your market and demonstrate why you feel that level of penetration is achievable; include

- market share and number of customers
- geographic coverage
- over what time period? and
- rationale for market penetration estimates. Can you cite similar product/technology histories?

Purchasing behaviors of potential customers: How customer needs are identified and what is the evaluation process. Final selection responsibility and authority (executives, purchasing agents, engineers, etc.).

Sales cycle dimensions (days, weeks, quarters, years).

Order dynamics: Lead times (time between customer order placement and product delivery), initial orders and re-orders, and volume purchases.

Secondary target markets: Identify and size, briefly, "next" target markets. Are there linkages to your primary target market?

Will your product change as you move to your next target? How?

3. *Market feedback to date:* Potential customers contacted, information/demonstrations given to potential customers, reaction of potential customers, importance of satisfaction of targeted needs, test group's willingness to purchase products/services at various price levels.

Industry and competition

This section addresses the industry and the risk inherent to this industry. Like the marketing section, this section is straight from the feasibility assessment described in the business assessment segment. This section describes the industry, how value is currently distributed across the industry, where your firm will fit into that value system, how you know that this is a high-value problem, and how your firm will alter that distribution. This discussion will include your PVC analysis. It will also discuss the likely industry competitive response to your firm's launch.

1. *Industry description and outlook:* Description of your primary industry. Current value distribution and why this is the case. Your position in value system.

    Size of the industry, number of sellers (concentrated, diffuse, standards-driven, etc.) Historically? Currently? In five years? In ten?

    Influential value system players (e.g. dealer network for autos and auto accessories).

2. *Competition:* Identify competitors by name.

    Current market share, company status of existing major players (can you name five?). Indirect competition?

    What can you learn from the competition?

    Competitive advantages (strengths) and disadvantages (weaknesses) of key competitors:

    - ability to satisfy customer needs
    - market penetration
    - track record and reputation
    - staying power (financial resources) and
    - key personnel.

    Importance of your target market to your competition.

    Conclusion on the attractiveness of the industry based upon whether your company can make money in this environment.

    Can you capture "enough" of the value you have created for your customer? PVC positioning.

Offering

This is a detailed description of the offering, including the activities that the firm will perform in its creation and delivery to the customer. It will discuss the status of the offering's development. The offering's differentiation and its source, including intellectual property protection, are also outlined here. The long-term sustainability of that differentiation is also discussed. This offering description should avoid technical jargon. It should clearly show the alignment of your capabilities to the offering's features/attributes and how those attributes connect to the value proposition to the customer. This is also your opportunity to mention the product development process your team went through to discover and affirm that alignment. There is a note on the product development process and its alignment with the Entrepreneurial Arch in Appendix E of this book.

1. *Detailed offering description* (from the user's perspective):

    Specific customer benefits of product: Value proposition (better, faster, cheaper), cost avoidance. Can you quantify at least one order of magnitude (10 × or 1/10th) improvement?

    Competitive advantages, key product differentiators. Connect the business value proposition to your capabilities.

    Present stage of development (idea, prototype, beta, small commercial production runs, etc.).

    Product life cycle.

2. *Intellectual property: Copyrights, patents, and trade secrets:*

    Existing copyrights or patents. Anticipated and pending copyright and patent filings. Key aspects of your products that cannot be patented or copyrighted; aspects of your products or operations that qualify as trade secrets.

    Existing legal agreements with owners and employees; non-disclosure and non-competing agreements.

3. *Research and development activities:*

    Activities (and status) in process; future activities (include milestones). Anticipated results of future research and development

activities: New products or services, new generations of existing
products or services, complementary products or services,
replacement products or services.

Research and development activities of others in your industry.

Strategy and operations

While the previous sections of your plan contained content that was
developed during the business discovery process, the content in this
section is primarily new. That being said, the information presented in
this section is grounded in the knowledge acquired in the business
design and business assessment segments of the Arch.

Marketing and sales

This section contains information from the marketing section of the
feasibility assessment, but zooms in closer to a go-to-market launch
strategy. This section picks up where the marketing section ended
with the description of the target market segment or persona. It then
describes the positioning statement for that segment (below). Beyond
the positioning statement is a discussion of precisely how you intend
to launch your offering.

Clearly articulated positioning statement

For ... (target segment/persona)
The ... (product/service)
Satisfies ... (most important user need)
By delivering ... (key benefit or feature)
Through/via/created by our ... (underlying capability)

One of the elements of the marketing mix that you are developing is
price. In the assessment segment of the Arch you had an offering price
you hoped to attain at some future point in time. This does not mean
that this will be the price of the initial offering. You may need to adjust
the price to drive early adoption. Given that it is challenging to raise

prices later, you may want to consider early-adopter discounts. Providing a temporary 100 percent discount is not the same as your offering being free. Whatever pricing inducements you may make to accelerate adoption must also be reflected in the financial statements you will be creating.

1. *Overall marketing strategy* (e.g. cost leadership, product differentiation, specialization, etc.):

    Price: Strategic consideration (e.g. skimming, penetration, comparable); pricing approach: cost-based, market-based or value-based; gross margin target levels and industry comparables; and discount structure (volume, prompt payment, etc.).

    Promotion: Strategic direction (push or pull); methods to identify members in your target market (e.g. directories, trade association publications or government documents); methods to reach members of your target market (e.g. publications, radio/television broadcasts, tradeshows, scientific conferences, advertising, public relations, personal selling, or printed materials, etc.).

    Place (distribution channels): Methods that will be employed for distribution (e.g. original equipment manufacturers, outside agents, distributors, wholesalers, value-added resellers, third-party resellers, storefront operations, other retailers, franchises, internet, etc.).

2. *Go-to-market strategies:*

    Current status of sales: Beta customers (revenue; converting to revenue) and reaching new customers via these relationships; paying customers.

    Sales force: Internal vs. external; justification of your decision; size; recruitment, training and compensation.

    Sales activities: Average number of sales calls per sale; average dollar size per sale; average dollar size per reorder; number of sales calls made per period; identifying and prioritizing prospects.

Operations

This section speaks less to the five risks an investor may be weighing with respect to your firm (industry, market, product, team, and financing) and more to how you will move this company forward. The mitigation of these risks is addressed in the financials and risks section of the plan. This section is therefore of lesser interest to your potential investors, but remains important to keeping the efforts of your new employees in alignment. This is your "go-to-battle" plan; a summary of how you will get done all the things done you need to do in addition to marketing and sales for this company to be successful.

Details to consider in this section include:

1. *Production, service, delivery, processes and capacity:*
   Internal, external (contractors).
   Anticipated increases in capacity: Investment; new cost factors (direct and indirect); timing.
2. *Operating competitive advantages:*
   Techniques.
   Advantaged capabilities (know-how, assets, experience, etc.).
   Economies of scale, capital efficiencies.
3. *Suppliers:*
   Identification of the suppliers of critical elements of production: Primary and secondary, lead-time requirements, evaluation of the risks of critical element shortages, and description of the existing and anticipated contractual relationships with suppliers.
4. *Tactics for growth:*
   Horizontal (providing similar products to different users).
   Vertical (providing the products at different levels of the distribution chain).
   Internally driven.
   Acquisition.
   Franchise.

Strategic relationships

This is a close-up discussion of the key collaborators that you identified during the business design segment. It could also include partnerships that were formed if your firm was in the upper left-hand quadrant
of the PVC framework. Generally, strategic relationships are agreements between two or more enterprises to conduct specified business
processes, usually related to technology development, or marketing
and distribution efforts. Each party should gain from the partnership or
its viability is doubtful.

1. *Vendors, R&D relationships, value chain partners:*
   What is their motivation to engage?
2. *Define nature of relationship:*
   Give and take; risk and investment. What is the win–win
   proposition? On what terms will dissolution occur?

Ownership and management

Your management team's talents and skills are some of the few truly
unique aspects of your company. This section focuses on the team,
including advisors, and its capabilities as these relate to the firm and
the opportunity that the firm is addressing. Highlight key members of
the management team and explain why they are key, demonstrating
relevance through the capabilities.

1. *Management staff structure:*
   Three to six people (resumés should be in the appendix). Fewer
   and the team feels incomplete; more and it lacks focus,
   cohesiveness.
   Has this team worked together before?
   Are all issues of ownership agreed upon?
   Management and key staff organization chart with brief narrative
   description.
2. *Key managers* (resumés should be in the appendix):
   Name; position (brief description with primary responsibilities);
   unique skills and experiences that add to your company's

distinctive competencies; compensation basis and levels; salary, benefits and equity. Are levels reasonable – not too high and not too low – to retain key talent?

3. *Planned additions to the current management team:*

Position; brief position description, authority, primary duties responsibilities; requisite skills and experience; recruitment timing and process; compensation basis and levels.

4. *Legal structure and ownership:*

Corporation, partnership, proprietorship.

Ownership by name with percentage ownership and extent of involvement with the company if not addressed in the previous section.

Form of ownership (e.g. common or preferred stock, general or limited partner).

Option pool and outstanding equity equivalents (e.g. options, warrants, convertible debt, etc.).

Common stock (authorized and issued).

5. *Board of directors:*

Names and backgrounds of board members; extent of involvement with the company; contribution to the company's success, historically and anticipated.

Action plan

This plan with specific milestones is an important concluding segment to the operations section of your plan. It should summarize the major steps in the development of your firm and its offering. These development steps should be time-bound. This is essentially your company's Gantt chart without the graphics. Milestones should focus on items that are within the firm's control and are the firm's responsibility. Discussion of milestones should always include estimates for product launch and/or first sale date. Regulatory hurdles and reasonable time expectations should be included here despite the fact that the ultimate decision is not the company's responsibility. Milestones should be tied to activities that de-risk the firm. Anticipated funding infusions should also be included on this list and tied to accomplishment of specific milestones. Whether or not this section is part of your plan's "operations section," it needs to be called out in the table of contents of the document for easy location. While initially the investors may not be interested in the details of your operating plan, they will be interested in this list as it ties directly to funding.

Financials and risks

Risks and mitigation strategies

The critical success factors (CSFs) derived in the feasibility assessment are included here. Beyond the risks derived from the financial analysis, externalities that could deeply impact the firm's chances of success are also articulated in this section of your plan. The five major risks that investors assess – industry, market, product, team, and financial – need to be addressed somewhere in your business plan as do the specific strategies for mitigating them. Those items that are not addressed elsewhere should be covered here. My preference is to see the major risks and their mitigation strategies in a single location in the plan, but they must flow with the story you are telling. It is fine to refer back to other sections of the document (marketing and sales, for example) so as not to repeat yourself. Common specific risk categories include:

- *Technology:* What if the science or technology does not perform? Or, what if the technology does not perform in the final product?
- *Market:* What if customers do not pay (or pay less than expected) for your product? Or, what if the market adoption rates are lower than planned?
- *Competition:* What if there are more competitors than you anticipated? Or, what if their response is much stronger than anticipated?
- *Management:* What if you do not have the right people in the right roles?
- *Execution:* What if you are doing the wrong things to generate the required results?

- *Regulatory:* What if your product will not satisfy current or pending regulations?
- *Financial:* What if you end up with insufficient funds to continue or the next round is in question?
- *Other externalities:*
  - Regulators (e.g. FDA for drugs and devices): Methods, cost and time involved for meeting the requirements.
  - Anticipated changes in regulatory requirements.
  - Governments and anticipated legislation.

Financial discussion

The financial analysis performed in the business assessment segment of the Arch aimed to determine the feasibility of the firm. That analysis was also used to elucidate the firm's CSFs. The factors in the operation section focus on cash flow and its management. These are two very different analyses which serve very different purposes. The assessment analysis focused on the potential return on investment. The analysis here focuses on how much money the firm will need to accomplish particular tasks over given period(s). It is an operational view of the use and generation of cash. That operational view will tell you nothing about the feasibility of the firm, just as the feasibility financial analysis will tell you nothing about the specific burn rate the firm will incur during its product development. Once investors have decided your firm is worthy of investment, they will focus on the amount of capital, and time, you will need to accomplish your next milestone. That is a cash-flow view of the business. As a result you will need to create five-year cash flow pro formas (income statements, balance sheets, and statements of cash flows). The first year of the five-year pro forma statements is typically reported in months or quarters, while the more distant years are reported in years. These statements are typically inserted in the appendix of the business plan and discussed in this section of your plan. These pro forma statements need to tell the same story as the text in your business plan; they simply use a different language in telling the tale.

Preparing the pro forma statements is a difficult and time-consuming task. Since the creation of pro forma statements is typically taught by extending existing statements, even those with backgrounds in finance balk at their creation from a blank spreadsheet. Take heart, you know more than you believe. In your feasibility assessment you projected revenue. You also projected EBITDA margins at some future point in time (typically at your firm's exit). Start at that future point and build your pro forma income statement by working backwards from there to the present. Keep in mind that resources must precede revenue. You may have projected that your SG&A costs, for example, will run at 35 percent of sales. Since you need the resources in place before the sales, you cannot put SG&A costs at 35 percent in each period as the firm transitions through a period of accelerated growth. One approach is to assume that SG&A costs will be at 35 percent of the *next* period's sales. Since the sales are growing, this will make it a significantly higher percentage of the current period's sales. Using this working-backwards technique will allow you to build a rational pro forma statement.

1. *Historical financials:*

   Discussion of performance to date; include current levels of profit, margin, cash flow, etc. If appropriate, note the name of your accountant and level of involvement (e.g. audit, review, compilation, etc.).

2. *Prospective financials:*

   Discussion of next twelve months.

   Discussion of the following four years.

   Summary of significant assumptions. This summary is of critical importance to any future discussion and will impact on all future discussion topics including valuation. What are the bases of the management's forecasts?

   Analysis: Discussion of historical and prospective financial statements. The statements themselves will be in the appendix.

   Sensitivity analyses: "What-if" scenarios, tied to assumptions.

Funds and uses

Any new or additional funding reflected in your prospective financial statements should be discussed here. Alternative funding scenarios can be presented; however, your preferred situation should form the bulk of the discussion. Investors will invest an amount of money to get you to the next significant milestone. Accomplishing milestones de-risks your business, time does not. Never ask for funding solely for a specific period of time; always to pass a specific milestone. Of course the milestone will be time-bound, but it is passing the milestone that is important to the investor, not the passage of time.

1. *Current funding requirements:*
    Amount and timing.
    Type (e.g. equity, debt, mezzanine, etc.).
    General overview of key terms.
    What milestones will be achieved and what risk will be
        mitigated?
2. *Use of funds:*
    Capital expenditures.
    Working capital.
    Other start-up costs such as equipment, leases, legal issues
        (licenses, permits, insurance), utilities, pre-revenue salaries.
    Debt retirement.
    Acquisitions.
3. *Funding requirements over the next five years:*
    Amount and timing
    Type (e.g. equity, debt, mezzanine, etc.).
    General overview of key terms.
    Primary purpose(s) of subsequent rounds of funding; that is, what
        milestones will be achieved and what risk will be mitigated?
4. *Long-range financial strategies a.k.a. exits:*
    IPO, i.e. going public.
    Acquisition; be sure to name likely acquirers and refer to current
        acquisition activity.

Management buyout or dividend distributions.
Liquidation of the venture.

Business plan summary

Every story, and therefore every business plan, will be different. While
the elements of every business plan are similar, the story they tell is
quite unique. The story of your business should be interesting and
compelling. Yes, it should be interesting. There are many, many details
to include in the plan, absolutely, but it should retain the passion you
have for the venture. Do not allow that passion to get lost in the details.
Imagine your parents writing the story of the first few years of your life,
shortly before you were born. Would it be boring and dry? Would it
focus on the number of diaper changes? The sleepless nights your
parents will suffer? Absolutely not! It would be positive, optimistic,
and full of passion. It would be realistic; it would not say you were
going to win a Nobel Prize at age five. Nor would it avoid the challenges you will face. But it would be touching, poignant, and passionate. Feel that when you are writing the story of your business.

THE PITCH

Pitching is fundamental to entrepreneurship. That does not mean,
however, that it comes naturally to entrepreneurs. To most it does
not. Like any of the skills of entrepreneurship, the skill of pitching
improves with practice. Large firms have marketing departments, in
small ones every single employee is marketing the company to one
extent or another. At the very least they are raising awareness of the
company. One of the questions most interviewees dread is "tell me
about yourself." Any time you are with a group of people and work
for a small firm you will be asked to "tell me about your firm."
Every employee at every level will get this inquiry. Clearly answering this query is most important to the firm's leadership, but every
employee that answers it will leave an impression of the firm
behind. That means every employee must be become skilled in the
art of pitching.

There are three different types of business pitch: The core concept opener, the elevator pitch, and the investor pitch. We will start with the core concept opener, which will be your initial response to that "tell me about your firm" question. It is always worth searching YouTube for some pitching examples. You will find good, bad, and ugly ones. Once you have reviewed the material below you should able to recognize the difference easily. Humor can be your friend in these pitches, but do not overdo it for you want to make sure you and your business are taken seriously. You also want to make sure the pitch you make is true to your personality. If you give a disingenuous pitch, the listener may translate that to an untrustworthy business.

Core concept opener

This is the introduction of your firm. It is also an invitation for your audience to ask for more detail. This is one or two sentences about your business that can ideally be expressed in one breath. It should always end with an invitation to discuss what your firm does in greater depth. The trick is to make it compelling without getting into too much detail. Every early employee in the firm should be provided with the core message the management wants delivered in the core concept opener.

When people ask what I do, I say:

> I teach courses and create experiential learning programs that accelerate the development of the next generation of serial entrepreneurs and venture investors. I'd be happy to tell you more, if you are interested.

You want to make it easy for your audience to ask a question. These are the hooks. If your summary is complete, there is simply no place from which the conversation can begin. One of the hooks in my opening sentence is "experiential learning." Many people outside academia are not familiar with "experiential learning." I do not define it in my single sentence, but it creates a natural opening for many people to ask their first question – "what is experiential learning?" Then the conversation has begun.

Elevator pitch

The elevator pitch derives its name from an elevator ride. If a person asked you to tell them about your firm as you were stepping onto an elevator, you would have to be able to finish before you exit. The elevator pitch is generally considered to be one to three minutes in length. Many universities have competitions for this type of pitch and make the contestants finish their talk within three minutes. Wake Forrest University used to run a very creative pitch contest in which they actually made contestants give their pitches while riding an elevator!

To have a very tight, yet very complete elevator pitch, it is useful to first write it down. Some guidelines are helpful. The first guideline is that average speech rate in the United States is about 150 words per minute. If you are excited about what you are discussing, that rate might increase to 200 words per minute. That means your three-minute pitch cannot contain more than 600 words. Of course, you *can* talk faster, but your audience will not be able to absorb all you say if you talk that briskly. They will either pick out parts of your talk as important or miss your message entirely in the verbal onslaught. You are in a much better position than your audience to pull out the important aspects of your business, so do that work for them.

On one hand, putting all the individual aspects of your business into a 600-word description is a challenge. On the other hand, three minutes is a long time to hold your audience's complete attention. Begin your pitch by giving a reason why they should pay attention to the rest of the two-and-a-half minutes or so. As was the case with the executive summary, you could capture this compelling connection by zooming out – putting your firm in the context of a larger picture. You could also make this connection by zooming in – personalizing the impact that your firm will have. In the executive summary section of this chapter I gave you an example of how to create an emotive connection between your audience and a medical device firm by zooming out. The following example is crafted by first zooming in, personalizing the message, before zooming out:

> We have all been touched by a cancer death. My first loss came when
> I was seven and my grandmother died of breast cancer. She was my
> card-playing buddy – that loss was devastating to me. The statistics –
> 7.6 million die of cancer every year – do not begin to capture the pain
> and loss felt by those left behind. Where are the new cures? Lost in
> the research labs. My firm is developing a unique device that will
> allow medical researchers to sort out the promising drug candidates
> from the thousands being evaluated, quickly, accurately, and
> inexpensively; a task that is expensive and painfully slow today.

That short introduction is 106 words, or about 32 seconds at 200 words
per minute. It zooms in by personalizing the problem in a way that
every audience member can understand. It then zooms out to capture
the scope of the problem, followed by a brief introduction of the firm's
first offering. Now that your audience has some context, it is more
likely to be receptive to hearing the details of your business. The best
feedback for an elevator pitch, as it was for your core concept pitch is
"tell me more." The worst is showing no understanding of why the
business is being created in the first place. I once heard a judge in a
pitch competition say to a team, "I understand your product, its costs,
and how you plan to produce and market it. I simply do not understand
why anyone would care." That's painful feedback. Remember, people
need a reason to do something differently than they are doing it now.
Your new offering will more than likely force them to change their
behavior in some way. There must be some compelling reason, some
motivational force, to overcome the inertia. If not, they simply will not
change.

Beyond the introduction of the opportunity, the elevator pitch
should cover an overview of your business. While the elements of your
business model should be included, the order will be that which best
fits your story. These elements include:

1. *Customers:*

    What is your target persona? (Need-based market segment?)
    What is the compelling need/desire? Value proposition?

What willingness to pay has been shown?

Size the market (number of buyers, units sold, currency value of sales).

2. *Offering:*

What precisely is your product/service?

How much will it cost to produce?

Is it unique? How will you stay differentiated?

What does the company do in the creation of this offering? How does this align with the team's capabilities?

3. *Collaborators:*

Why will they collaborate with you? What value do you create/ problem do you solve for the your customer and collaborator?

4. *Financial:*

How does your company make money (revenue model)?

What type and how much funding do you believe will turn this plan into reality? Are the projected returns congruent with the investor type?

Financial feasibility is dominated by what business elements?

Keep in mind that, if pitching to potential investors, they are thinking of their five risks: industry, market, team, product, and financial. Recall that investors typically pre-screen deals based on industry, so their focus, if they are in your audience, will be on the other four risks. That is, the order listed is the order they are most immediately concerned about, so do not spend your entire pitch talking about the product when they are more interested in the market and the team. Clearly you will have to make choices about what to leave in and what to leave out given the time constraint. If collaborators are not a huge element of your firm's success, leave that piece out. If, on the other hand, you need to establish key partnerships in order to be successful, you may want to focus on progress to date in the development of those partnerships. As you can see, it all depends on the specifics of your firm. Discussing your new firm is idiosyncratic and contextual, making it impossible to state specifically what "must" be included in your presentation.

Investor pitch

After you have prepared a three-minute elevator pitch, preparing for a fifteen- to thirty-minute investor pitch may seem easy. After all, you have so much more time! That is the downfall of many teams – trying to tell their *entire* story. Even if you are given thirty minutes to present at an investor's office, you should plan on using twenty minutes. Something will go wrong. The partners will be late or need to leave early, the projector will malfunction, your carefully planned demonstration will lock up, you will be interrupted by questions, etc. Something will happen. You want to make sure you complete your presentation. There is nothing worse than being on slide eighteen of a fifty-two-slide deck when the meeting ends. (Of course you should *never* have a fifty-two-slide deck, but we will get to that.)

The first thing you need to know to prepare your presentation is how long you will have to present. Honor that time. Do not be that entrepreneur who thinks the time limit does not apply to them. Guy Kawasaki of Garage.com has written and talked extensively about investor pitches. It is worth reviewing some of his materials before your presentation, particularly his 2013 blog entry that includes an example slide deck – eleven slides! That's right, he does not use the thirty slides you think he should. You should think minutes of presentation per slide, not slides per minute. Remember, frames per second is how they describe movie projection rates. You do not want your slide show to be a continuous blur to your audience. Instead, make it a series of captivating still photos; you want each frame to be memorable.

The content of your investor pitch will be the entire business plan as outlined at the beginning of this chapter. Of course, you cannot review your entire plan in that time. You will need to tailor that presentation to your audience. You need the right message for the right audience, clearly articulated and delivered with passion!

The remainder of this section will discuss the things you should consider before you present, keys to building a successful presentation, the actual delivery, a few tips to creating compelling visual slides, and finally some tips on handling questions.[2]

Before you present
Any communication should begin with the audience and the pitch is no different. Who is your audience? Are they business professionals or investors familiar with the area in which you are launching your business? If so, you can skip a great deal of fundamental background. If you do need to provide that education, do so in a way that does not have the slightest hint of condescension.

What is the purpose of your pitch? Are you trying to attract potential employees to the firm? Demonstrate the ability of the management team? Convince investors of the value of your business? This will allow you to focus. Understand that if you cannot deliver a focused presentation, the audience will assume you cannot manage a focused company. This is an important judgment when focus is critical to any new venture. You may think that unfair, but it is real.

What is the occasion of your presentation? Is it a business plan contest? A venture or growth capital event? Are you presenting to bankers or investors in their office? Understand the format that goes along with the occasion. The time, which I mentioned before, is the most important. Show respect for your audience by adhering to the allotted time. Can you expect questions to come at you throughout your presentation or will they be asked only after you have completed your talk? Is this a formal occasion or more casual? Will you be projecting your slide presentation or walking through copies of your slides one-on-one or one–one–few?

Building the presentation
Like theater productions, presentations generally have three acts: The introduction, the body, and the conclusion. The introduction should only take 10 percent of your speaking time and the conclusion only 5 percent. That's one or two slides (maximum) for the introduction and one for your conclusion. The remainder is dedicated to the body of your

presentation. This presentation approach is sometimes described as "tell them what you are going to tell them," "tell them," "tell them what you told them." Simple but effective. Most importantly, it contains the key element of persuasion – repetition.

The introduction needs to capture your audience's interest. It should get their attention, state the goal of the presentation (including an outline of the agenda for the remainder of the presentation), and introduce the team. The introduction is your opportunity to manage expectations. There is no one in the room with a deeper knowledge of your business or more passionate about its success than you.

The body of your presentation contains the key elements that you need to communicate to this specific audience. You have your entire business plan to pull from in the creation of this portion of your presentation. The elements you choose to emphasize should be consistent with both the audience and your objectives for the presentation. If you are pitching for an investment, you must talk from the investor's perspective. I have heard too many entrepreneurs tell investors that they can "help us build a great company." Yes, angel and venture investors are in the business of building businesses,[3] but they are primarily seeking a return on their investment (Chesbrough, 2003, 2006; Hamermesh, 2002; Osterwalder and Pigneur, 2010; Kawasaki, 2004). It is a huge miss to ask for money and not talk about how that investment will help the investor.

The heart of your presentation will draw on the same elements as outlined in the elevator pitch. While you will have more time to talk about these elements in more detail, you will still have limited time. As was the case with the elevator pitch, you will need to choose the elements that must be included, and of those, which will be expanded upon and which will only be highlighted. Like the elevator pitch, the order of the elements presented will be determined by the approach you are taking to tell the story of your business. Keep the risk factors in mind. The investors first invest in the tide (market) as a strong tide will raise all ships. They then look at the crew (the team) because a skilled crew will be able to make the on-the-fly adjustments necessary for the ship to reach its final destination through uncharted waters and unpredictable storms. Lastly they look at the ship (product). This is last because a good crew will understand that they will need to make adjustments to the ship as they proceed. Most entrepreneurs instinctively want to pitch in the opposite order. Ignore your instincts and follow the lead of your audience.

The body of your presentation will hammer your point home in many different ways. Mixing facts, statistics, research, and customer quotes allows you to vary the illustrative supporting data. Varying how you visually present the information, in addition to the type of information, will allow the presentation to be visually interesting.

The conclusion is your chance to create a final and lasting impression. Restate the goal, review the main points, and clearly state your call to action. That call to action is typically an "ask" of some kind: Asking a potential employee to join your team, or asking an investor to invest in your firm. Of course, neither is going to agree to do so on the spot. The details of "resourcing" will be covered in the next chapter and include a section on due diligence. This "ask" is but a step toward the end result you are seeking.

You will get questions. No presentation is so complete that it leaves no questions unanswered. On the contrary, questions are a sign of interest. Embrace them, anticipate them, and prepare back-up slides to answer them. When preparing your presentation anticipate questions you may receive. Much of the detail that you believe should be in your original presentation should be in back-up slides in case you receive those questions.

The delivery

Your presentation starts well before the moment you stand up to speak. Are you asked to sit in the lobby and wait for a bit? Do you show signs of nervousness and general unease or do you exude confidence? It is, of course, natural to be nervous, but you are the world's expert on the topic you are about to discuss – your firm. Be confident. We are all always learning, so there is no need to be arrogant, but you have every reason to be confident. Look to the role you are projecting. Are you are a scientist striving to be the CEO of your new firm? Then enter the meeting looking like a startup CEO and not as though you spent all night in the lab. You may be one of those that shirk at the 'dress for success' approach, thinking they will clearly see how brilliant you are. They may, but why do you want to start with an image you have to overcome? Why not put yourself in control of the first impression you desire to make? After you have made your first billion you can wear whatever you want and people will think you are eccentric. Before that first billion, they simply think you are odd.

Remind yourself that presentations are part theater. Of course you want to be genuine and passionate, but you also need to keep your audience's attention for fifteen to thirty minutes. To do that you must have variation in your delivery pace, your tone, and in the slides you are presenting. Be conscious of your posture and body language. Glaring at your audience with your arms crossed when they ask you a "dumb" question will not get you any points. Part of what investors are assessing is whether or not they can work with you. They want to know whether you are "coachable." They do not have the time or interest to constantly butt heads with an intransigent first-time entrepreneur. There are other deals in their pipeline, other fish in the sea. Be the hungriest, most attractive fish, not the ugliest and most ornery one.

Eye contact is extremely important. In the sciences it is often said that an introvert looks at his own shoes while an extrovert scientist looks at the other person's shoes! Look into their eyes. Read the non-verbal cues. Do they "get" the message you are intending to deliver with the slide you are on, even though you had more to say? If they understand, move on. Remain upbeat and energetic. Passion and energy sell. When you enter a room to present, own the room. Introduce yourself and your team. Project confidence.

Credibility is crucial. You are assumed to have it when you enter the room. Do not destroy that. Check the math on your presentation slides. You will constantly be updating your market numbers, your cost estimates, and your financial projections. Make sure these numbers all get transferred to your presentation. Investors pick up on math errors and inconsistencies. Do not get caught with one number for your market size on slide 3 and a different value for that market on slide 5. They will notice. Do not use the "we hope," "we think," or "we believe" phrases. Use evidenced-based arguments. "Our preliminary market research suggests ... " is much stronger than "we believe." Remember you are being tested on your ability to change if the data suggests your current hypothesis is incorrect. Investors are not looking for a leader that simply "believes." When asked a question you do not know the answer to, avoid two common responses: Answering a different question from the one you were asked, or saying "I don't know." The first response gives you the appearance of being evasive, which will kill your credibility. The second could make you appear ignorant. Of course, you may not know. It is certainly fine not to know, but saying "I don't know" suggests that you have not even considered the point or do not think it is important. The asker thinks it is important. If you need clarification on the question, ask for it. If you have looked into the question, but have not reached a conclusion, say so. It is much more powerful to say "that is a very important issue for the firm and we are still in the process of getting our arms around that" than to simply say "I don't know."

Finally, when presenting, have fun. Be honest, be passionate, and be enthusiastic. Just as every person is not going to be a customer to your company, not every investor is going to be interested in providing funds for your firm. You are looking for a good match, a long-term investment partner. Take your time and try to enjoy the dating process. This is your dream, savor the ride.

COMMON MISTAKES

Part of what makes the creation of a good business plan so difficult is the number of goals the plan is trying to achieve and the number of audiences at which it is aimed. First and foremost, it is an operating document, used to guide the internal workings of the firm. The biggest mistake entrepreneurs make is forgetting that primary purpose. Instead, they treat the creation of the document as an item on a check-list that must be performed, but is not terribly important. That attitude results in a very uninspired plan that will make it unnecessarily difficult for the entrepreneur to attract any resources (people or capital).

As an operating document, it will capture the strategies and tactics the firm will use to mitigate identified risks. Of course, before articulating the mitigation strategies, the plan must first discuss the risks and their impact on the firm. In doing this, the plan summarizes the feasibility assessment. The plan, however, is not a feasibility study and cannot replace one. The financial assessment in a business plan is completely different from those performed during the assessment phase. It is a mistake to confuse the two.

Entrepreneurs sometimes forget that the plan, particularly the executive summary, is selling the firm. Not the product, not the team, but the entire firm. Instead, they get focused on a single element of the firm, such as product details, and forget the big picture: What's the problem, who owns it, how are you solving it, and how will you make money doing so?

The financial section of the business plan causes many entrepreneurs fits. The financials will never be correct, but they do need to be rational. You want to avoid losing credibility with your spreadsheets. Many first-time entrepreneurs show cash flows that never go negative. That is a big credibility destroyer, as such a situation is just not possible. There are always expenditures that are incurred before sales revenue is booked.

In presentations, common mistakes usually stem from trying to say too much in the allotted time. This leads presenters to talk too fast, put too much detailed information on each slide, which causes them to use too small a font (anything less than 18 point is too small). Less is more is the mantra. Put all that detail in back-up slides you may use in answering questions. Focus on communicating your main message.

If you have more than one slide in your presentation, please put numbers on all the slides. How do you expect anyone to ask you a specific question regarding a specific slide if there are no numbers on them? There is nothing more awkward in the Q&A session after a talk than to hear someone ask "Can you go back to the slide with the green graphic on the bottom?" You do not want to be the entrepreneur nervously fumbling through their slides looking for that particular slide. Make it easy on yourself and your audience; put numbers on your slides.

Finally, make sure everyone in your firm can articulate a clear and consistent core concept opener; one or two sentences that describe(s) the essence of your firm. This will be the best marketing investment you can make as a young firm.

SUMMARY

The business plan makes your business real. It marks the transition from business discovery to business execution. Before the creation of the plan, you may have been doing much of your work in stealth mode. Maybe it felt more like a project you were working on and less like something that was going to be real. The plan makes it real. The plan provides a means for you to start communicating the essence of your business. You need to attract customers, collaborators, and resources. You will need the plan and various ways to pitch your business. Accordingly, this chapter talks about the business plan as a communication tool and discusses the three types of pitch:

- *Core concept opener.* One or two sentences that describe the essence of your firm. This ends with an invitation to discuss the new venture in more detail.
- *Elevator pitch.* One- to three-minute monologue that provides a brief overview of the aspects of your firm: The issue the firm is addressing, your solution, the size of the opportunity, etc. Ends in a "happy to tell you more" offer.

- *Investor pitch*. Fifteen- to thirty-minute presentation with visual
  aids that details the opportunity, the company, and the team.
  Typically ends in a specific ask, a call to action.

The chapter also provided a detailed outline of all the elements that
could be included in your business plan. Given the uniqueness of every
business every plan will be different. In the preparation of your plan,
you will need to determine which of these detailed elements are
important to include in your plan, which should be no more than
twenty to thirty pages long. An outline of those plan elements is
given below.

- *Summary/introduction:*
    Executive summary; company description.
- *Industry, market, and offering* (i.e. the feasibility overview):
    Market; industry and competition; offering.
- *Strategy and operations:*
    Marketing and sales; operations; strategic relationships;
    ownership and management; action plan.
- *Financials and risks:*
    Assessment of risks (from feasibility assessment) and mitigation
    strategies; detailed financial discussion (note this is different from
    the feasibility financials).

The business assessment segment of the Arch completed the business
model and performed a feasibility assessment. It told you what the
business was and what elements had the greatest impact on its success
or failure. It did not tell you how the business would operate, nor how
you would mitigate those risks. The business plan does that. Before you
can actually execute that plan, you need to acquire resources. Those
resources will come in the form of human and financial capital.
Resourcing the business is the next segment of the Entrepreneurial
Arch and the subject of the next chapter.

NOTES

1. Technical description of the BD Accuri C6 flow cytometer from BD
   Biosciences website. Retrieved November 11, 2013 from www.
   bdbiosciences.com/instruments/accuri/features/index.jsp. To be fair, this is
   not BD's marketing pitch for this product, but sadly sounds like a pitch made
   by many technical founders of startup companies.
2. Many of these tips originated with Paul S. Kirsch, my long-time colleague at
   the University of Michigan (2003–13). They are included with his
   permission.
3. Ian Bund, Plymouth Venture Partners, personal communications.

6   Resourcing the business

You have a plan for executing your business, but that plan is dependent upon resources. This segment is about marshaling the resources you need to launch your business. The resources that you will need will, in turn, depend on human and financial capital, the emphasis of this chapter. The final segment of the Entrepreneurial Arch, managing growth, will cover the challenges involved in the continued addition of people and resources to the firm as you grow beyond the first five years. This chapter will focus on acquiring the resources you need to survive those critical first five years.

Entrepreneurs tend to focus on obtaining the financing for their business, but financiers tend to focus on the management team. Clearly you need both in order to launch a successful firm. It is a chicken-and-egg problem for those launching new firms. Jim Collins, author of *Good to Great*, said that great leaders start with people (Collins, 2001b). They "get the right people on the bus, the wrong people off the bus, and the right people in the right seats." He summarizes why in this way:

> First, if you begin with "who," you can more easily adapt to a
> fast-changing world. If people get on your bus because of where they
> think it's going, you'll be in trouble when you get 10 miles down the
> road and discover that you need to change direction because the
> world has changed. But if people board the bus principally because of
> all the other great people on the bus, you'll be much faster and
> smarter in responding to changing conditions. Second, if you have
> the right people on your bus, you don't need to worry about
> motivating them. The right people are self-motivated: Nothing
> beats being part of a team that is expected to produce great results.
> And third, if you have the wrong people on the bus, nothing else

matters. You may be headed in the right direction, but you still won't achieve greatness. Great vision with mediocre people still produces mediocre results (Collins, 2001a).

This chapter will begin with a discussion of people. It will be followed by a discussion of capital. Due diligence will be a part of the discussion on acquiring capital as no institution will provide your team capital without some level of due diligence. Start with people, then money.

PEOPLE

Assembling your initial team is critical to a successful start. Clearly, you want team members that have complementary skill sets and will drive the success of the business, but think of skills needed now *and* in the future. Will your team be able to grow with your business? Hire people as you need them – you do not want your payroll to be any larger than it needs to be. When you are recruiting employees, think about the alignment of your team's objectives with your own. Does your partner wish for a three-person business, while you want to grow the venture quickly? Ask questions, discuss visions. Do not assume everyone's career and personal ambitions are the same as your own. "Being successful" can mean different things to different people.

Beyond your personnel, your company also needs specific, formal and informal, business relationships – from business advisors to suppliers to beta customers to web designers to bankers to accountants and corporate lawyers. Think of these relationships as extensions of your company. Keep them consistent with the goals, values, and needs of your venture.

You know that the business is not going to unfold exactly as you wrote it up in your business plan. That plan is your best projection based on your current understanding. Your knowledge will increase once the business launches. As your understanding changes, you will need to adjust your plan accordingly, just as von Moltke said about first contact with the enemy. This adjustment may come one mile down the road and not ten! You therefore need people that can adjust, that are

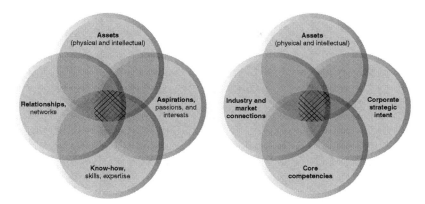

FIGURE 6.1 Personal or team capability map

flexible. This is why investors repeat the mantra that an "A" team with a "B" idea will outperform an "A" idea with a "B" team.

You will need people that align with the capability needs of your firm. The capabilities are shown in the capability map in Figure 6.1.

The vertical spheres represent "hard" capabilities: Assets and know-how. The horizontal circles represent "soft" skills: Relationships and aspirations/passion. What matter are the capabilities of the entire team, including the advisors. Advisors are particularly useful in expanding your networks. Every startup should have a set of advisors. These can range from informal advisors to formal advisory boards. Regardless of how they are organized, your firm should have some. When asking someone to advise your firm, frame the commitment for them. How many times can they expect to be contacted (daily, monthly, quarterly)? How long are you asking them to serve in this capacity (six months, a year, forever)? For early-stage startups, the advisors are typically uncompensated. You will be pleasantly surprised how many will be willing to help you should you only ask.

One capability that is often emphasized is "passion." Many claim to have it. What they really have, I believe, is temporary excitement. Passion is the willingness to give up some semblance of a "normal life" to achieve your goal. This is very different from the transient state of "excitement" in that it takes personal sacrifice. You need to know where your team will be when the going gets tough, because it will get tough. You need team members that are dedicated to achieving results, not simply having a job.

I learned this personally early in my career. I was leading a technical team that was developing a new material. We had been at this development for approximately four years and were now making test samples at a pilot-scale facility. The company decided not to pursue the project any further, so we were preparing to sell the technology. The facility ran twenty-four hours a day as it took nearly thirty-six hours from the initial start of the facility to seeing a final product emerge out the back end. We had just completed the shutdown of a long run when we received word that a potential buyer was coming early in the morning to view the plant. The buyer, of course, wanted to see the pilot facility in full operation. It was mid-afternoon. We did not have thirty-six hours. We had less than half that time. Getting the plant up and running safely in half the normal time was going to take some imagination and dedication. Most of the team was energized by the challenge. A few suddenly realized that their children had soccer practice and opted to leave. Those that stayed, and stayed all night, did so willingly and enthusiastically. Those that remained had passion. They felt a deep responsibility to achieve results. We were not working a job. As a team, we achieved our goal with an entire hour to spare! There is simply no substitute for a dedicated and capable team.

Passion, while important, is certainly not enough. Passion without the other capabilities does not accomplish much. The converse is also true; all the skills in the world with no motivation to use them will accomplish nothing. Knowing without doing is the same as not knowing.

Hiring

Advisors are important and need to be included as part of your firm's capability assessment. Hiring, however, will be the most pronounced method by which you will expand your firm's capability set as your firm grows. One of the biggest challenges of the first hires is that the organization is still rapidly evolving. Although you have a plan, you know the future will not roll out before you exactly as you have envisioned it. It is therefore impossible to hire "task performers." I have never worked in HR, but have hired dozens of people over my career. I am constantly amazed how many rapidly growing firms try to hire people to do specific tasks. They then look for candidates that have performed those tasks in the past. Here's the problem. Yes, those tasks need to be done and the person you hire should have the capability to accomplish them. But that is not nearly enough. The scope of the tasks that you will want this potential hire to perform will evolve and most certainly grow. Worse yet, those tasks that you desperately need done today may not even be relevant six months from now. Hiring by defining tasks and looking for evidence of an ability to perform those tasks is a waste of time for your early hires.

You need to hire by capability. The hard-skill capabilities are the easiest to measure – does the candidate have relevant skills and know-how? However it is the soft capabilities – networks/relationships and aspirations/passions – that are the most important in the long run. Clearly you are looking for capabilities that complement the existing team and that align with the vision of the firm. Too often, rather than expanding the team's current capabilities, teams instead "hire themselves": People with backgrounds and attitudes similar to their own. The candidate simply "feels right" to them. Of course they "feel right;" the candidate is a reflection of the hirer. Sometimes companies get more sophisticated in describing this "hire-by-feeling" method and claim the candidates are a good "cultural fit" in the company. I am not saying that establishing a corporate culture is not important – it is extremely important. Nor am I saying that hiring people that will help establish that culture is not important – it is. What I am saying is to be careful not to get caught up in some rationalization for justify hiring someone that looks like a younger version of yourself.

Interpreting resumés

Before launching into the specifics of what to look for in a candidate, it is worth spending a few moments on interpreting resumés. The resumé will likely be the first information you will see regarding a candidate. It will also serve as a yardstick for culling prospective candidates. Learning how to interpret them properly will expand your potential pool of new hires. There is this notion, for example, that only people with startup experience can work in startups. Going forward, professionals will flow seamlessly from small firms to large firms and back throughout their careers. This means that startup firms will need to be able to interpret the resumés of those with large-firm experience and vice versa.

Young, rapidly growing companies can have annual corporate growth rates twenty or more times the rate of their more established brethren. As the change over time in a position's scope and responsibility is impacted by this growth, the relative differences in growth rates must be accounted for in comparing candidates from large and from startup companies. Due in part to the disparate company growth rates, for example, the development pace of an employee that holds a particular position at a fast-growing startup over a five-year period is equivalent, in terms of increasing job complexity and responsibilities, to that of a counterpart at a moderately growing, large corporation who had multiple-level promotions during the same period. This relativistic nature of the growth of positions within these two types of company can mean that positions and responsibilities in resumés from startup-company candidates must be interpreted quite differently from how they would be assessed on the resumé of a large-corporation candidate. The following are examples of two different types of innovator.

Functional specialists Inside large organizations, these employees have very recognizable, stable-looking resumés. They tend to stay in positions within organizations for long stretches of time. However, in young, fast-growing companies these same individuals appear to the uninitiated to be unstable job-jumpers. Since the responsibilities for a given job rapidly expand in high-growth companies, these individuals must constantly change companies in order to keep a position with a relatively constant level of responsibility.

High-potential leaders Those fast-trackers who move frequently to positions of increasing responsibility in a large firm, look quite the opposite in smaller, high-growth companies. In the smaller, high-growth firms those same fast-trackers tend to stay in one position longer, but the company's hyper-growth drives rapid expansions in the scope and responsibilities of their job. When these individuals do move from one small company to the next, unlike the specialists, changes in position title tend to accompany the move. The entrepreneurial career path they will take may start as new business development specialist in one firm, then to new business director in the second firm, business development VP in a third firm, etc.

Candidate evaluation

Keeping in mind the relativistic differences between the look of the resumés, we will proceed with how to discern background factors and personal characteristics of a potential candidate. The background factors are the most direct and the easiest to interpret. Care must be taken to zoom out and assess capabilities and not to fall into the trap of only considering resumés from candidates that have been VP of Sales in another electronic component firm, when you are looking for a VP of Sales for your electronic component firm. The relevant background elements include education, industry experience, company experience, functional experience, and level of responsibility. The next sections of this chapter will review each of these attributes, starting from the widest field of vision. Keep in mind that, when hiring from a capability perspective, you are using these traditional measures as proxies for the capabilities the firm really needs. Be careful not to mistake the proxy for the real need. This happens far too often.

Education
Certain degrees, and the training that underpins them, are necessary to
perform certain jobs. I would not want anyone without a civil engineering degree responsible for the technical aspects of a bridge-building
project, for example. It is the knowledge of statics, soils, and other
specific know-how that is really required for a bridge-building project.
The degree represents a proxy for that knowledge. Zooming out and
thinking about the skills and know-how that are necessary for the
position will help you avoid hiring a degree and not the capabilities
you actually need.

Industry experience
As discussed on the business discovery half of the Arch, much of the
knowledge the firm needs to be successful is tacit. There is no better
way to attain the tacit knowledge of an industry than by being
immersed in it. The downside of being immersed in an industry is
that innovations tend to come from people, not from the established
industries but from those that have not completely bought into the
norms of that industry. They are willing to question "that's just how it
is done" industry standards. Industry experience is a double-edged
sword. What exactly are you looking for in a candidate with "industrial
experience?" Zooming out and looking from a capabilities perspective
will be helpful. What you may be looking for when you think you
need "industry experience" is relationships or connections. Or are
you looking for insights into customer needs? Or something else? As
was the case with education, focus on the capability you need to hire
and not its proxy.

Company experience
Company experience is relevant for candidates that are moving from
one part of a large firm to another. This is a proxy for understanding
the company work processes and culture. When hiring for a new firm,
this could be relevant in two ways. First there are the items previously

discussed in evaluating resumés of those from large vs. startup companies. Second are the capability proxies that are often inferred from previous startup experience. If a candidate has startup experience on their resumé, it is assumed that they are comfortable with ambiguity, are self-directed, and have the know-how to get things done with very few resources. A startup company manager often views large-company experience, on the other hand, as an implication that the candidate is a bit coddled and needs lots of infrastructure/support/help to achieve results. These are all overgeneralizations. Some positions in large firms operate very independently with very few resources. Do not rely on these proxies for the capabilities you require. Decide what the company needs when hiring a candidate and ask questions directly to those points. If you need to hire a person that can get things done with few resources, ask the large-firm candidate for examples of that in their history. You might be surprised to learn that the candidate successfully led a skunk-work project within a large firm.

Functional experience

Functional experience is a proxy for know-how. Does the candidate have the know-how and skills required to do the tasks at hand. Just because you have never built a bird-house before does not mean you do not have the skills to do so. Have you built other similar items? Do you know how to use the tools essential to building a bird-house? It is pure laziness to consider only those that have built bird-houses when hiring for that job. More importantly, even if they have built bird-houses in the past, does your candidate have the background that would suggest they are interested and flexible enough to do other things? Your plan calls for your firm to grow rapidly; that bird-house job will expand quickly. In addition, the company could change course. If the company comes to realize that the market needs cat-cages instead of bird-houses, does that candidate have the relevant, transferable skills? I could have said managing a group of app developers instead of building bird-houses, but the logic is the same and often more easily pictured when the task is tangible. Here again you are looking at the more general capabilities, not the specific tasks.

Level of responsibility

The job's level of responsibility is often a proxy for scope of decision-making responsibility. It could also be used as a proxy for the breadth of impact the candidate had on the firm. Did the candidate set budget or simply follow it? Set strategy, operationalize the strategy, or simply execute it? Managing people is another dimension of responsibility. A friend of mine was recently turned down by a firm because he had not managed one hundred people before; he currently had ten direct reports. Now, no one can realistically have one hundred direct reports. You likely manage ten, who in turn manage ten each. The relevant experience is not a quantitative one, but one of managing managers. The relevant experience is directly managing people and indirectly managing them through others.

The key is to evaluate candidates against the capabilities you desire. There are two challenges that prevent firms from this approach. The biggest impediment is that they have not crafted the company from a framework of capabilities. The firms neither know what capabilities they have nor realize which ones they need. As discussed in Chapter 2 above, this is largely a zoom-in, zoom-out exercise. The challenge is to think of the positions in terms of capabilities instead of activities. Again, this entails a zoom-out exercise. List the activities or tasks that need to be done and then determine the capabilities that enable their successful completion. When reviewing candidates it is then much easier to judge them on how well they align with this capability match than to engage in the typical apples-and-oranges comparisons that inevitably follow from comparing proxies to these capabilities.

The next set of elements, while critically important, cannot be pre-screened via a resumé review. They need to be teased out in an interview. These are the personal attributes of the candidate that they will bring to the firm. It is these soft skills that are often the difference between success and failure on the job. These include intellect, personality, and motivation. As before, these attributes will be reviewed in turn, starting from the broadest perspective.

Motivation

As noted in the discussion on passion earlier in this chapter, none of the candidates' other attributes elements matter if they are not motivated to get the work done. This is why I always start with motivation when talking to a candidate I am interested in hiring. The mistake is in thinking this is the only attribute that matters. It is not. Motivation, or passion, is a necessary, but not a sufficient condition upon which to base a new hire. If the candidate is motivated and intelligent many of the other elements (short of a personality mismatch between them and the firm) can be developed over time. That assumes, however, that you have that time. Most startups do not. In the end, for any firm, it is about results. The potential to achieve results does not cut it. You need someone that will make it happen. Having a "less talented" or "less experienced" person that actually performs is far superior to having a perfect candidate that does nothing but track the performance of their personal stock portfolio all day.

How does the open position in your firm align with their personal goals? Is the candidate's response to that inquiry consistent with the career arc displayed in their resumé? What are their personal interests? Do these align with their career goals? What is the candidate's energy level? Are they high-energy, attack-the-problem people, or cautious and reserved, waiting for specific direction? New ventures need self-starters, highly motivated people. Just make sure that what they are motivated to do is in alignment with your vision for the firm you are building.

In Bud Caddell's 2009 post "How to be happy in business" a Venn diagram illustrates how you want your position to align with your ideal candidate. Of course, you want them to have the skills and know-how to perform the required tasks. You also need the achievement of results to be what they want to do.

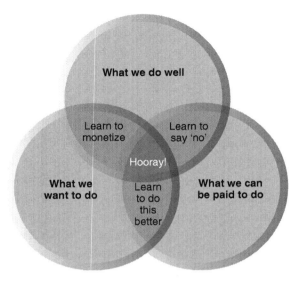

FIGURE 6.2 How to be happy in business
Source: Bud Caddell, "How to be happy in business", 2009.

Samuel Zell, Chicago commercial real-estate entrepreneur, is fond of saying, "W-O-R-K = F-U-N." If work is fun, he would say, you will never work a day in your life. Obviously every position comes with a balance of "things you love to do" and "things you need to do." You need that love:need ratio to be a positive one in the mind of your potential candidate.

Personality
As you build your firm, you are also building the culture of the firm. The personalities of potential new hires must align with the culture you want to create. Do you want a "democratic" culture in which everyone feels that their voice is heard on every decision or are you creating an ultra-responsive culture in which designated leaders are given autonomy to make significant decisions on their own? The decision-making style of your new hires must align with that vision. A dominant personality type would fit well in the second structure and

destroy the first. A more patient person would thrive in the first and not in the second. The same goes with formality. Are you creating a formal structure with titles or a more casual one? A researcher that insists on being called Dr. Jones will be a better fit in a formal organizational structure.

A serial entrepreneur friend of mine expresses this sentiment this way. He says that nirvana to him is "doing the things I like to do with the people I like to do them with." He promotes a friendly, respectful working environment in the companies he builds. Hiring a talented but abrasive employee can weaken the entire company. Be wary of this proverbial bad apple. Stanford professor Robert Sutton, in his book *The No Ass-Hole Rule*, argues vehemently against the rationalization that these "difficult personalities" are very talented and therefore worth keeping (Sutton, 2007). They poison the well, Dr. Sutton argues. If you want to hire people that can become part of high-performance teams, then you need to create an environment that supports that. You want a culture in which each team member enables the performance of everyone around them to be better, and does not discourage and demotivate by their behavior. This environment requires unselfish, achievement-of-results orientation vs. one driven by individual recognition.

Intellect

Intellect is an important part of one's personality. Education and grades or standardized test scores (800+ on the GMAT) are often used as proxies for this element. Intellect can be divided into two categories: Analytical ability and creative ability. Analytical ability is the more easily measured of the two. As far as creativity, I think firms are really looking for "applied creativity." Applied creativity is not just the ability to dream something up, but the art of implementing the unorthodox in an organization. As before, candidate interview questions should prod candidates to express examples of each. How did you solve a problem in a way not done before in your organization/industry? This question also speaks to those dedicated to achieving results, mentioned at the beginning of this chapter, rather than those only interested in being nonconformists.

These soft-skill candidate attributes – motivation, personality, and intellect – are the most difficult to evaluate. As with the other attributes, the key is to zoom out and determine first of all the needs of the organization. Do you want an organization driven by small, high-performance teams or individual stars? Do you want an ultra-responsive organization or a democratic one? The other challenge is to understand whether your candidate is being forthright or is simply skilled at interviewing. Looking for congruence between their responses and their resumé is one method to determine this, but it is by no means fool-proof. Your odds of selecting the best candidate can be improved by having multiple interviews with multiple people assessing the same capabilities in different ways. It is that second part, assessing the same capabilities, where most firms fail during the interview process. Understand what attributes you desire in a candidate at the widest level and communicate that to all who interview them. You will then have a common basis on which everyone can compare the candidates.

Compensation

Before your potential new hire will join your team, you will need to agree on compensation. When your company is first starting out, you will not be able to pay market rate for most of your positions. You are selling the bigger dream of the company; the opportunity to change the world. You are also, more than likely, offering equity, future stock options, or revenue sharing as part of the compensation package for key hires. Early on in company formation, first-time entrepreneurs sometimes treat equity as candy – giving it away to everyone. They give it to their employees, their web-development firm, and on and on. Equity represents ownership in the company. Equity is certainly not the only way to align effort with the ultimate success of the firm. Do you want all of these service providers to be co-owners of your firm? To be your partners in this venture? The answer may well be yes, but before you randomly print and distribute stock certificates be sure you are buying a long-term contribution to your firm. At the very least all equity distributed to employees should come with a vesting schedule. You do not want to provide an employee 10 percent of your firm the day you hire her only to have her quit the next month. It happens. Make sure there is a significant vesting period – at least eighteen months, up to five years – for the equity offered. If employees leave during that vesting period they may only get a fraction of the potential equity offered, based on the vesting schedule you have determined.

As Jim Collins said at the beginning of this chapter, the goal is to "get the right people on the bus" (Collins, 2001b). Determining who is "right" is the challenge. Capabilities and corporate culture should be your measuring stick for making those choices. The second challenge is getting the financing you need to launch your firm.

FINANCING OPTIONS

Financing typically comes with people in the form of board members, advisors, and the like. As a result, part of your evaluation of financing sources will include an evaluation of the people that you will acquire with the financing. Financing that comes with well-aligned advisors is what is referred to as "smart money." Many first-time entrepreneurs seeking equity financing make the mistake of taking the highest initial valuation. The result is that these firms end up with board members that are a poor fit for the firm. These board members either do not add to the firm's capability set or are not in alignment with the firm's vision. Either way, it is trouble. This is known as "dumb money." Smart money is the goal. This is yet another reason why the people evaluations should come before the financing evaluation.

The investment potential framework, shown in Figure 6.3, was introduced in Chapter 4 to guide you toward the type of investment that optimally aligns with the potential of the firm you are building. The implications of various funding sources for the future of your firm are also detailed at length in Appendix C. That information will not be

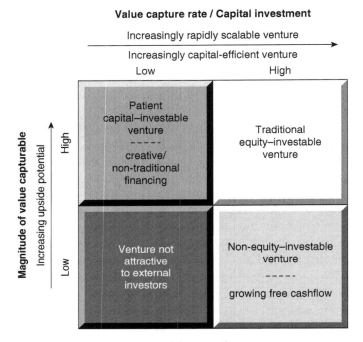

FIGURE 6.3 Investment potential framework

repeated here. Rather, this chapter will focus on the financier's perspective. This chapter will focus on how various financing agencies make decisions. By understanding this perspective better you will be in a better position to attain the type of funding you have determined is optimally aligned with the business you desire to build. Clearly, the business plan and the investor pitch that were outlined in Chapter 5 will be incredibly important. Finding and getting an audience with the investors you want to fund your business can also be a challenge and will be discussed in this chapter as well.

Lower half of investment potential framework

If the investment potential assessment put your firm in the lower half of the investment potential framework, then you are not seeking an equity investment in your business. If you are in the lower left-hand quadrant, then you will need to self-fund this company. Your other option is to obtain a grant that would further the development of your firm and make it attractive to non-equity investors. We will therefore start the discussion with grants and move to more traditional non-equity financing.

Government grants

A great many regional economic developers are turning to "economic gardening" as a means to increase employment in their region. Economic gardening is simply the strategy of growing locally created firms as opposed to attempting to relocate established companies to your region. While this is a new trend for some regions of the globe, others, such as Enterprise Ireland, have had a focus on economic gardening for decades. Grants to launch and grow firms typically form part of those economic development efforts. Check with your region's economic development office and make an appointment to see the administrator in charge of your local program.

In the United States, the Small Business Administration offers a number of services and programs for the fledgling entrepreneur. With local offices around the country, it is worth the entrepreneur's time to talk to a local representative about programs relevant to her business that may be available nearby. The Small Business Innovation Research (SBIR) program and the Small Business Technology Transfer (STTR) program are just a part of the US government programs that support the launch of high-growth potential businesses. Leverage these grant monies to get to some kind of sales as soon as feasible. Focus on creating the MPV, the minimal product that a customer is willing to purchase. Purchase orders, or better yet, actual sales and revenue are vital to acquiring loans and lines of credit (see later in this chapter for details).

Friends and family

This funding category is better known as the 3Fs – Friends, Family, and Fools! Founders seeking this type of financing often seek it in the form of long-term loans. From a strictly business perspective the interest rates on these loans should be well in excess of what the investors could attain at their bank or in low-risk money market investments. The emotional ties of the relationships, however, often prevent deals from being assessed strictly as market-based transactions. From the entrepreneur's perspective, the proverbial "rich uncle" is good to find – especially if he cares more about you than his money!

Bank loans

In normal times, bank loans, which include revolving lines of credit, are fairly easy to attain for profitable going concerns. While lending institutions will follow slightly different specific criteria for judging your firm's creditworthiness, all typically follow the five C's: Character, capacity, capital, conditions, and collateral (PNC, n.d.).

Character In his book, *Integrity is All You've Got*, serial entrepreneur Karl Eller emphasizes the character issue that banks assess (Eller, 2005). How do you fulfill your obligations – to your employees, your suppliers, as well as your customers? Do you have a history of fulfilling your obligations in a timely fashion? Does your credit history and scores validate this supposition? The banks will definitely be reviewing your personal credit history as part of their assessment.

Capacity This is your firm's ability to make your loan payments. There are various financial ratios that banks may use in this valuation, but the Times Interest Ratio is sure to be one of them. This measure is a ratio of your firm's EBITDA (earnings before interest taxes, depreciation, and amortization) to its minimum loan payment obligation. The bank would like to see this ratio be at least 1.5. This is why generating revenue is so important. Without sales, there is no loan, as most startups do not have much in the way of tangible assets.

Capital How much investment has gone into the business? Is the firm well capitalized? Silicon Valley Bank, among other firms, will provide loans to firms financed by venture capital. Because they are venture-backed, these firms are well capitalized. If anything should go wrong the equity holders are subordinate to the debt holders, making the bank first in line to make itself whole in a bankruptcy.

Conditions As any small business person that was trying to get a loan during the 2008 recession will tell you, the macro-economic conditions play a significant role in debt financing. Even firms qualified in all other respects found bank loans impossible to get in 2008.

Collateral Given that a company's cash flow is the primary source of loan repayment, capacity will be the first screen for a firm's ability to acquire a loan. However, should the firm have a hiccup in its cash flow, the bank will look at secondary sources of loan repayment. Collateral represents company assets that could be leveraged to pay off the loan if necessary. That is why, unless you have a business with a proven repayment record, you will almost always be required to pledge collateral. If the firm does not own any tangible assets, you may be asked to pledge some personal ones (such as your house). This is why loans are dangerous waters for entrepreneurs.

Crowdfunding

Crowdfunding is a relatively new source of capital for new firms. The term 'crowdfunding' refers to the use of a social network to raise small amounts of money from a large number of contributors. In aggregate the amount raised by this method can range from hundreds to tens of thousands of dollars, although the typical amount raised is usually a few thousand dollars. Many of the efforts of entrepreneurs utilizing crowdfunding sites (Kickstarter.com and GoFundMe.com, among others) have been to leverage the social impact of the work they put in. Others have offered incentives to contributors via future product sales. While this may be a mechanism to get your firm moving, you will likely need to leverage this source with other funding.

A team that was interested in opening a restaurant based on a unique, health-oriented menu needed to test the market before launching. Their MPV was a food cart where they could test the menu, people's willingness to pay, and their assumptions of repeat customers. The team raised roughly $5,000 on one of the crowdfunding sites that helped launch their food cart. With the success of the food cart behind them, they were able to raise the funds necessary to open the restaurant.

You are not limited to one type of investment. You may need to bridge to the "ideal" investment in your firm. The bridging activity should also de-risk the firm as this example illustrates.

The current mode of crowdfunding has the firm retaining 100 percent ownership of the funded work. The JOBS Bill passed in the United States in April 2012 paved the way for crowdfunding to be used as an equity investment. On September 23, 2013, the US Security and Exchange Commission implemented Title II of the JOBS Act by lifting a decades-old ban on the mass marketing of private security offerings. However, as of this writing, how entrepreneurs can legally raise funds under this law is still up for significant debate (Brummer and Gorfine, 2013).

Upper half of investment potential framework

If your firm was assessed to be in the upper half of the investment potential framework illustrated in Figure 6.3, then you are building a firm that is attractive to equity investors. That does not mean, of course, that you desire equity investment, only that it is likely available should you seek it out. As discussed in Chapter 4, equity financers will need to sell the firm or have it go public in order to transform their equity stake in your private firm to something more liquid (either cash or stock of a publicly traded firm). This may not be in alignment with your aspirations. If not, you should avoid this type of financing.

Venture capital firms and angel investors make up the primary equity investors for startup firms. Both types of investor predominately participate in the "traditional equity" quadrant of the investment potential framework. These investors have relatively short investment time horizons (three to seven years). VC firms invest other people's money with the goal of returning capital to their investors plus a return significantly greater than the investors could achieve by other investments (stocks, bonds, etc.). Angel investors, like VC firms, tend to invest in startup firms that show high growth potential.

Government economic developers, on the other hand, typically have longer time horizons and the goal of job creation rather than wealth creation. That longer time horizon puts them in the "patient equity" quadrant. Funding in this quadrant tends to be non-traditional. The creativity used to fund firms in this quadrant increasingly includes the creation of Public–Private Partnerships (PPPs) (DeWulf, Blanken, and Bult-Spiering, 2012). If you have a firm that has the potential for significant job creation and that falls into this quadrant of the investment potential framework, you should have a long and serious discussion with the economic development agencies in your area. If this type of funding is not available, you will have to reposition the firm by iterating back to the business assessment segment. Since patient capital financing tends to be unique to the region which the firm is located, this section of this chapter will focus on how to obtain the more traditional equity financing.

Equity financing
Selling a portion of your company in exchange for cash is known as equity financing. Unlike loans that can get paid from the cash generated by the profitable operations of the company, a private company's equity – an illiquid asset – can only be turned into cash or some other liquid asset by two means. One way to transform private equity is to sell the entrepreneurial company to another entity for cash or publicly traded stock. A second way is take the private company public through an initial public offering (IPO) on a major stock exchange (NYSE, London Stock Exchange, NASDAQ, etc.).

Angel investors and VCs are the two primary groups that make equity investments in nascent private companies. Each will be described in more detail below. Those investor groups that are interested in taking an equity stake in an entrepreneur's company will not want to have their investment tied up for very long. Typically, their target time from first money in to liquidation is three to seven years. As a result, the entrepreneur seeking this type of financing should anticipate the sale of the startup within that time window. The entrepreneur can also expect any group taking an equity position in their firm to perform significant due diligence on the firm before investing. This due diligence will be overviewed at the end of this chapter.

Angel investors "Angel" investors derive their name from Victorian England where the term was used to describe wealthy individuals who provided money for theatrical productions. High-net-worth individuals (a common definition is individuals with liquid assets of $1 million or more) are "qualified" angel investors (in government terms). It is important to note that angel investors are investing their own money. They are often retired entrepreneurs or executives, who may be interested in angel investing for reasons that go beyond pure monetary return. But make no mistake, such investors are definitely interested in obtaining a substantial return on their investment. Other motives for these investors include wanting to keep abreast of current developments in a particular business arena, mentoring another generation of entrepreneurs, and making use of their experience and networks on a less-than-full-time basis. Accordingly, in addition to funds, angel investors can often provide valuable management advice and important contacts.

Angel investors are equity investors, meaning that they exchange their capital for an ownership stake in the company. The challenging question becomes how much ownership should the angels receive for a given injection of capital. The only way to answer that question is to place a value on the company at the time of the investment. There are two relevant and related company valuations: Value before and after the investment. The "post-money company value" is the company's valuation immediately after receiving an investment, while the "pre-money value" is its value immediately before receiving the investment. If the company is worth a million dollars after a quarter-million-dollar investment, then the post-money value is $1 million dollars. Since the quarter-million-dollar investment represents one-quarter of the value of the post-money valuation of the company, the investor should receive 25 percent of the equity in the company for the investment. In this example the pre-money value of the company, the value of the company before the investment) was $750,000 (post-money value less the investment).

One of the most significant difficulties in taking an ownership stake in an early-stage company is determining the value of that company at the time of the investment. Angel investors that anticipate follow-on VC investment will typically defer the valuation question to the VCs. In these cases, angel investors will take "subordinated debt" in lieu of a direct equity investment in the company. (It is called "subordinated" debt as it has lower priority than bank debt in a liquidation, meaning the bank debt will be paid before the subordinated debt holder.) This debt is typically structured to convert to equity at a follow-on investment round of the company. For this reason, such an investment is also called "convertible debt," as it "converts" to equity at a later date. The hope is that the valuation of the company will be easier to determine during the follow-on investment round. The VCs prefer to value the companies themselves and therefore prefer this valuation to be deferred by the angel investors.

If the angel investors take convertible debt in lieu of equity, this debt will convert to equity at the next (often VC) financing round. To compensate the early, angel investors for taking on the initial financing risks, the conversion terms typically include one or more investment incentives or "kickers." One common investment kicker is for the interest on the convertible note to be compounded and considered part of the investment at the time the debt converts to equity. So, if the angels invest $1 million at 10 percent annual interest, and if this debt is converted to equity a full year after the investment, the angels will get credit for a $1.1 million investment. A second common incentive for angel investors is either getting warrants for extra shares or pricing discounts on shares they purchase. Either way, they end up with more shares per dollar of investment than the investors in the follow-on round. For example, if the angel investment agreement allowed them to convert to equity during the follow-on investment round at a 20 percent discount to the price offered to next-round investors, and if the follow-on investors were paying $1 per share, then the angel investors would convert their $1.1 million in investment and interest to shares at $0.80 per share, thus receiving 1.375 million shares for their initial $1 million investment.

Entrepreneurs seeking early-stage equity funding would be remiss in ignoring angel investors. The VC investment level went through a significant bubble in 2000. In 1998 the aggregate of capital investments by venture capital firms in the United States was slightly over $21 billion (National Venture Capital Association (NVCA) website, retrieved 2013). This figure jumped to more than $100 billion in 2000, before falling back to just over $22 billion in 2002. Since the bubble burst in 2000, the total investments by angels and groups of angels has been slowly increasing to the point where the aggregate amount invested by both groups is nearly the same. In 2010 in the United States, angels invested $20.1 billion in aggregate in approximately 61,900 deals while their VC brethren invested approximately $22 billion in 2,750 deals (Angel Capital Association, 2012). Angel investors also tend to fund firms at an earlier stage than do VC investors. Angels funded 79 percent of seed-stage deals that were either angel- or VC-funded in 2010. The magnitude of investment by angel investors is not trivial either. According to a 2012 survey conducted by the Angel Capital Association, 67 percent of Angel Groups invested $150,000 to $500,000 per deal (Angel Capital Association, 2012).

Angel investors are private individuals that often want to retain their privacy. There is no directory of angel investors. Private companies seeking to meet potential angels have several options including referrals from sources and other business contacts the investors trust, at investor conferences and symposia, and at meetings organized by groups of angels where companies pitch directly to investors in face-to-face meetings. Increasingly, angel investors are collaborating and forming organized groups or "Bands of Angels." These groups can be ad hoc all the way up to quite professional, having websites and other support systems in place to allow their members to connect with entrepreneurs. Do your homework, and network at local entrepreneurship and economic development forums. Angels are out there and increasingly want to be found.

Venture capitalists Venture capitalists are professional investors who work for firms that invest other people's money in companies with high-growth potential in exchange for equity in those companies. The National Venture Capital Association (trade association that represents the US VC industry) describes these professional investment firms as firms that manage pools of risk-equity capital dedicated to high-growth, entrepreneurial companies (NVCA website, 2008). Another way to describe these firms is that they are in the business of building businesses (Bund, 2006).

Venture capital has obtained a lot of press and notoriety, since it has been instrumental in financing many well-known firms from Sun Microsystems to Google to Facebook. As a result, many entrepreneurs equate startup funding with venture capital. This could not be further from the truth. The types of company that fit the VCs' investment model are very limited. This model is limited to a narrow range of companies showing growth that can be greatly accelerated by a significant infusion of capital. Clearly, many companies, and companies that end up being very successful, do not fit this investment model. As an example, in 1999 during the dot-com frenzy when the perception was that "everyone" in the startup world was obtaining venture capital, an inspection of *Inc Magazine*'s Inc. 500 told a different tale. The Inc. 500 lists the fastest growing, privately held, US-based, independent companies. To qualify these companies must have a minimum of $200,000 in annual revenue for at least four years (*Inc. Magazine*, 2008). Annual compounded growth rates for these companies are in excess of 30 percent per year. In short, these are very good companies. Given their growth rates, this data set of companies should be skewed more toward that VC investment model and at a time (1999) when venture capital was setting investment records (*Inc. Magazine*, 1999). Yet only 6.3 percent of this set of high-growth companies received VC money. Today, that fraction is significantly smaller. The vast majority of the startup capital for new firms (over 75 percent) comes from personal savings. The point is that receiving venture capital is rare, even for very good companies in the best of times. This is less a reflection on the entrepreneurial company than it is on the VCs' investment model.

Venture capitalists have investment targets for both rate of return and return magnitude. The earlier the stage at which the VCs or angels invest, the greater the risk and the greater the expected return on investment. Venture capital firms attain their funding from limited partners. An early-stage VC fund may have sold its limited partners on the concept that the fund will yield, in aggregate, a 25–35 percent annual return on their investment. For the VC fund to be an attractive investment to the limited partner, that return rate must be more than the limited partners could achieve from other, less risky investments (stock market, mezzanine funding, private equity investment, real estate, etc.). Given the high failure rate of investments in early-stage firms, each specific investment must potentially return well in excess of the overall fund return target to cover the losses on the failed investments. A VC fund making investments in ten early-stage startup companies, for example, may see one of its portfolio companies delivering tremendous returns, two or three of the ten "going sideways" (returning their investment, plus a nominal profit), and the rest going bust, being written off as total losses. As a result of the low probability of success and the need to make a significant return on the entire fund for their limited partners, VCs expect extremely high rates of returns on each investment.

An investment's internal rate of return, IRR, is not the only consideration for a venture capitalist. The magnitude of the return is also important. A small investment with a high IRR will not return enough capital to satisfy the investors. Given the low probability that portfolio companies will succeed, as a rule of thumb each investment must have the potential to "make the fund." This means that each investment portfolio company must be able to potentially return an amount of capital to the VC firm roughly equal to the size of the VC fund. If the VC fund is worth $350 million, then each startup that the VC invests in will need to have the potential to return at least

$350 million to the fund. That is a high bar to hit. Most startups do not have that kind of upside potential. Even if your company has the potential to return fifteen times the capital invested, but only requires $1 million of investment, it will be considered too small to attract VC as that potential $15 million return will be significantly less than their fund size.

Venture capitalists generally place a new venture's risk in one of four categories: Market (will there be demand for the offering?), team (can the team perform?), product (will the product be sustainably differentiated, attractive to customers?), and finance (will there be follow-on financing available to the firm to drive it all the way to success once we get it started with our early investment?). There is a fifth risk factor, the industry, that the VCs do not explicitly talk about, but it is core to their investment thesis as their firms tend to invest exclusively in specifically defined industries. Given that their investment thesis was based on particular industries, this is the first risk the VCs actually consider. This goes back to what was discussed in Chapter 2, that most business failures are attributable to launching in unattractive industries (Shane, 2008).

There are local and national listings of VC associations. Most invest in specific industries at specific investment stages. Do your homework before approaching a VC firm. They prefer warm introductions to business plans mailed to them without references. (They will almost always ignore those plans tossed over the transom.) A warm introduction means that you will be introduced to a general partner of the VC firm by someone known to the firm. Network, network, network to find these links. Social media sites, like LinkedIn.com, make finding these links easier, but it is still an effort. When you do get that warm introduction, have your three pitches that were described in Chapter 5 ready to go!

Part of doing your homework includes understanding the VC's business model. Even among successful companies, as just discussed, the so-called "VC-backable" or "venture-grade" companies represent a very narrow band of entrepreneurial companies. This is more of a reflection of the VCs' business model than on the entrepreneurial firm itself. To understand better why this is the case, we need to understand better how VC firms operate.

VC firm investment model The simplest way to understand the VC firm's business model is to follow the money. Venture capital firms raise investment capital from other investors who become limited partners (LPs) in the venture firm. These limited partners are typically investment funds such as pension funds, university endowments, retirement funds; wealthy individuals; or fund-of-funds (investment funds raised explicitly for investment in VC firms). Large investment funds such as pension funds and endowments typically allocate their investments to stock, bond, and real-estate holdings with a small fraction allocated to "alternate" investment classes. Venture capital is part of this "alternate" investment class. A venture firm will raise investment capital from a number of LPs. The VC fund will have a set target value (say, $300 million) and a fixed life: A typical venture fund has a ten-year life. This means that, during those ten years, the general partners (GPs) in the VC fund will invest the money raised from its LPs and return its profits to those LPs within that ten-year window. The LPs do not turn over the capital they have committed to the venture firm all at once, but commit to do so whenever they receive a request, known as a "capital call," from the VC firm.

The VC firm invests the capital raised from the LPs in startup companies. Successful startup companies that VC firms invest in must go through some kind of liquidity event – be purchased or become publicly traded companies – in order for the VC firm to transform the equity stakes they have purchased in these private companies into cash that they can redistribute between the firm's investors. Since the life of the VC fund is ten years, this process must all happen within a ten-year window. Since the VC firms will make investments in new companies over the life of the fund (i.e. not all on the first day of the fund), the VC investors are typically looking at companies that will exist, from first investment to liquidation, for between three and seven years.

Venture capital firms typically make money in two ways. The first way in which they normally generate revenue is from a management fee; the second way is from the "carry." The management fee, which usually is not very large, is typically aimed at keeping the VC firm open – paying employee salaries for support staff, renting office space, etc. This management fee is typically based on the total size of the venture fund and is negotiated between the VC firms and their LPs. It is typically around 2 percent of the fund per year. A $300 million fund would therefore charge $6 million per year in maintenance fees. This is a great advantage for large funds, as a small fund of say $10 million would only net $200,000 per year making it difficult for this small fund to pay much for supporting staff. Venture funds have a fixed number of general partners. These GPs are the ones that make the investment decisions and often become board members of the startup companies in which the VC firm has made an investment. Small VC firms may have only two GPs while large VC firms may have five to ten.

The fund's maintenance fee is just that – maintaining the venture capital firm's organization. The real profits come from the "carry." The carry is a percentage that the VC firm receives from the positive investment return from a specific investment. Like the maintenance fee, the carry is a number negotiated between the VC firm and its LPs. The GPs in the VC firms typically receive around a 20 percent carry on successful investments. The carry works like this: $10 million of the LP's capital was invested in startup Company A. Company A ultimately is sold to a large corporation. Let's say the investment firm's equity stake in the startup returned $100 million from that sale to the VC firm. The VC firm now must redistribute its earnings from this investment among the limited and general partners.

The first thing that typically occurs in a successful VC investment redistribution is that the original amount invested in the startup, $10 million in this example, is returned to the LPs. In this example, that leaves $90 million in profits on the sale of Company A. Of that $90 million, the VC firm retains its carry of 20 percent (or $18 million) and redistributes the remainder ($72 million) between its LPs. In this way both parties share in the upside of the investment.

The carry profit-distribution methodology is not perfect from the LP's perspective. Limited partners tend to grumble when there is no upside to share; VC firms do not share equally in investments that do not work out. When $20 million is invested in startup Company B, for example, which then goes bankrupt and is shut down (not an atypical outcome), the LPs get nothing in return, and have lost their $20 million investment. While the profits of an investment are shared between LPs and GPs, there is no proportional loss for the GPs on a startup company investment that goes wrong. The LPs grumble that, even if an investment goes badly, the VC firms still get their maintenance fees, and therefore never have a "loss." Despite this conflict between the LPs and the GPs, the overall investment returns on investments in VC firms have generally been large enough to appease the LPs.

As in all businesses, the manner in which VC firms make money, as described above, drives certain decision-making behavior. In this model, the venture capitalists make the greatest returns by investing in startups with huge upside potential – the so-called "home run" model. This model is supported by the facts that, first, for the VC firms there is no downside to investments in companies that end up ceasing operation, and second, the maximum profits for VCs are obtained when the difference between the exit value and the invested value is maximized.

Looking at the investment strategies of two hypothetical $100 million VC funds will demonstrate this phenomenon. Each of the hypothetical funds invests $20 million in each of five startup companies. Each VC fund will draw a 20 percent carry from the investment profits. In this example, illustrated in Figure 6.4 below, the "conservative" investment model invests in startup companies that can return two times their investment. The "home run" investment model invests in riskier startup companies that have the potential to return ten times their investment. Figure 6.4 illustrates the investment returns to the VC firms and the LPs if all of the "conservative" firm's investment

"Conservative" investment model			
Startup investment	Exit value	LP profits	VC carry
$20m	$40m	$16m	$4m
$20m	$40m	$16m	$4m
$20m	$40m	$16m	$4m
$20m	$40m	$16m	$4m
$20m	$40m	$16m	$4m
	TOTAL	$80m	$20m

"Home run" investment model			
Startup investment	Exit value	LP profits	VC carry
$20m	$200m	$144m	$36m
$20m	0	0	0
$20m	0	0	0
$20m	0	0	0
$20m	0	0	0
	TOTAL	$144m	$36m

FIGURE 6.4 VC investment comparisons: Conservative vs. home-run models

decisions are correct and the "home run" firm only gets only one in five correct. Note that this example is only a comparison of investment returns and does not include the maintenance fee costs.

As the tables clearly illustrate, even if all of the investments in the "conservative" model are successful, the profits made by the LPs and the "carry" drawn by the GPs of the VC firms are much lower (80 percent less!) than what the "home run" model returns. And that is assuming that the "home run" investors get only 20 percent of their investment predictions correct. The table clearly shows that one home-run and four strike-outs will return more to the VC firm's GPs than will five singles or doubles (startup investments with small, but positive investment returns). This heavily skews VCs to invest in companies that can potentially deliver huge upsides. This is why the "home run" model dominates the venture capital industry. This example also illustrates that, while LPs may grumble about the carry model, they have no financial incentive to change it.

There is a second, more subtle, impact of the so-called "home run" investment model. It illustrates why each firm invested in by VCs has to return enough capital to make the fund. This "make the fund" investment criterion means that if only one of the portfolio companies in a fund has a positive exit (the rest go bankrupt), the exit of this one must return enough cash to provide the LPs with the targeted overall return for the entire fund. In the example discussed above, the exit value of each investment in the "home run" model must be greater than the size of the VC firm's investment fund – much greater – in order to provide the LPs with the desired overall return on their investment. Those return rates will likely range from 20 to 35 percent or more, depending on the investment stage on which the VC fund focuses its attention.

The result is that the "home run" investment model, which has been adapted by virtually all VC firms, drives investments in startup companies that have the potential to produce huge investment returns (by increasing their valuations by at least ten, and maybe fifty times or more). In addition to having this great upside potential, these firms must fall within the ten-year window of a VC fund. The result is that every startup firm that VCs consider investing in must be able both to increase its valuation by ten to fifty times *and* either go public (have an IPO) or get purchased within three to seven years after the initial investment by the VC firm. These criteria create a very narrow set of successful entrepreneurial startup companies that are considered "venture-backable" or "venture-grade" by VC firms.

Mitigating investment risk Venture capital funds have several ways to mitigate their investment risk after committing to invest in a startup firm. The first is that VC firms do not provide one lump-sum injection of capital to entrepreneurial startup companies and then step back and wish these companies well. Quite the opposite: Once the entrepreneurial company is selected for investment, then that company is actively guided by the VC firm's GPs. Actively managing their investment typically means that one of the firm's GPs will sit on the board of directors of the startup companies in which the firm has invested. These startup firms typically have monthly board meetings. It is estimated that 20 percent of GPs' time is spent identifying a startup to invest in, while the other 80 percent is dedicated to helping guide their portfolio of startup companies.

The heavy time commitment of the VC firms in coaching and guiding their portfolio companies is one reason why the VC firms will invest in syndication with other firms. By investing with other venture firms they know and trust, the GPs can split their board duties with the GPs of other investment firms. For example, if VC firm X and VC firm Y both invest in startup companies A and B, then a GP from firm X can sit on the board of startup A, while a GP of VC firm Y can sit on the board of startup B. Doing so leverages the precious time of the GPs of each VC firm. It also spreads the VC investment risk, by allowing them to spread their fund's capital among more startup companies.

The second method by which VC firms mitigate their investment risk in startup companies is by investing in "stages" or "rounds." These investment rounds have the objective of de-risking the firm and thereby increasing its value. Rather than providing all the capital a company may need to become successful all at once, the capital is dispersed from the VC firms to the startups in smaller amounts. These incremental infusions of capital into startup companies are referred to as investment rounds. Entrepreneurs make the mistake of asking for a specific amount of money to fund them for a year. The value of your firm will not increase just because it is a year older, but only because during that year you successfully passed milestones on the company's development path. Typical investment milestones were discussed in Chapter 4; I list them again below.

Pre-seed investment stage

This investment stage seeks answers to questions such as:

- Is the science repeatable?
- Have you created a working prototype of the idealized product?
- Is there substantial intellectual property (IP) to protect the proposed product?
- Does the company have the freedom to practice this IP?

This milestone is targeted at mitigating the technology risk.

Seed investment stage

Beta-product development.

- Can a quasi-commercial product be created?
- What is the market's reaction to this product?

This milestone is targeted at mitigating the product risk and obtains the first market feedback.

Startup investment stage

Create commercial product.
Obtain first sales.
Compare product costs and margins to those projected.
This stage targets more of the market risks.

First-stage investment

At this stage the aim is to accelerate growth.

- Can the product manufacturing and sales be scaled?
- What are the cost and speed of customer acquisition?
- Are there limits to growth on the supply side (availability of product) or demand side (product adoption rates by customers)?

More market risk mitigation is sought.

Second-stage investment

This stage focuses on profitability:

- making the company profitable
- accelerating profitable growth and
- mitigating market/execution risk.

Mezzanine or bridge investment

The firm seeks capital to extend/expand operations to grow the company to make it a good acquisition target or IPO candidate. It can require the acquisition of smaller competitors. Many companies can complete this phase only with the use of company profits.

Each VC investment round is referred to by a letter: The first round being the "A-round," followed by the "B-round," etc. The stock issued at each investment round will be "preferred" shares. The original company's "founders' shares," which are not associated with an investment round, are converted to "common stock" upon the first investment that triggers the issuance of a series of preferred stock. The preferred share preferences are typically related to priorities on liquidation should the company be unsuccessful. Typically, the later investors will want to get their investment back first following a last-in, first-out scheme. These liquidation preferences typically go away if the firm is sold for a profit, meaning all the preferred shares will convert to common shares. These preferences are definitely something the entrepreneur has to be aware of: you should have an attorney experienced in these type of agreement review the terms.

The price per share sold at each investment round will ideally increase as the company moves forward and passes its designated milestones (see above). The consequences of missing a milestone are severe. In the extreme, the startup will not be able to attract follow-on funding and will end up going out of business. The remains of the firm, whatever those may be, will be sold and the proceeds distributed to the shareholders. This is the time when the liquidation preferences of the various investment rounds are fully leveraged. If the company is able to obtain follow-on funding, say where the milestone was passed but not within the timeframe envisaged, then the next round will likely be priced lower than the previous. This means that the price paid for each share by the investors in the new funding round will be lower than the price-per-share paid by the previous investors. Such an investment round is called a "down round." The investors in the prior rounds are often said to get a "haircut" in such cases. While the terms are humorous, the results are not. Down rounds have a significant impact on ownership and therefore on the potential for early investors to achieve their targeted rates of returns. It also greatly impacts the value capture potential of the entrepreneurs as we shall see in an upcoming example. Before delving into that example, let's first review cap tables and valuations.

Valuations and cap tables

Equity investing requires a valuation of the company at the stage of the investment. In Chapter 4 we discussed how you could estimate an exit value for your firm. That estimate was challenging. Now imagine determining a value for your firm after every investment milestone. That is what must be done before every round of equity financing.

Nowadays pre-seed investments are typically made primarily by angel investors. Angel investors and VC firms have long been at odds over valuing early-stage companies. The initial valuation has significant impact on both the investors and the entrepreneurs, as will be illustrated in a later example. The compromise the two groups have arrived at over time is that typically the angels will not value these companies. Instead their pre-venture investments will typically be made as convertible debt, as previously mentioned, rather than equity. The debt will be converted into equity at a round priced by the venture capitalists.

Capitalization tables, more commonly referred to as "cap tables," track company ownership over time. Multiple capital infusions will be required as a company grows. Each new equity investor will be issued shares of stock in the private firm. In a practical sense, what happens is that the entrepreneurial company will issue new stock certificates to new investors. The issuance of new shares increases the number of total company shares issued. The addition to the total number of shares "dilutes" the percentage of the company owned by the shareholders prior to the new investment. Founders are often too fixated on "dilution." There are two points for the entrepreneur to keep in mind. First, a percentage is not a unit of currency. Second, 100 percent of $100 is worth far less than 1 percent of $100 million.

As the company moves toward commercial success, milestones are passed and investment risks are reduced. Investors that invest at a later date cannot therefore expect to attain the same rates of return on their investments as earlier-stage investors. Since at the company's exit all shares will be valued at the same share price, this means that ideally later-issued company stock should be sold to investors at a higher price per share than the earlier-issued stock. A cap table is created to keep track of all of these details: Who owns what, what quantity of stock was issued, when that stock was issued, what price per share was paid for that stock, and ultimately what return on investment is achieved by all the investors.

Cap tables keep track of each investment round's pre-money value, investment, post-money value, and the number of shares issued at each round. Entrepreneurs often believe, falsely, that the only valuations that matter are the pre-money value at the first investment round and the post-money value at the end of the process (i.e. the value at which the company is sold). The rest of the valuations, these entrepreneurs believe, are simply number games that venture capitalists play with each other. Nothing could be further from the truth. Every valuation at every investment stage impacts the return for those investors as well the ultimate value the founders will capture from the firm, as the example below illustrates.

In this example, we will look at three different investment scenarios and see how those changes impact the investor's return from each investment round. The example will also highlight the financial return to the founders. In the example below, each case has an identical initial pre-money value ($1.0 million). Each case has five investment rounds. In each case the company will be acquired for $350 million a year after the fifth investment round. The amount and timing of the investments are also identical in each case. The only difference between the cases is the company valuation for the intermediate rounds. The ratio of the pre-money value in an investment round to the post-money value in the prior round is called the "step-up." The round-by-round step-ups are shown for each case. In none of the examples are employee stock options taken into account.

Case 1 is the ideal case where the step-up is greatest in the early investment rounds. As you can see in the summary table below, in Case 1 the return rates for the investors decrease in each round: One would expect this, as the risk that the subsequent investors take on decreases.

Table 6.1 *Case 1: Step-up greatest in the early investment rounds*

Investment round	1	2	3	4	5	Sale value
Pre-money valuation ($m)	$1.0	$5.0	$20.0	$80.0	$180.0	$350.0
Investment ($m)	$0.5	$5.0	$20.0	$50.0	$100.0	
Post-money valuation ($m)	$1.5	$10.0	$40.0	$130.0	$280.0	
Round-to-round Step-up		3.3	2.0	2.0	1.4	1.3
IRR by round	87%	62%	51%	32%	35%	

Table 6.2 *Case 2: Step-ups fairly similar in each investment round*

Investment round	1	2	3	4	5	Sale value
Pre-money valuation ($m)	$1.0	$2.0	$10.0	$45.0	$140.0	$350.0
Investment ($m)	$0.5	$5.0	$20.0	$50.0	$100.0	
Post-money valuation ($m)	$1.5	$7.0	$30.0	$95.0	$240.0	
Round-to-round step-up		1.3	1.4	1.5	1.5	1.5
IRR by round	44%	46%	48%	47%	46%	

In Case 2, the round-to-round step-ups are fairly flat. The mid-round valuers may be cautious so as not to overvalue the company. The result in this case is that most of the increase in the value of the firm comes at the end of the process. In this case the IRR that the investors receive are fairly similar, meaning that not all the investors are achieving a return commensurate with their investment risk.

In the third scenario something has gone wrong. There is a down-round after the second investment round. The step-up for that round (round 3 post-money value divided by round 2 pre-money value) is less than one. The company ends up recovering and selling at the same time and price as in the other two scenarios, but the investors before the down-round are poorly rewarded.

Table 6.3 *Case 3: Third round is a down-round*

Investment round	1	2	3	4	5	Sale value
Pre-money valuation ($m)	$1.0	$2.0	$3.0	$30.0	$100.0	$350.0
Investment ($m)	$0.5	$5.0	$20.0	$50.0	$100.0	
Post-money valuation ($m)	$1.5	$7.0	$23.0	$80.0	$200.0	
Round-to-round step-up		1.3	0.4	1.3	1.3	1.8
IRR by round	10%	5%	42%	48%	75%	

Table 6.4 *Summary of the three case studies*

Investor's IRR	Case 1	Case 2	Case 3
Round 1 investors	87%	44%	10%
Round 2 investors	62%	46%	5%
Round 3 investors	51%	48%	42%
Round 4 investors	32%	47%	48%
Round 5 investors	35%	46%	75%
Founders' % of exit value	6.6%	1.8%	0.5%

A summary of the three cases, shown in the table above, shows the devastating effects of the down-round on the investors in the first two rounds in Case 3. The first two rounds' investors would normally expect returns in the order of those for Case 1. Their returns are significantly diminished in this scenario. The impact on the founders is equally significant. The percentage of the company that the founders own at the time of sale drops more than an order of magnitude from Case 1 to Case 3 despite both cases having identical initial valuations, final firm acquisition price, and identical investments at the same times.

The lesson in these three scenarios is that those intermediate valuations matter. Those intermediate pricings are like the American game show *The Price Is Right*. Those that win are able to estimate the price nearest to the actual price without going over. Underestimating the intermediate values shifts the value capture to the later investors. Overestimating the intermediate company valuations could cause a down-round which will devastate all the investors prior to that round. First-time entrepreneurs tend to go with venture firms that provide them with the highest pre-money valuation for their firm. No doubt those valuations boost the entrepreneur's ego. They well might, however, pinch their pocketbook if the early valuation proves too high.

Equity stakes

Entrepreneurs always want to know "how much of my company will I have to give up in order to get VC financing?" First of all, that is the wrong question. Entrepreneurs do not "give away" equity stakes in their companies; they sell those equity stakes for the capital they need to grow their businesses. Because venture capital is very expensive capital, entrepreneurs with another way of raising the amount of capital required should pursue it. The fact is, entrepreneurs often do not have an alternative source for the kind of capital required.

The question remains, how much equity does the typical entrepreneur sell in each investment round? That question is impossible to answer with any degree of certainty as each startup is different and each investment deal is unique. That said, some insight can be gained by looking at the national venture investment numbers. Figure 6.5 below shows VC investment data for the USA in the first quarter of 2007 (NVCA website, retrieved 2013). Beyond the VC investment bubble period, that data has been fairly consistent over the years. This

Investment round	Median investment per round	Median pre-money valuation	Median equity purchased per round	Entrepreneur's cumulative post-investment ownership position
Seed	$1 m	$1.5 m	1/(1+1.5) = 40%	100%×(1−40%) = 60%
First	$4.9 m	$5.2m	4.9/(4.9+5.2) = 49%	60%×(1−49%) = 31%
Second	$9.5 m	$18.2 m	9.5/(9.5+18/2) = 34%	31%×(1−34%) = 20%
Later	$12.1 m	$41.0 m	12.1/(12.1+41) = 23%	20%×(1−23%) = 16%

FIGURE 6.5 Venture capital investment stages and median equity stakes for 1Q07 investments

data suggests that entrepreneurs typically sell 40 percent of the equity in their company in a seed-stage investment. First-round investors typically acquire 49 percent of the remaining firm. Assuming that the startup was owned 100 percent by the entrepreneurs before the seed investment round, then the entrepreneurs would retain 60 percent of the company after the seed round, 30.6 percent (60 percent × 51 percent) after the first round, etc., as shown in the table. Recall that every round issues new stock. That means that, while the equity purchased in each round cannot be more than 100 percent, the sum of all these investment rounds, shown in the fourth column of the table below, can indeed exceed 100 percent.

DUE DILIGENCE

All investors will do some type of due diligence. They will not simply be so impressed with your business plan or pitch that they will immediately write you a check. Obtaining money for your firm is a process: Plan, pitch, then due diligence. Since VC funds are investing other people's money they will have a formal due diligence procedure that requires significant documentation. Angel investors' due diligence process will often be less formal, but there will still be a process. You can plan on spending weeks if not months in the due diligence process with venture capitalists. It may also cost your firm tens of thousands of dollars in time and material to complete, even if you are unsuccessful at eventually obtaining funding. While it may feel good to have many, many firms considering investment in your firm, the reality is that it will be very expensive to you to have them all perform due diligence on your firm. Due diligence is a serious process that should not be started without serious thought.

There are many good reference books on the due diligence process. The due diligence on your firm will cover a wide range of topics ranging from your incorporation documentation to relevant insurance policies. The outline below is not meant to be exhaustive or completely inclusive,[1] but representative of the types of issue that you can expect to be investigated during the process (Camp, 2002; Zygmont, 2001).

1. *Legal structure, agreements, and ownership:*

Articles of Incorporation and by-laws of the company
and seller.

Corporate minute books and stock transfer records of the
company.

Federal and state tax returns and related reports of the company
including:

- income tax returns,
- audit reports of taxing authorities including descriptions of
any open issues,
- real estate tax bills and payment records,
- personal property tax bills and payment records,
- franchise, license, capital stock, doing business, and similar
tax reports, and
- other material documents.

Agreements and arrangements between the company and seller
or any affiliate of the company or seller, including:

- stock subscription agreements,
- loan, line of credit, or other financing arrangements,
- tax-sharing agreements or arrangements,
- overhead-allocation agreements or arrangements,
- management services or personnel loan agreements or
arrangements,
- guarantees or keep-well arrangements for the benefit of
creditors or other third parties, and
- other.

Shareholder agreements relating to stock of the company or
stock owned by the company.

Documents imposing restrictions or conditions on stock
transfer or merger, including any arrangements
granting rights of first refusal or other preferential
purchase rights.

Third-party or governmental consent or authorizations required
for merger or acquisition.

2. *Financials:*

Financial statements, including audited financial statements for all periods beginning on or after (date to be determined), consisting, in each case, of at least a balance sheet and income statement; interim, monthly, unaudited, financial statements for periods after the latest audited statements; and working papers relating to the foregoing.

Bank accounts and depositary arrangements.

Credit agreements and credit instruments including loan agreements, notes, debentures and bonds, and files relating thereto.

Performance and financial bonds.

Letters of credit.

Instruments or arrangements creating liens, encumbrances, mortgages, or other charges on any real or personal property of the company, including property held indirectly through joint ventures, partnerships, subsidiaries, or otherwise.

Receivables analysis including aging, turnover, and bad debt experience.

3. *Operations:*

Internal management reports and memoranda.

Policy and procedures manuals including those concerning personnel policy, internal controls, and legal and regulatory compliance.

Budgets, financial projections, business plans, and capital expenditure plans.

Contracts and arrangements for supplies or services, including the following which were entered into or under which work was done during the past [number] years:

- contracts for the sale or purchase of real estate,
- contracts for the purchase or sale of materials, equipment, or other personal property or fixtures,
- contracts or other arrangements for legal, accounting, consulting, brokerage, banking, or other services, and
- construction and engineering contracts or subcontracts.

Proprietary information and documents, including:

- patents and patent applications,
- copyrights,
- trademarks, service marks, logos, and trade or assumed names,
- non-patentable proprietary know-how,
- federal and state filings relating to any of the foregoing,
- licensing agreements relating to any of the foregoing (whether the company is a licensor or licensee), and
- confidentiality agreements relating to any of the foregoing.

Partnership or joint venture agreements to which the company is a party and any other arrangements with third parties concerning the management or operation of properties, facilities, or investments of the company.

Reports to management, board of directors, or shareholders prepared by outside consultants, engineers, or analysts.

Closing documentation and related files for each prior sale of company stock and each material asset purchase or sale by the company during the past [number] years.

Leases, deeds, and related instruments, including without limitation, office premises leases, equipment or vehicle leases, and any such instruments held indirectly through joint ventures, partnerships, subsidiaries, or otherwise.

Agreements or arrangements granting rights of first refusal or other preferential purchase rights to any property of the company.

Other material agreements or arrangements.

4. *Personnel:*

Corporate policies concerning hiring, compensation, advancement and termination.

Labor contracts together with a list of all labor unions that have represented or attempted to represent employees of the company during the past [number] years.

Agreements with individual employees, including:

- executive employment agreements,
- bonus, profit-sharing, and similar arrangements,
- post-employment agreements including "salary continuation" and "golden parachute" arrangements, and
- covenants not to compete by present or former employees.

Names of any officers or key employees who have left the company during the past [number] years.

Each of the following which the company maintains or contributes to, together with filings with the Internal Revenue Service, Pension Benefit Guaranty Corporation (PBGC), Securities and Exchange Commission, and Department of Labor, including without limitation, Forms 5500 and 5310, summary plan descriptions, summary annual reports, IRS determination letters (for qualified plans), and PBGC reportable events:

- union-sponsored multi-employer plans,
- defined benefit plans,
- defined contribution plans including:
  - money purchase pension plans,
  - profit-sharing plans,
  - stock bonus plans,
  - employee stock ownership plans, and
  - savings or thrift plans,
- health and benefit plans, including:
  - medical, surgical, hospital, or other healthcare plans or insurance programs including HMOs,
  - dental plans,
  - short-term disability or sick pay plans or arrangements,
  - long-term disability insurance or uninsured arrangements,
  - group term or other life or accident insurance,
  - unemployment or vacation benefit plans, and
  - other benefit plans,
- non-qualified deferred compensation arrangements including:
  - director or officer deferred fee plans,

- excess benefit plans (providing benefits in excess of Internal Revenue Code limitations for qualified plans), and
- severance pay plans,
- incentive or bonus plans including:
  - stock option plans,
  - stock bonus plans,
  - stock purchase plans, and
  - cash bonus or incentive plans.
5. *Insurance:*

   Insurance policies including those covering:
   - fire,
   - liability,
   - casualty,
   - life,
   - title,
   - workers' compensation,
   - directors' and officers' liability, and
   - other insurance policies.

     Claim and loss histories, correspondence with insurance carriers, and names of all insurance representatives relating to the foregoing.
6. *PP&E (property, plant and equipment):*

   List of real estate (with legal descriptions), equipment and other personal property owned, leased, or in the process of being acquired or sold by the company, with the cost and book value of each item.

   Real estate, equipment and other personal property leases, and conditional sale agreements.

   Information relating to title on all property listed in the items above, including motor vehicle title documents.

   Appraisals of real estate, personal property, and equipment.
7. *Regulatory:*

   Licenses, permits, filings, or authorizations obtained from, made with, or required by any governmental entity.

   Correspondence with any governmental regulatory authority.

Accident or injury reports to federal, state, local and foreign governmental entities.

8. *Litigation:*

Pending or threatened litigation, regulatory investigations, governmental actions, arbitrations, or notices of violation or possible violation, including proceedings in which the company is a plaintiff or claimant, and the names and addresses of legal counsel advising or representing the company in each matter.

Files and records relating to the foregoing including opinions and evaluations.

SUMMARY

The primary resources you will need to build a successful business come down to people and money. Get the right people on the bus, as Jim Collins says, then pursue the money (Collins, 2001b). This chapter began with a discussion of people. That discussion ranged from how to interpret resumés to how to determine a candidate's alignment with the firm you are trying to build. Focus and alignment are key. Do not get ahead of your plan when hiring and do not hire simply to accomplish tasks. Get the right people in place that will add value to your firm now and into the future.

First and foremost when pursuing funding for your firm, make sure that capital fits the type of firm you want to build. The investment potential framework assesses the type of financing you *could* attract. The type of financing you desire needs to be consistent with that framework and the long-term aspirations of your firm. Even if your firm falls within the "traditional equity" quadrant of the investment potential framework, you do not need to pursue angel or VC financing. This is particularly true if it is your desire to own the firm for decades. You will not be able to grow your firm as fast without that capital so you must assess what this may mean for your firm's future competitiveness. Slower growth may mean an opportunity for a competitor to launch and overtake your market position. You can also use combinations of capital. Perhaps you could obtain grant monies or funds from crowdfunding sites to do some early de-risking of your firm before seeking follow-on venture capital. The advantage to that is the further the company is de-risked, the more attractive it becomes to financiers.

Either way, you should consider the people that come along with the capital in the same manner you would a significant new hire. Investors, particularly equity investors, will become part of your firm for a long time. Alignment with the company you desire to build is paramount. Do not be seduced by the highest valuation. Not only may this backfire on you later in terms of what it means for company ownership, but that money may not come with the best people for your firm. People first, then money.

The launching of your business will be a hectic and emotional experience. Signing contracts and other agreements will make real what was once only an idea in your mind. Having moments of sheer exhilaration and great trepidation during this period of controlled chaos is normal. Follow your plan, stay focused, execute those tasks that lie along your critical path, and you soon will find yourself transitioning to the next phase of your company's growth.

NOTE

1. This list was compiled over time during my management of the Wolverine Venture Fund (2003–6), a student-run venture capital fund. Significant contributors to this list include Mary Campbell of EDF Ventures, Don Walker of Arbor Partners, and investor David Shelby, all long-time advisors of the WVF.

7 Strategies for managing growth

Growth is the number one concern of corporate executives, economic developers, and government officials desperately trying to reduce unemployment (Shleifer and Vishny, 1997; Ernst & Young, 2012). And why not, since growth is at the heart of economic prosperity – personal, corporate, or regional? Entrepreneurship is at the heart of growth. Growth is driven by entrepreneurs discovering new business opportunities from which they create new businesses and new lines of business within existing companies. Innovatively solving complex problems through organizations is what professional entrepreneurs do. As Archimedes said, "Give me a lever long enough and a fulcrum on which to place it and I shall move the world." Organizations are that lever, entrepreneurs are that fulcrum.

All companies rely on innovations to grow over time. In a presentation at Stanford University in 2005 Geoffrey Moore, author of *Crossing the Chasm* and *Escape Velocity*, said this about the connection between innovation and growth:

> Why innovation? It has to do with this notion that we are in a capitalist market; we are in a competitively driven market. The effect of competition-driven markets is, over time, to commoditize any differentiation a company has and thereby diminish its ability to win customers and win capital and to win sales at attractive margins; to create attractive returns.
>
> So the only way you can respond to that is to continually come up with new differentiation and to do that you have to innovate. So it is not rocket-science to understand why we care about this issue [innovation] (Moore, 2005).

The only way to maintain differentiated margins is to continue to drive innovative growth. Innovation is the tool of the entrepreneur (Drucker, 1985). Throughout this chapter we will draw upon aspects that were developed in other segments of the Entrepreneurial Arch. Growth is not simply about "marketing." It is not something that a single group in the firm can accomplish on their own. As this chapter will illustrate, growth is an aggregation of all the activities of the Arch that precede this one.

It would be a mistake to discuss growth without first reflecting on the original aspirations of the firm. Your approach to growth is very dependent on why and how you want to grow your firm. As Bo Burlingham pointed out in *Small Giants* (2005), bigger is not always better. Firms like Zingerman's Deli purposely choose to stay small and spin off related businesses (a community of businesses) in the Ann Arbor, Michigan area of the United States rather than create a global franchise (Zingerman's, n.d.). At the heart of this choice is the founder's aspiration to create a local socio-economic impact. Paul Saginaw and Ari Weinzweig, the co-founders of Zingerman's, could have easily created a national brand as Tom Monaghan did with Domino's Pizza (also first established in Ann Arbor, Michigan), but consciously chose not to do so. This chapter will provide strategies and pitfalls to growth, should you choose to make that choice for your firm.

Growing your firm requires a clear direction. Beyond a clear direction, growth requires focus and alignment. Many young companies get caught in the trap of chasing every opportunity that comes along. You do have to pay attention to the market. The product or service you believe is satisfying a need may not be the one the customer truly wants or values. You have to be able to listen and be flexible enough to adapt to what the market is telling you. However you have to do this in the context of a focused vision. You need to define and articulate the company vision in terms so simple that every employee can repeat them in their sleep. That means a clear and precise corporate vision, not some flowery mission statement. Keeping your rapidly increasingly employee base aligned to that vision will absorb most of management's effort as your company grows. You will be bombarded with ideas – all well-meaning – from employees to customers to casual observers. You need to adapt a culture of "admiring ideas, and worshiping execution." It is all too easy to have the organization's energy dissipated. Doing one thing well is better than doing many things in a mediocre way. A researcher friend had developed a unique process for nano-materials. He represented the paradox that many startups face. My friend told me that he could produce many different types of nano-material with his patented process. I told him he had to focus initially on one material and one application. "What if I pick the wrong one?" he asked. "Your business will fail," was my answer. "Then I won't do it. I'll continue to work on all materials and all applications," was his response. "Unfortunately, it works like this," I said. "If you choose my path, there is a probability the company will fail. If you stay on your path, your firm is guaranteed to fail." Unfortunately, that is the cold, hard truth of entrepreneurial life. A company that tries to be everything for everyone ends up being nothing for anyone. The elements on the left-hand side of the Entrepreneurial Arch, discussed earlier in this book, are designed to help you choose the commercialization path that improves the probability of your success.

Consistent with the approach taken throughout this book, we will discuss growth from a distant to a close-up perspective. That discussion will move from the vision-level perspective, to a strategic one, to an operational one. In this approach we will examine aspects of growth – corporate, offering, and personal. We will start with the external, demand-side view of the firm. We will then look inside the firm at particular features, specifically the maturation of work processes. From there we will move to the offering; first by taking a broad view of market segment-to-segment growth and then by zooming in and looking at the growth of a product across a specific segment. We will finish by zooming in on people – particularly the founders – and how they impact the firm's growth.

Consistent with the mistake most firms make in identifying opportunities in the first place, the sole focus on growth tends to be on the current offering. That is a paralyzing mistake. The offering is nothing but a current manifestation of the company's capabilities that satisfies a current market need. Offerings will be transient. The half-life of that transience may be quite long for commodity raw materials and very short for consumer electronics, but all are transient nonetheless. We will start the process by zooming out to obtain the corporate perspective. Both internal and external factors will be examined from a corporate growth perspective. The examination will then zoom in to people, with particular focus on the founders, and then focus on the offering.

CORPORATE GROWTH

The corporate vision should be the least malleable aspect of your new venture while the offering should be the most. The detailed vision for the new venture was articulated in the operationalization segment of the Entrepreneurial Arch. This vision sets the direction for the firm. It is its North Star. Every other aspect of the firm can and should be measured against this vision. Every employee at every level should be able to answer the question "How does this activity help us move toward that vision?"

Throughout this book we continue to view the segments of the Entrepreneurial Arch through the lens of capabilities. Examining growth will be no different. Large organizations tend to focus on being efficient. For these firms, it is all about execution – maximizing the output from the firm's capabilities. In new, growing firms, it is as much about capability growth, and the leveraging of those new capabilities, as it is about execution. Differentiated products are built upon differentiated capabilities. As a result, entrepreneurial firms must continue to expand their capabilities, and be aware of how these are expanding, in order to continue to create the differentiated margins associated with differentiated products.

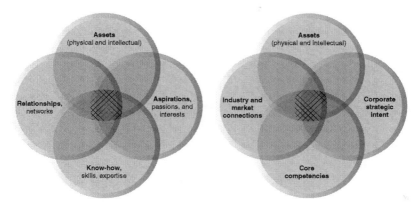

FIGURE 7.1 Team and corporation capability maps

Capabilities have been defined very specifically throughout this book. Figure 7.1 shows both team and corporate capability maps. The firm operates at the nexus of these maps. The difference between doing and dreaming is the ability to take action regarding your vision. The nexus of these capabilities represents the sweet spot for the entrepreneurial firm. Opportunities that fall outside that nexus are outside either the entrepreneurial firm's scope or its interest. In other words, if any of the elements are missing there is no way to implement the business concept or no interest in doing so. The entrepreneurial firm includes everyone associated with the firm, from founders to advisors. As the firm progresses across the Arch it expands its capabilities. It did so through the addition of people and through the expanding experiences of the people in the firm. Established or new, all organizations are constantly leveraging and growing their capabilities. The firms may not, however, be aware of this expansion of their capability. That lack of awareness limits future growth, as would the lack of capabilities themselves.

Innovative new businesses, whether new lines of business in existing companies or new startup companies, are, by definition, moving into new arenas for the organization. Like young college graduates, these young entities have high ambitions, but limited capabilities.

Even if the corporation housing the new line of business has expansive capabilities, these capabilities will be limited with respect to the new line of business. If that is not the case, it is likely that the proposed new business line is not all that innovative. The key question, as every new college grad quickly learns, is "How do you leverage the capabilities you do have to grow into the area where you want to be?" To do so you need to understand which skills are transferable into the new space, which are differentiating, and which you will need to acquire or leverage from those around you.

The best career counsel I ever heard given to students was by my friend and colleague Alec Gallimore (2010). He tells students to approach the workplace with a "learn and contribute" attitude. Contribute to the prosperity of the firm – execute on your current capabilities – and also learn – expand your capabilities. By doing so, you will become increasingly valuable to the firm or other firms, thereby increasing your personal marketability. There is no growth in contributing without learning and no financial viability to learning without contributing. New ventures would do well to heed the same counsel. If your firm is not expanding its capabilities it has very limited potential for future growth. If the firm is not making products that contribute to the firm's financial viability, it will not be long for this world.

Growth strategies must extend beyond thinking about the adoption of a single product. Instead they should extend to the adoption of a series of products based on current and growing capabilities. The first product a new firm releases will not always be the product they ultimately imagine, but it will be the one they can produce the quickest that someone will buy. This minimum viable product (MVP) was first discussed in Chapter 3. A new firm's initial product needs to put it on a path to future products. The company Rain-X is a perfect example of this methodology. Rain-X offers a line of consumer automotive and surface care products. The firm introduced its original windshield "wax" that forces water to bead and roll off of the windshield, often without needing the wiper, in the late 1990s. While the product worked great, it took some effort to apply. That meant that the segment willing to purchase the product would be relatively small – auto enthusiasts. Some years later the company released a combination 2-in-1 glass cleaner and window protectant that was easier to use, and had broader customer appeal, but was much more difficult to create and manufacture. The combination 2-in-1 glass cleaner and window protectant was likely the ideal product Rain-X had envisioned from the start. However, the development time for that product was both challenging and substantial (the original Rain-X product warned that glass cleaners would reduce the effectiveness of their product!). Rather than going into a long period of product research and development with no income, the company launched the first product, which you could think of as their MVP. This product launched the company and fueled the research that led to the launch of the second product, the 2-in-1 cleaner/protectant. In other words, Rain-X leveraged its current capabilities in the launch of its original product. It built new capabilities in the development of its follow-on product. The firm also increased its manufacturing know-how, in addition to developing relationships with distributors and retail outlets along the way. All these additional capabilities were leveraged in the new product. More recently, Rain-X leveraged the brand it had developed over decades of creating leading-edge windshield-related products to introduce windshield wiper blades. The company's growth can be succinctly summarized to illustrate how it built upon expanding capabilities. First it had the formulation polymer (patented composition of matter), the windshield "wax." It then developed an improved mechanism for delivering the polymer – aerosol spray mixed with cleaner. Over time it established a brand that it could leverage to differentiate itself in launching a commodity type of product (windshield wipers). Note that with each new or improved capability came a new offering, differentiated by the new (or improved) capability. Each product, in turn, broadened the firm's customer base and growth potential.

Leveraging capabilities: PVC

The Positioning for Value Capture (PVC) framework is detailed in Appendix A. In Chapter 2 we discussed using the PVC framework (Figure 7.2) to reposition your firm in order to optimize its potential to capture value. As outlined in that chapter, the initial success of the firm is dependent on capturing a healthy share of the value your firm creates for others. Now we will use the PVC as a framework for positioning the firm for growth.

Your organization's ability to capture value is dictated by the combination of how difficult your capabilities are to replicate and how easy the complementary capabilities are to obtain. In the two-by-two PVC framework, the vertical axis describes your capabilities. Specifically, it defines how easy those capabilities are to imitate or reproduce (i.e. appropriate). Specialized capabilities are difficult to reproduce. It is not that they are impossible to reproduce; it is simply

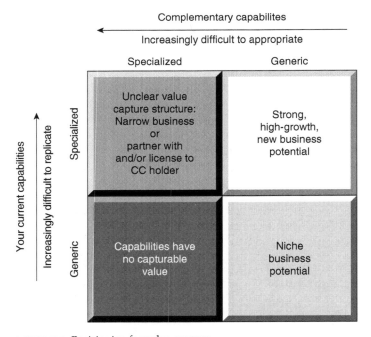

FIGURE 7.2 Positioning for value capture

that it would take considerable time, effort, and/or money to do so. Generic capabilities, on the other hand, are more common and can be easily appropriated. The PVC framework compares your capabilities to those complementary capabilities (CC) that you will leverage from the ecosystem.

The ideal position for a strong new business with high growth potential is to be in the upper right-hand quadrant of the PVC diagram shown in Figure 7.2. Organizations in this quadrant have specialized, differentiated capabilities and only need generic, complementary capabilities; capabilities that are easy to appropriate. While starting in the quadrant is ideal, it is not the only quadrant in which new firms are launched. Clearly, if the firm is in the lower left-hand quadrant it should have been repositioned. Any of the other three quadrants are viable starting points for new ventures. In the next three sub-sections of this chapter we will discuss growth starting from each of the three positive quadrants of the PVC diagram.

Growth strategies from the niche business quadrant

As we discussed in Chapter 2, firms that were initially located in the upper left-hand quadrant (unclear value capture) often reposition themselves to move to the niche quadrant. If the firm has specialized assets, the move creates a "specialized niche" business. However, despite some specialized assets, the firm is still lacking significant complementary capabilities necessary for it to become a business with high growth potential. One can imagine Rain-X, for example, starting here with a proprietary polymer formula that could be good for "waxing" windshields, but not much else. From the niche quadrant, the firm needs a growth strategy to allow it to grow into the upper right-hand quadrant.

Finding yourself in the lower right-hand quadrant generally means that you principally have generic capabilities but only need generic complementary capabilities to enable your business. The main defense of your business in this quadrant is being small. For example, say I have a small IT consulting business. Let's say my annual revenue is around $200,000. For the sake of this example, let's say that my skills and capabilities are pretty generic. I know a little networking, and a little about web development but nothing out of the ordinary. I am able to capture some value because of the niche business space that I fill. IBM, on the other hand, is also in the IT consulting business. Its revenue is measured in the tens of millions. IBM has an established brand and many patented and non-patented processes. IBM is clearly in the upper right-hand quadrant while my small firm is in the lower right-hand quadrant of the PVC diagram. Is my firm a threat to IBM? Will they come after my little firm, by either attempting to acquire me or in some other way drive me out of business? No, absolutely not. My firm is simply too small for them to worry about. Smallness is my firm's defense. However, if I decide to grow my business without developing any specialized capabilities I could, in theory, reach a size that could become be a threat, or at least an annoyance, to IBM, by negatively impacting on their market share. In that case, IBM would most certainly take aggressive action against my firm. If my capabilities were still generic, it would be difficult for me to respond and hard for me to capture any value.

Many firms that begin in the niche business quadrant have grander ambitions. The issue is how to grow the business strategically and move from the lower right-hand quadrant to the upper right-hand quadrant of Figure 7.2. To move to the upper right-hand quadrant you need to develop specialized capabilities that the firm is currently lacking. While this development usually occurs over time, it begins with a vision of your future firm. That vision must then be translated into goals, objectives, and specific activities that drive the venture forward. The easiest way to think about this is through a specific example. Consider McDonald's hamburgers in the late 1940s. During that post-war period in the United States there were many hamburger restaurants in many small towns across the country. McDonald's started as just another small, "me too" hamburger restaurant. It did not have any particular differentiated or specialized capabilities. How did it grow and become the global chain that we know today, serving 68 million customers daily in 119 countries around the globe (Wikipedia, n.d.)? They did this by identifying a user need and developing several specialized capabilities. Certainly, today they are one of the most widely recognized brands in the world. While brand is an important, specialized asset and building a brand is important, it usually occurs with the development of other capabilities. McDonald's leveraged the disruption of increasing consumer mobility. In the postwar era in the United States automobiles became more accessible and affordable. People were taking advantage of this new asset to explore their surroundings. The "Sunday joy ride" was becoming commonplace. This disruption created an opening in the fast-food business. While you may know the quality of food in hamburger bars in your own town you may not have any knowledge of the hamburger restaurants in surrounding towns. What McDonald's discovered was that people wanted consistent food. They did not want to be surprised. When they pulled into a hamburger place, they wanted to know what they were getting. What McDonald's developed was a process for making hamburgers and french fries that could be easily replicated from restaurant to restaurant. That process produced consistent food. This process is a specialized capability.

The second capability that McDonald's developed was in finding store locations. They became experts at locating their stores in areas of growth and new road development. The result was that, when you drove into a new town, their store was one of the first restaurants you saw. The two specialized capabilities moved them from the niche business quadrant to the high-potential-growth business quadrant.

One can imagine Rain-X starting as a couple of polymer chemists selling their solution to car enthusiasts via ads in car magazines. Perhaps at first they could only manufacture small batches in their kitchens and package these themselves. They may have found contract manufacturers to which they could outsource the manufacturing and distribution. They then likely started developing relationships with retailers (specialized capability) that would increase their distribution outlet to car-part retail stores and then to big chain stores. The firm's growth potential likely remained limited until the development of the 2-in-1 product (another specialized capability) that appealed to the masses. However, by the time this was developed, the other important relationships were already in place, making the firm's accelerated growth possible. While I do not know this to be the case with Rain-X, I have seen enough other, less-well-known, startups follow this path to know it is a very typical way forward for technology-based startup firms.

Moving up from the lower to the upper right-hand quadrant of the PVC is about much more than marketing and market share. It is about "learning and contributing" – developing new capabilities while generating revenue from your current ones. It is also about keeping your firm in a position to capture a significant portion of the value you are creating. In Rain-X's case, as with many other startup firms, it also lies in defining a growth path from an MVP that may only be attractive to a small market segment, to a product with wider market appeal.

Growth strategies from the specialized–specialized quadrant

Firms with specialized assets, particularly intellectual ones, often find themselves in the upper left-hand quadrant of the PVC framework, since they often lack the specialized complementary assets necessary to create the finished offering and deliver it to their customer. This quadrant is often referred to as the "licensing" quadrant, although that is just one of the options for a firm positioned here. The fundamental issue is how to capture the most value from your capabilities, which could mean, as discussed in Chapter 2, initially repositioning your firm. As previously discussed, the repositioning could be directly to the upper right-hand quadrant, but is more likely to travel through the niche business quadrant.

Since the previous section discussed growth from the niche business quadrant, this section will focus on growing from the upper left-hand quadrant directly to the upper right-hand quadrant. Chapter 2 discussed the special case of a product development firm that would sell its product (or partially developed product in the case of a new pharmaceutical after completion of Phase II of the US FDA's approval process) to the CC holder. That case will not be discussed further here, therefore. Instead, this section will focus on growing your way to the upper right-hand quadrant.

The reason that you are in the specialized–specialized quadrant in the first place is that you require specialized capabilities that you do not have and cannot appropriate. These capabilities are specialized because they take considerable time or money to develop. The issue, therefore, for moving directly from the upper left to the upper right is how to obtain the commodities necessary (time and money) for you to appropriate these specialized assets. One way to buy yourself time is to keep your day job while you work on your business on the side. This tactic may work if what you are primarily missing is relationships. It may also be a possible path forward if what you primarily need is know-how that you can acquire over time on your own. Unfortunately, neither is typically the case in this quadrant. If the firm has the potential for high growth, then that usually means there is a relatively small window of opportunity in which you need to get your business launched and growing. Miss that window and someone else will grab that brass ring before you. All of which means you need money, and a considerable amount of it, in order to acquire the specialized capabilities you require.

Finding a considerable amount of financing for a business that has questionable potential to capture value sounds like a non-starter. In opportunity identification, I urged you to reposition firms of this type as you were never going to be able to attract outside financing. However there is an alternative. What if the financing did not need to come from the outside? What if there was a way for you to produce it? While this sounds crazy, it is possible. The approach you need to take to gain the money needed to move from the upper right-hand to the upper left-hand quadrant is a variation on the "narrowing your business" strategy discussed in Chapter 2. In that chapter we discussed repositioning the firm from, say, tire manufacturing to tire design. The idea was to define a business that emphasizes your specialized capabilities, yet only requires generic CCs to realize. Now we want to think about acquiring the specialized capabilities we need, so we need to think of "narrowing" the business in a different way.

Most firms in the upper left-hand quadrant have some sort of intellectual asset, yet lack the other capabilities required to exploit it. Intellectual assets can have many fields of use. I had a friend that developed a technology that could be the foundation for a mini-CT scanning device. His aspiration was to see the device commercialized for medical use. He envisioned dentists and otolaryngologists using a device based on his technology in their offices to examine teeth and sinuses. Beyond the patented invention there were many specialized CCs that my friend simply did not have. He needed a significant amount of cash to acquire them. Like most fundamental intellectual assets, this one had a wide variety of uses. It could potentially be used in the field, for example to examine physical equipment (engines, pipelines, etc.). My friend had no interest in pursuing these uses. He therefore licensed his technology to firms that were interested in developing the technology for uses outside of healthcare. He needed cash, so instead of the typical license agreement of a royalty on future product sales, he licensed his technology for a one-time, up-front cash payment. Those cash payments were significant, but proved to also be a good deal for the licensees as they were significantly lower than they would have paid in ongoing royalties. With the licenses sold, my friend now had the cash he needed to acquire the capabilities necessary for him to build the company he desired. Creativity and a clear vision of what you want to build is required for growth from this quadrant.

Strategies for growth from the high-growth-potential quadrant
Firms in this quadrant are positioned for high growth. Realizing that potential is the challenge. The examination of these firms will take both external and internal vantage points. We will start with the external, demand-side, view of the firm. This will be followed by an internal, supply-side, view, specifically focusing on the maturation of work processes.

Demand-side (external): Growth and renewal strategies Firms in the other quadrants know they are not optimally positioned on the PVC framework. As a result they understand that they need to make adjustments to their strategies in order to grow. Firms in this quadrant may get complacent, and think they have arrived. They may presume that all they need to do is continue to grow their business; meaning expand the sales of their current offering. After all, they have optimized the firm based on the first five segments of the Arch. The danger in that thinking is that their success may be short-lived. If the objective is to flip the firm, demonstrate rapid revenue growth and then sell it, there may be no need for the current team to think longer-term. If the objective is to continue to operate the firm over an extended period of time, you need a longer-term vision. Certainly, the acquirer in the flip case also needs a longer-term strategy. That vision must extend beyond the adoption of the current offering: Rather, the long-term growth strategies should extend to the adoption of a series of products based on current and future capabilities. We are examining the future of the company, but once again doing so through the lens of the organization's dynamic capabilities.

Envision a series of offerings that develop over time, each new offering building on the capabilities developed through the creation and sales of the previous offering. Grow and contribute: This is the essence of the market adoption roadmap shown in Figure 7.3. Clay

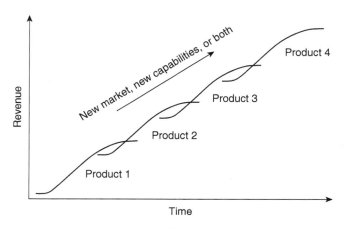

FIGURE 7.3 Market adoption roadmap, customer and product changes

Christensen showed a similar series of s-curves when discussing technology innovations over time in his book *The Innovator's Dilemma* (1997). The concept of the market adoption roadmap is broader, in that it represents a series of offerings based on all of the firm's growing capabilities; all capabilities, as they have been defined in this book, not just advances in technology.

These additional, revenue-producing opportunities fall in either of two categories: Market adjacencies or capability adjacencies. Market adjacencies allow the firm to leverage its deepening and broadening knowledge of the market and its needs. Capability adjacencies let it leverage its deepening and broadening capabilities to create offerings for markets quite different from those currently being served. Market adjacencies are more common, and will be addressed first.

Market adjacencies   One of the tasks in the business assessment part of the Arch was to segment the market. A go-to-market methodology was then crafted in the operationalization segment. After a positioning statement was developed for the segment, an appropriate marketing mix (4Ps) was designed. Finally, sales and profit objectives were developed for the segment. First, a target market segment was identified. Now it is time to move to the next segment. That requires the new business to return to the business assessment segment of the Arch and identify the next appropriate segment. A positioning statement, an appropriate market mix, and sales and profit targets have to be developed subsequently. It is certainly feasible that the business may have to loop back all the way to the business design segment of the Arch and perform more elicitations if the underlying needs of the next target segment are not precisely known.

The choice of the next targeted segment should be connected to the segment the company pursued initially. You are building an integrated company, not a holding company of unrelated businesses. All four P's of the marketing mix (product, price, place, and promotion) need to be re-evaluated for the new segment. The product is the one element of that mix that many small firms forget to consider as needing to morph as they move to the next segment. Rain-X, for example, started out as a relatively niche business, leveraging its specialized water-repellent window-coating polymer. By developing new capabilities that allowed it to deliver this window "wax" in concert with a window cleaner the firm's market expanded to another segment. Along the way it grew new capabilities and a significant brand, which it leveraged in the introduction of wiper blades to another new market segment.

SurveyMonkey is another example of how developing capabilities over time allows a firm to grow into adjacent markets. The firm began as an online survey company. Its website made it easy for individuals to create surveys and analyze results. Individuals still had to create the surveys and find appropriate surveyees, but the creation and dissemination of the survey was much simplified by SurveyMonkey's website. The company gained expertise in the creation of surveys through all the examples it was exposed to over time. In addition it learned, from interactions with its clients, how to attract appropriate surveyors. The company has manifested these new skills in a new offering aimed at an adjacent market. The firm will now design surveys for clients and even find appropriate people to take the surveys.

Classic upstream and downstream integration also fall into this market adjacency category. This could occur when a widget manufacturer moves upstream into the raw materials supply space or vice versa. The value system you created in the opportunity identification segment will tell you both the potential and the barriers to making such moves.

Capability adjacencies   The lesser utilized of the two growth strategies, but one leveraged by some very well-known, innovative companies, is capability adjacency. This strategy involves leveraging your firm's current and growing core capabilities in completely unrelated markets. 3M Corporation and Dyson Ltd are great examples of how this strategy can be effectively implemented over a long period of time.

Dyson's core capabilities include air flow movement/manipulation and industrial design. The firm's strategic intent is to create simple, elegant appliances that are easy to use. The firm began by creating specialty vacuum cleaners based on their cyclone air-flow technology. These products attacked the biggest market pain – people avoid changing vacuum cleaner bags. The consequence of not changing the bag is an ineffective machine. If the firm had pursued a typical market adjacency tactic, Dyson likely would have moved from a vacuum cleaner to other floor-cleaning products. Instead, they leveraged their core technology, elegant air flow manipulation, into the design of a bladeless fan. Further product launches from the company include the hand-driers found in many public restrooms. Very different markets than vacuum cleaners and fans, but a strategy solidly grounded in their air-flow expertise.

Capability adjacencies are not simply the domain of focused, founder-driven, young firms. 3M Corporation has been using this strategy for decades. The company's first successful product launch was sandpaper. The capabilities underpinning the creation of quality sandpaper are a uniform dispersion of fine particles (silica) and the ability to fix those particles to a flexible substrate. The company has been leveraging those two capabilities (particle dispersion and adhesion) for decades in everything from Scotch tape to DVDs. The adhesion technology is continually evolving as is the size and type of particle being manipulated, but the commonality among the products is not the markets but those underlying capabilities.

Supply-side (internal) growth As the firm grows, it is not enough to focus entirely on expanding into new markets and introducing new products. The firm will also face increasing challenges *within* the company as it grows. As the company grows, you will need to ensure your company continues to keep its increasing resources, including its people, focused on performing tasks consistent with the business today and tomorrow. As your employee base grows (rapidly), keeping it aligned with the company vision and working in a coordinated manner will consume an increasing amount of management's effort. Again, the starting place is a clear vision of the future of the business. Share that vision with every new employee. Challenge them to ask themselves in their daily decisions whether the choices they are making are consistent with getting the company closer to that goal.

The "everybody does everything" chaotic dance of a new startup has to shift quickly to something more coordinated as the firm grows. Many entrepreneurs resist the necessity for increased structure and more formalized work processes. The "bureaucracy" is abhorrent to them; that's why they do not work in corporations, they will assert! The fact is that as companies grow they need to keep employees organized; to divide up the workload. That requires coordination, work flow, and work processes. In a study of seventy-eight high-growth US companies, the research of Antonio Davila and George Foster thoroughly dispelled the myth of the free-for-all startup. They learned that quite the opposite is true. Firms can actually grow faster with strong internal planning and control systems. In their study, 80 percent of the successful firms had financial planning processes in place by year five, 62 percent had strategic planning systems, 57 percent had HR planning systems, and 48 percent had formal financial-evaluation work processes (Davila and Foster, 2012). This is not the mythology of a startup, this is its reality. Companies need structure in order to grow.

Davila and Foster's work was consistent with the classic paper of Neil Churchill and Virginia Lewis. Churchill and Lewis proposed that new firms go through five stages of growth, listed in Figure 7.4. The first two phases describe the firm early in its existence when it is simply trying to obtain enough sales to survive. It is during stages three and four, in which the company starts its accelerated growth, that structure becomes critical. The first step along that path is delegation

Stages of Growth	Growth by...
Existence	Creativity
Survival	Direction
Success	Delegation
Take-off	Coordination
Maturity	Collaboration

FIGURE 7.4 Five stages of growth for a new venture
Source: Neil Churchill and Virginia Lewis, "The five stages of small business growth", 1983.

from the founders to the new staff (Stage 3), followed by coordination through structured processes (Stage 4) (Churchill and Lewis, 1983).

Business needs structure in order to grow. Overburdening a young firm with too much structure will have it collapse under its own weight. No structure leads to chaos which decreases productivity. The art is to find the right amount of structure. That amount will continue to increase as the company grows. The fatal mistake many firms make is having no structure then, out of frustration, instituting over-prescriptive policies. If Jack's open shirt is causing a distraction in the workplace, it is better to talk to him about buttoning up his shirt and revealing his chest less than to suddenly institute a dress code that bans garments with more than three buttons from the workplace. Many policies are overgeneralizations of specific situations. Create the structure needed to keep the golden eggs of your firm being laid, but do not kill the goose in the process.

Renewal: Completing the arc

Companies that last know how to reinvent themselves. They do so by leveraging their capabilities. To leverage its capabilities a firm has to know what these capabilities are and how they are changing over time. Self-awareness, on a corporate level, is a beneficial attribute. Whether leveraging new knowledge of the customer or new know-how within the organization, both market and capability adjacencies are really leveraging the expanding capabilities of the firm (as these have been defined in this book).

From the perspective of the new capabilities, the firm must again zoom out and assess where else these capabilities might be applicable. This exactly the approach taken in Chapter 2 in this book. This is, in its essence, the corporate renewal process. This renewal brings you all the way back to the first segment of the Arch: Opportunity identification. Renewal is very similar to capability adjacencies in that both do that. They are also similar in that you will likely shift industries. The difference between them is subtle. Capability adjacencies continually leverage the company's core capabilities. Renewal hits the company reset

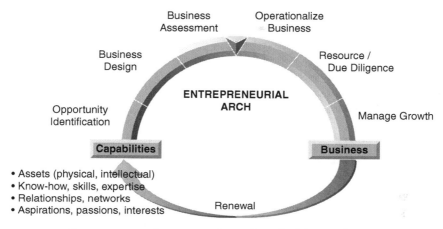

FIGURE 7.5 Corporate renewal: Restarting the Arch methodology with renewed capabilities

button and begins again from the start, forcing the firm to re-evaluate its entire capability map and start again, as Figure 7.5 illustrates.

Renewal, therefore, is not some mystical process that can only be performed by the few. It brings the company back to its roots and forces it to start again. Companies like Dyson and 3M have demonstrated over the short and long term that this is possible if it is part of the strategic intention. It is not that large firms are incapable of renewal; at one time they did precisely this. For most firms, however, that was long ago and that competency has been lost. Large firms focus on operational efficiency, focusing on the execution side of the Entrepreneurial Arch. They need to rediscover the business discovery side and begin again.

OFFERING GROWTH

In Step 2 of Chapter 3, we discussed the five attributes involved in identifying an initial target market segment. The first is that the customers are extremely motivated to buy your product. This means that they are extremely motivated to change. This implies that there is a large discrepancy between their need or desire and the benefit that current offerings provide. The pain they are experiencing through this discrepancy is enough to motivate them to change. The second feature of the perfect initial segment is that the customers are willing to buy quickly. The combination leads to a fast adoption rate with a relatively low cost of sales. The drivers of this quick adoption of new products are the perceived attributes of the innovation (Rogers, 1995, Chapter 6). These attributes consisted of the relative advantage of the product, compatibility with previous product, complexity, scope to try them out, and observability.

The third piece of the perfect initial segment is that the customers have the capacity to pay. Motivation and willingness to buy will not translate into fast sales if your customer cannot pay for your offering or needs multiple levels of approval before doing so. The fourth element of the initial perfect segment is that this segment of customer requires the lowest amount of product sophistication. Or put another way, the customers are willing to buy your MVP. The early adopters of Rain-X windshield wax are good examples. These customers were willing to do what they needed to do to make it work. The later adopters were waiting for the ease of use of the 2-in-1 product.

The fifth and final attribute of the perfect initial target segment is that these customers are on the development path to subsequent segments. This attribute of your initial target segment is the funda-mental ingredient of segment-to-segment growth. You segmented your market in the opportunity identification segment of the Arch and devised a go-to-market strategy for the initial segment in the operationalization segment. You likely will need to return all the way to the business design segment to carry out more elicitations in order to understand better the secondary needs of your next target segment. I refer to "secondary needs," as the customers likely share the same primary needs as the initial segment. However, the secon-dary, decision-making needs of this group are not currently being addressed. These needs could be information or an attribute of the product that is currently missing. If information is one of them, you need to understand how this segment acquires information. Are they looking for references before making a purchasing decision? Where do they look for references? Through continued elicitations you will be able to ascertain that knowledge of your customer. In the Rain-X example, certain product attributes were missing. All the target segments for Rain-X's windshield "wax" were the same – to be able to see more clearly when driving their car in the rain. The secondary need – ease of application – was very different when we compare the first target customer with the mainstream customer. Attributes of the product needed to be changed to address this need. No amount of "marketing" was going to cause these customers to buy the original product. They wanted the 2-in-1 glass cleaner that left the rain-repelling polymer on their windshield without any further effort on their part.

Persona development, as was discussed in Chapter 3 and Appendix B, can be a useful aid in articulating the differences between your target segments. According to the company's former CEO, Ann Taylor stores model two distinct personas to which they sell (Merrick, 2006). The segments that company targets are personified as "Ann" and "Loft." "Ann" is a more sophisticated, less price-conscious consumer who buys clothes for business that can equally be worn to a dinner meeting. "Loft" is more fashion-conscious, more fun, and more price-conscious. "Loft" is younger than "Ann," but will likely become "Ann" one day. This works for the progressive segmentation of Ann Taylor stores in that they can attract "Loft" to the brand and keep her with it as she matures. The two segments are connected. When Ann Taylor was selling to "Loft" it did not decide to just put some hipper, cheaper clothes in its store. It went back to the market segmentation of business assessment. The company realized that it could attract a younger audience that it could keep as they aged. "Loft" is likely 20–30 years old and an aspiring professional. "Ann" is an established professional. This makes for a perfect sequence. Once the "Loft" segment is identified, the next step is to drop back to the business design segment and understand the needs of that segment and then craft an offering that satisfies those needs. This is not a random walk, but a process of directed discovery.

Growth within a segment

In Step 4 of the business design methodology I addressed the homogeneities of a seemingly homogeneous market segment. That discussion will not be repeated here. This challenge is discussed in great detail in Geoffrey Moore's iconic work, *Crossing the Chasm* (1991). Short descriptions of the five subcomponents of what appears to be a homogeneous segment are described below:

- *Innovators/technology enthusiasts:*
    This group is eager to try new offerings. They have the ability to work with complex new offerings and the expendable income necessary to try things that may not work out for them.
- *Early adopters/visionaries:*
    They are more connected to the early majority than the innovators. They love to propagate information. This is the group that tweets and posts reviews.

    –The chasm –

- *Early majority:*
    This group is cautious and deliberate in its decision making.
- *Late majority:*
    This group motivated by peer pressure and economic necessity. The opposite of the innovators, the late majority have limited expendable income and need to make every expenditure count. As a result, they tend to be quite conservative in their decisions.
- *Laggards:*
    Traditionalists that are focused on the past. This group tends to be quite skeptical.

    It is essential to provide and emphasize the offering attributes necessary to move across the chasm. For example, the early majority will need references. The early adopters enjoy advocating products and services. Your young firm must leverage these qualities in the two groups. Have you created a mechanism for those early adopters to easily provide feedback on your offering? Is that information in a form and place that makes it easily referenced by the early majority? If a customer need is information, you need to create flow channels for this information. Amazon does this well. They know the early adopters loves to post product reviews. They also know that the early majority will not likely buy a product without a review. The company therefore provides an easy mechanism for customers to create and read reviews.

Product marketing

No chapter on growth would be complete without a discussion of product marketing. Your company strategy can be aligned, your product strategy be well thought-out, but if your potential customers are not aware of your products and the advantage these have for them, all will be for naught.

Often the marketing program – advertising, PR, sales force, partnerships, alliances, channel partners – is more important than the technological advantage, but comes at considerable expense.

The fundamentals of marketing still apply to innovative new companies. Sometimes startup firms forget this. They tweet, Facebook, and make other social media connections but forget the fundamentals of marketing – knowing your audience. Resources are scarce in any new firm, so nothing can be wasted. This requires tireless focus. Unlike their large corporate brethren, new companies have minuscule marketing budgets. It is therefore paramount that the startup leverage as many as possible no- or low-cost means to get their message out. Leverage PR as much as you can in lieu of advertising dollars. Start newsletters and other targeted, low-cost methods to build consumer awareness for your products or services. The critical element in all these initiatives, however, is to understand the target at which these initiatives are aimed, and to understand the result for the firm that the initiative is intended to gain. Without this understanding there is no means by which to measure the impact of the initiative and therefore no reasonable way to address whether or not it is successful. No startup has the resources, in time or money, to continue to do things with questionable outcome.

Customer acquisition time and cost are also critically important to the new firm. In addition to the adoption issues previously mentioned, there are issues related to the buying process of the customers that could cause significant delays. What is the purchase cycle of your customer? Does purchasing your product have to go through the budget cycle? If so, how long a lead time does that customer's cycle contain? Is your product part of a new offering for the firm? How many years in advance is a firm planning to incorporate your product or service? Are other regulatory issues involved? What approvals (internal and external to the customer) need to be addressed? Do tests need to be run inside with your buyer? Do these tests have to be scheduled? I knew an energy recovery startup that had significant technology related to capturing waste energy from large industrial facilities. It turned out, however, that no firm was going to purchase this offering without significant internal testing. In addition to the testing, any purchase had to be synchronized with the large firm's budget process. The combination made the offering's adoption time, the customer acquisition time, in excess of five years! That lengthy customer acquisition time, not to mention the costs associated with that, are killers for any startup company. It is worthy of note that some sales are simply more costly to attain than the profits that sale could generate.

PERSONAL GROWTH

This section addresses the most sharply focused growth perspective: The personal growth of the founders.

For startup firms, rapid growth has significant implications for the founders. As the entrepreneurial firm rapidly grows, its needs could exceed the skill-set of the founders. It is a rare entrepreneur that has the skills to transcend the growth of a business from a garage to a Fortune

500 company. There are examples, of course (Steve Jobs, Bill Gates, Michael Dell, Jeff Bezos, to name a few), but it is difficult to name more than ten. In his book, *The Entrepreneur's Survival Guide*, Mark Paul calls it the "rubber band theory" (Paul, 2003). Mr. Paul suggests that the founder and their firm are connected by a rubber band. More often than not, the vision, drive, and energy of the founder pull the nascent new venture up. The company's needs, however, increase as it grows. Unless the founder's entrepreneurial skills can grow at the same rate the company is growing, the relative position of the company and the entrepreneur on that rubber band will eventually flip. When this transition occurs, the founder is actually impeding the growth of their own firm, as illustrated in Figure 7.6. The bottom line is that your role in your business may change over time. It is good to think about that at the beginning rather than be shocked and hurt by it later.

Every MBA student that graduates from the University of Michigan is expected to participate in a field project. These seven-week Multidisciplinary Action Projects (MAP) take place all over the world with companies of all sizes. The University, primarily through my friends and former colleagues Professors Andy Lawlor and Len

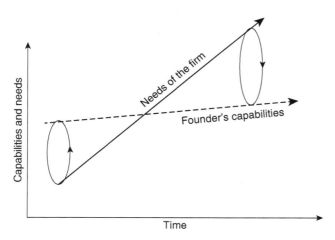

FIGURE 7.6 The rubber band theory
Source: Mark Paul, *The Entrepreneur's Survival Guide*, 2003.

Middleton, has a long-standing relationship with Enterprise Ireland (EI) and has completed many MAP projects with them (Middleton, 2010). EI has been active in economic gardening for decades. One of the many projects undertaken by the students for EI focused on new growth. One of the phenomena EI had observed was that their companies would reach a certain revenue size and then plateau. There are many factors, of course, including the structural elements noted in the previous section. A significant component, however, was traced right back to the rubber band effect. The founders' capabilities were limiting the firm's growth. There are times when the founder needs to step aside or take a 'lesser' role in the firm for it to continue to grow. There is a huge emotional component to this reality. The founders put everything into the launching of their new business: Their heart and soul and in many cases their personal finances. They are truly "all in," to use poker parlance. Once the firm is successful, and the founders find themselves with a large stack of chips sitting in front of them, it is often very difficult emotionally to go "all in" again, which might be required to take the company to the next level. Capabilities certainly play a distinct role, but founders are also human beings so there is a distinct emotional component to this.

SUMMARY

The three attributes of the growth of a new firm or a new line of business were examined in this chapter. These were the corporate, offering, and personal elements. Corporate growth was examined by leveraging the PVC framework first introduced in Chapter 3. Opportunities and threats were examined from both external and internal perspectives with respect to the new firm.

Growth and renewal are not isolated activities. Quite to the contrary, growth and renewal are intimately connected to the other five elements of the Entrepreneurial Arch. As in the other segments of the Arch, there are iterations that take place within this segment and iterations that need to take place between segments. Growth, therefore, cannot be looked at as an "add-on" to existing operations, but instead requires the firm to iterate back and through segments across the Arch. Corporate renewal is the most difficult challenge as it completes the arc of the Entrepreneurial Arch, causing the company to re-evaluate its capabilities and start again at opportunity identification.

The outline below illustrates the elements of each of the segments of the Entrepreneurial Arch that impact growth. The outline also includes the aspects of growth covered in this chapter and how they loop back to the other Arch segments. There is no doubt that growth is not simply a matter of marketing.

1. *Opportunity identification:*
    Opening (for you; alignment with capabilities).
    Industry selection.
    Constructing a value system; identifying a high-value problem.
2. *Business design:*
    Elicitation – discovery of needs.
    Persona development.
    Adoption profiles across a homogeneous segment (crossing the chasm).
    Offering development: Connection of offering attributes with value proposition, MVP.
    Position statement for the segment.
3. *Business assessment:*
    Market segmentation: Connection between segments.
    Market quantification.
    Market adoption analysis.
    Pricing: Revenue, sales and profit objectives for each segment.
4. *Operationalization:*
    Corporate vision.
    Marketing strategy.
    Marketing mix 4Ps (not product, which was covered in business design); for each segment:

- price:
  - how will the price change over time?
  - how to get from zero to the long-term profit objectives described in assessment? Is there a pricing path (e.g. systematic reduction of early adopter discounts)?
- place (channel), and
- promotion.

5. *Resources:*

Are the right people in place to forward the growth strategy? Is their compensation aligned with this objective? What other resources are necessary?

6. *Growth:*

Corporate:
- market adjacencies (return to business design)
- capability adjacencies (return to opportunity identification with improved capabilities), and
- renewal – start from scratch with opportunity identification using broader set of capabilities.

Offering growth:
- segment-to-segment (return to assessment), and
- growth within a segment (return to business design).

Personal.

8   Summary

The Entrepreneurial Arch is a graphic representation of a methodology to discover and develop a new financially sustainable organization. The methodology also guides you to a business that aligns with your capabilities; a new venture that both creates and captures value. The systematic reshaping and de-risking attributes of the methodology are aimed at increasing the odds of your post-launch success. There are a lot of moving parts to contend with in discovering and building a new business. Teams often get overwhelmed by the process. Some try to use the structure of the business plan or other dashboard appliances to help them establish some semblance of order during the process. Unfortunately these can cause more harm than good as they typically represent a hodgepodge of activities that range from discovery to operations. By contrast, the Entrepreneurial Arch lays out a rational order for the activities necessary to create and simultaneously de-risk your potential new venture. The method outlined in this book has six segments. These segments represent the dissection of the process of business discovery and launch into manageable parts. This assists in keeping teams on track, so they are not worrying about the kind of financing they may need, for example, when they are still in the business design stage. The tools necessary to perform the activities of each segment appropriately are introduced and described as part of the overall methodology.

The first half of the Arch is focused on discovering a viable, high-value business that your team or organization can act upon. This is a learning process that involves identifying, describing, reshaping, quantifying, and ultimately assessing potential new ventures. The second half of the Arch focuses on implementing the discovered

250

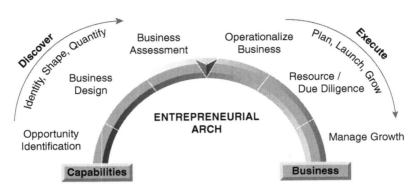

• Assets (physical, intellectual)
• Know-how, skills, expertise
• Relationships, networks
• Aspirations, passions, interests

FIGURE 8.1 The Entrepreneurial Arch

business. The actions described here are segmented into planning, launching, and growing the firm.

Successful serial entrepreneurs do not randomly conjure up new businesses. They have a methodology they follow. Their methods may be highly instinctual to them, but there is structure to their approach. The Entrepreneurial Arch replicates the structure I have observed in interviewing hundreds of successful serial entrepreneurs. It is not a random walk, nor is it a linear march to a successful new venture. The method is highly iterative and stochastic. It keeps the entrepreneur focused on the appropriate tasks by dissecting the overall method into manageable segments. The approach also incorporates a "fast fail" thought process, which allows the entrepreneur to discover just enough information to make a decision before moving forward (or backward). This will help avoid getting locked into a specific idea too soon. The discussion of the discovery section of the Arch includes a summary of common mistakes made in each segment. Avoiding them will help you spiral in toward a viable new business more quickly.

Many programs teach half of the Arch, focusing only on how to operationalize a business concept. The method of this book includes the critical business discovery process elements of entrepreneurship. This is not the typical "brainstorm and filter" process that is often seen, but a rigorous method of directed discovery. Discovery is a learning process; you will learn as you travel across the Arch. That learning will cause you to rethink and reshape hypotheses that were constructed in earlier stages. This allows you to move quickly to avoid falling in love with a bad idea. The methodology requires a constant zooming out and zooming in, evaluating the big picture, then the small detail, and back out. The methodologies are aimed at guiding the entrepreneur toward better decisions. Entrepreneurs' time is their most precious resource. More ideas can be hatched. More money can be found. But entrepreneurs never get back their time. The entrepreneur should therefore spend it wisely, investing it on those ventures that have the greatest opportunity of making an impact on the world through their success. That is the ultimate purpose of business discovery.

The entire methodology is viewed through the lens of the team or organization's capabilities. Team and organization capability maps are illustrated in Chapter 2. The maps define the intersection of four different competency categories. The four categories are shown below in individual and corporate terms. The nexus of these four categories represents the optimal operating space for the team or organization.

The capabilities are the basis of what an organization can accomplish. It is the difference between dreaming and doing. That said, you will never have all the capabilities you need to create your offering and deliver it to your customer. You will always be levering the ecosystem. You must, however, bring something to the table if you are going to successfully capture any of the value you create.

The initial stages of business discovery involve finding an opening for a new business, determining whether that opening is right for you or your organization, understanding whether that business would solve a high-value problem, deciding whether it has the potential for you to capture value, and finally determining whether it is investable. This series of evaluations and repositionings takes on four different perspectives; that of the entrepreneur, the customer, the industry, and

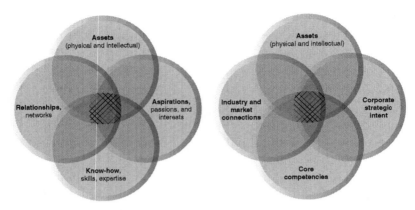

FIGURE 8.2 Team and corporation capability maps

the financier. No view of a new business is complete without all four perspectives.

To determine whether there is an opening, a wide-angle view of the opportunity being considered is evaluated against Drucker's seven sources of innovation (Drucker, 1985). Those sources, which were detailed in Chapter 2, are unexpected occurrences, incongruities, process needs, industry and market changes, demographic changes, changes in perception, and finally new knowledge. Drucker suggested that new knowledge is the most difficult opening to exploit. The Entrepreneurial Arch reveals the reason why this is true, as doing so forces the team or organization to go all the way back to a capability assessment before proceeding to identify opportunity. This involves the most iterations of the methodology, since multiple industries will likely need to be assessed.

By the end of the opportunity identification segment of the Arch you know what issue you are trying to solve. You have not yet drilled down to a specific customer and customer need, but understand the segment of an industry that is struggling with the high-value issue. You have identified the *concept* for a solution, not a precise offering, a specific approach to addressing the issue. That solution concept is in alignment with your capabilities. There are five generic approaches for crafting a solution: 1. create a "me too" product; 2. create a substitute product; 3. aggregate/consolidate a segment of the industry ecosystem; 4. collapse the industry value system, and 5. create a new segment in the value system that makes the entire ecosystem more efficient. These were outlined in Chapter 2. Creativity is essential to successfully navigating this portion of the overall process.

The business design segment of the Entrepreneurial Arch transforms this specific opportunity into a qualitative business description. It does so by zooming in on the specific opportunity. A five-step method was outlined in Chapter 3 to identify each of the most sharply focused details of the proposed new venture. By the end of business design you will have a precise description of the proposed new venture's offering. You will know what activities the company will perform in the creation and delivery of that offering to your customer and what activities will leverage the business ecosystem. You understand how the activities your firm will perform align with your capabilities. You will be able to explicitly describe both your customer and any collaborators. You will also understand why each will engage with your organization; the value you create for both. You will know how your proposed offering compares to the customer's current solution in the mind of that customer. The connection from your capabilities through the product attribute(s) to the underlying unmet or under-met customer needs will be established. Finally, clear and precise customer and collaborator position statements will be crafted at this stage.

Common mistakes at the business design stage stem from not being precise enough in the description of the firm. It is assumed that the venture does everything; it will not. Another common error is that the design does not distinguish between customers (those that pay for your offering) and end users. Often value is created for end users, but not for direct customers. Part of this overgeneralization is that the offering is still too vaguely defined and is essentially still the concept for a solution. The other mistake is that the offering is described as the perfect product you hope to produce "someday," rather than the minimum viable product you can create and sell quickly.

The final segment of the business discovery section of the Arch is business assessment. This segment has two objectives: To complete the business model by quantifying the elements of the business design, and to perform financial assessments and sensitivity analyses to determine critical success factors for the proposed new venture. Feasibility is too often thought of as bimodal; either feasible or not feasible. In business discovery, assessment is about finding the conditions under which this business can be viable. Once that is accomplished the team must then judge whether or not those conditions represent a reasonable risk and warrant moving forward. If they do not, then the team needs to return to earlier segments of the Arch to reshape the venture. If the conditions warrant moving forward, we go on to determine the type of financing that is in alignment with the company that is being proposed. In this analysis, the financier's perspective is taken. The type of funding, however, also impacts the new venture's founders. While Chapter 3 takes the financier's perspective of the proposed venture, Appendix C discusses the impact of various types of investment on the founders. By the end of this segment, all the elements necessary to write a feasibility report on the proposed venture are known.

The next section represents the transition from the discovery section to the execution section of the Entrepreneurial Arch. The first step toward successful business execution is to create an operational plan. The architectural view of the business is known after the business discovery segment, but how that business will be constructed is not determined until the operationalization segment of the Arch. Consistent with the entire methodology, this section also takes both close-up and wide-angle points of view. From a high level, the document describes what kind of firm you aspire to be. Low-cost provider? Creator of leading-edge products? In addition, it describes the high-level strategy you will employ to maintain your firm's differentiation in the marketplace. Closer up, this section of the Arch creates a detailed plan that articulates how the business will proceed during its first five years and how the risks identified in the assessment segment will be mitigated. This planning process is important in and of itself. Beyond the learning that the process provides, the plan provides a roadmap for development and, as such, creates a benchmark to measure the firm's progress. Chapter 5 provides a detailed outline of all the elements that could be included in your business plan. Given that every business is unique, every plan will be unique. It is the entrepreneur's charge to determine which of these detailed elements are important to include in your twenty- to thirty-page plan.

Chapter 6 describes how to attract the resources necessary to launch and grow the firm. Those specific resources will vary greatly from firm to firm although they can typically be reduced to money and people. Get the right people on the bus, as Jim Collins says, then pursue the money (Collins, 2001b). This chapter began with a discussion of people. That discussion ranged from how to interpret resumés to how to determine a candidate's alignment with the firm you are trying to build. Focus and alignment are key. Do not get ahead of your plan when hiring and do not hire to accomplish tasks. Get in place the people that will add value to your firm now and into the future. When approaching funding sources, make sure that capital fits the type of firm you want to build. The investment potential framework assesses the type of financing you *could* attract. The type of financing you desire needs to be consistent with that framework and the long-term aspirations of your firm. You must also keep in mind that people usually come along with financing. The funders will often become advisors or board members. You want to make sure these people add to the value of the firm. Evaluate them as you would other new hires. Combinations of capital may be useful in moving through the early de-risking steps. Perhaps you could obtain grant monies or funds from crowdfunding sites to perform some early de-risking activities before pursuing follow-on capital from banks or equity investors. The advantage is that the more the company is de-risked the more attractive it becomes to later-stage financiers.

Finally, the last section of the Arch surveys the strategies for managing the venture's growth. Most entrepreneurs erroneously equate growth with marketing. While marketing is important, every segment of the Entrepreneurial Arch impacts growth. Chapter 7 covered three types of growth: Corporate, offering, and personal. Corporate growth was evaluated from both external and internal vantage points. Both market and capability adjacencies were examined from an external perspective. Rain-X was used as an example of market adjacency growth while Dyson illustrated capability adjacency growth. Internally, the analysis focused on increasing the structure a new firm must adopt as it expands. Growth of the firm's offering includes modifying the offering to meet the demands of additional market segments, particularly their secondary and tertiary needs. Corporate renewal completes the arc of the Arch, by returning to the capabilities and subsequently back to opportunity identification. Growth and renewal are intimately connected to the other five segments of the Entrepreneurial Arch. From a personal perspective, the unfortunate news for the organization's founders is that the needs of the firm often outstrip their ability to lead it as the venture grows. At that point the founders either limit the company's growth or must find a way to step into a different role. Growth is much bigger than product marketing and therefore cannot be looked at as an "add-on" to existing operations. Instead, it requires the firm to iterate back and forth through segments across the Arch.

This is the entrepreneurship era. We need to move past the lottery mentality of quick riches and be serious about how to leverage one's strengths in the creation of viable, new, sustainable businesses. The world needs more professional entrepreneurs that know how to:

- identify clear opportunities and threats from a confusing, chaotic, constantly-changing environment
- formulate potential businesses that take advantage of these opportunities
- assess the feasibility of these proposed business ventures

- create practicable, operational plans from disparate and incomplete information for these new business opportunities
- acquire and align the resources necessary to launch the business (these resources will be both in and outside of the organization's immediate control), and
- implement the plans in a manner that focuses on driving accelerated growth for their organizations.

It is my sincere hope that this book moved you forward along your journey to become one of them.

Appendix A   Positioning for value capture framework

Successful businesses capture a significant share of the value their firms create. Clearly you must create value in the marketplace, but though a necessary criterion it is insufficient. What new entrepreneurs often fail to realize is that their business can fail while providing goods for an exceptionally attractive market if the business is not able to capture any of the value created.

Your organization's ability to capture value is dictated by the relative robustness of your capabilities. In judging the outcome of any competitive sporting event, it is not enough to evaluate the talent of your team; rather, that talent must be evaluated in comparison with that of your opponent. No organization is an island. It takes an industry to serve a customer. You will need capabilities outside your firm to create and deliver your solution to your customer. Your capabilities relative to those in the ecosystem that you need to leverage will determine your organization's share of that created value. David Teece, in his seminal paper, discussed the ability of firms to capture value from their intellectual property (Teece, 1986). The positioning for value capture (PVC) framework, Figure A1, broadens that work beyond intellectual assets to include the firm's entire capability set.

In the two-by-two PVC framework, the vertical axis describes your capabilities. The four categories that are your capabilities are shown below in individual and corporate parlances. The nexus of these four categories represents the optimal operating space for the team or organization.

The PVC forces you to assess how easy those capabilities are to imitate or reproduce (i.e. appropriate). Specialized capabilities are difficult to reproduce. It is not that they are impossible to reproduce, it is simply that it would take considerable time, effort, and/or money to do this. Generic capabilities, on the other hand, are more common and can easily be appropriated.

The PVC framework compares your capabilities to those Complementary Capabilities (CCs). The CCs consist of all those things necessary, in addition to the capabilities you control, to create the product/service your customer desires and deliver it to them. Your firm will always need CCs. Do not think of the CCs as the capabilities you currently do not have, but will soon acquire or develop. While you will increase your capabilities over time, you will always need complementary ones. Like your own capabilities, advantaged or specialized CCs are difficult to

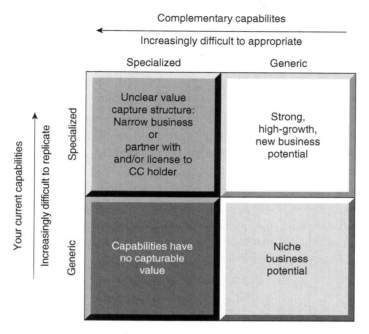

FIGURE A1 Positioning for value capture

imitate, reproduce, or acquire. In short, they are increasingly difficult to appropriate. Advantaged CCs fall into three of the four capability categories (assets, know-how, and relationships). Like your own capabilities, CCs are very specific to your offering and the industry in which you will be operating. It is therefore impossible to create a comprehensive list of all CCs. A few, typical, advantaged CCs are shown in the list below.

- *Physical and intellectual assets:*
  - brand name
  - manufacturing plants
  - unique or proprietary distribution channels
  - intellectual property (IP), especially where it prevents your freedom to operate, and
  - significant resources (e.g. deep financial reserves).
- *Know-how and relationships:*
  - manufacturing or design capabilities
  - sales and service expertise

- exclusive sales channels, and
- customer relationships.

SPECIALIZED–GENERIC QUADRANT: HIGH-GROWTH POTENTIAL BUSINESSES

The ideal for a strong new business with high growth potential is to be in the upper right-hand quadrant of the PVC diagram as shown in Figure A1. In a sporting analogy, your team is strong, while your opponents are weak. Residing in this quadrant is your best opportunity to win. Organizations in this quadrant have specialized, differentiated capabilities and, in turn, only need generic CCs that are easy to appropriate. An example may be a patented and differentiated medical device with low regulatory requirements that can be manufactured and distributed to your customers easily. In this example, let us say that you do not have the manufacturing or distribution capabilities. Since the manufacturing of the device is simple in this example, that manufacturing capability may be out-sourced to a number of potential vendors. Alternatively that know-how could be acquired and brought in-house. Either way, the firm can find a way to manufac-ture the device and will not have to cede an extraordinary amount of the value of the device in order to accomplish that task. Firms in this quadrant have strategic options.

GENERIC–SPECIALIZED QUADRANT: NO VALUE-CAPTURE POTENTIAL

This is the worst-case sporting analogy; you are an amateur team playing the professional world champions. You have almost no chance to win. In this scenario you only have generic capabilities and you need highly specialized CCs in order to produce your offering and deliver it to your customer. You envision, for example, that you will leverage your generic website-creation capability into being an online retailer that will sell another firm's highly differentiated products. You have virtu-ally no chance of capturing much or any value in this situation unless you have the ability to reach a new audience for the product producer, and to be the only retailer doing so; which would be a differentiated, not a generic capability. Note that this is independent of the market or needs analysis; this conclusion can be reached entirely on the relative strengths of your capabilities vs. the merchantry your firm will be opposing.

The upper right-hand and lower-left hand quadrants are fairly straightfor-ward. One is ideal, the other is death for your business idea. Initially finding yourself in either the upper left-hand quadrant or the lower right-hand quadrant, however, is fairly uncommon. Moving to the upper right-hand quadrant generally takes repositioning.

GENERIC—GENERIC QUADRANT: NICHE BUSINESS POTENTIAL

The sports analogy for this case is the face-off of two weak teams. Your team will likely win if it is highly motivated to do so. Being in the lower right-hand quadrant means that you have generic capabilities but only need generic CCs to enable your business. The main protection of your business in this quadrant is being small. These firms operate in niche areas that are impractical for the big players to service. Trying to grow without simultaneously growing your capabilities, however, can create a scenario in which the big players would see your firm as a threat. In that case, they would most certainly take aggressive action against your firm, making it difficult for you to capture value.

Specialized niche business

In any simplistic two-by-two framework, there will be exceptions. One exception is a niche business enabled by specialized capabilities. For example, you may have a very specialized offering that is enabled by your specialized training and know-how. However, this business is not scalable in its current form because you and only you have the know-how required to perform the firm's services. It is a niche business, but based on specialized know-how. As a result, you would place such a business on the top end of the niche box, because it is not a scalable business in its current form. To become a scalable business, you could develop training materials and methods in order to "franchise" your specialized know-how to other employees of your firm, thereby increasing the scalability of the business. The materials and methods would be specialized capabilities that would push your firm into the upper right-hand quadrant of Figure A1.

SPECIALIZED—SPECIALIZED QUADRANT: LICENSING, PARTNERING, AND MORE

In the sports analogy, this is a battle between top-ranked teams. In such battles, the experienced team will most often win. If you are a startup going against seasoned incumbents, despite the outcome in this quadrant being labeled "uncertain," you will likely lose. New firms with specialized assets, particularly intellectual assets, often find themselves in the upper left-hand quadrant of the PVC framework as they typically also need specialized CCs. Perhaps there is background technology that someone else controls that blocks your freedom to practice (or freedom to operate) your IP. Alternatively, your product or service may only be sold bundled with other related equipment to which you do not have access. There are a number of reasons why you need specialized CCs. The fundamental issue is how to capture the most value from your capabilities, which could mean repositioning your firm to the upper right-hand quadrant – the "high-growth startup" quadrant. There are many options available from this box, including multiple repositioning paths. A reposition path could take you directly from the upper left-hand to the upper right-hand quadrant of Figure A1. The more common pathway, however, is to move to the upper right-hand quadrant through the "niche" quadrant (lower right-hand quadrant of Figure A1). We will review each of the options for capturing value from this position.

New firms finding themselves in the upper left-hand quadrant have three options: 1. license their specialized assets to the CC holder; 2. partner with the CC holder, or 3. reposition the firm, typically by narrowing its scope. Established firms seeking to expand into a new line of business have a fourth option: Acquiring the CC holder. Of the three options for new firms, licensing likely captures the lowest value. All three require a redefinition of the customer and potentially alliances with collaborators, which means rediscovering their needs via more elicitations. If licensing, for example, you need to understand why the licensee would license the technology and how developed the technology must be (bare patent, working prototype, beta product, commercial product, turn-key facility) before they are likely to license it.

Partnering is another option. If partnering, as Pixar did with Disney to distribute its films in the early days, you may need to shore up your capabilities to get a better partnership deal. Pixar went public and raised a lot of capital to show they were not completely dependent on Disney to distribute their films (Isaacson, 2011). While this is not an option for most startups, increasing your options relative to the CC holder does increase your negotiating position.

Repositioning your firm typically involves narrowing its scope. Instead of being an automobile company, are you better positioned relative to the strength of your capabilities if you become a tire design firm? In some cases a repositioning of your firm can move you directly to the "high-growth" quadrant, in other cases you may become a niche business on your way to becoming a high-growth company. For example, instead of creating a medical device, your firm creates a specialized component that it then sells to the device manufacturer. On the other hand, you may become a specialized design firm, such as the specialized niche business previously discussed. The issue then becomes what further specialized capacities your firm must develop or acquire over time to reposition it in the high-growth quadrant.

Product development companies

One reason you may land in the specialized–specialized quadrant is that your firm is a product development company. You may be developing a product, but not have the capability to finish it, to deliver it to the market, or perhaps to monetize it. Pharmaceutical discovery and development is the classic example of a product development company. Your firm likely has very significant and difficult-to-replicate skills and know-how in developing new pharmaceuticals. It may also have a patent on a new drug formulation. What your firm does not have is the means to get the drug all the way through the United States Federal Drug Administration's (FDA) approval process or the ability to manufacture or distribute the drug. Product development companies are eventually sold to the CC holder. In pharmaceutical development, this sale typically takes place after completion of Phase II (efficacy studies) of the US FDA's approval process. This is because the cost of the remaining studies is prohibitively expensive. In fact it is estimated to cost over $1 billion to bring a new drug to market in the USA; beyond the reach of most biotech startups (Keating, 2002). Developing a product and selling it to the CC holder can be lucrative. It is a high-risk, high-reward venture. It is not, however, business development. You have no options should the CC holder choose not to purchase your product, no way to monetize your capabilities beyond the sale of the rights to your product. YouTube, Instagram, and other software products purchased by Google and Facebook, respectively, are non-pharmaceutical examples of product development companies. These firms have little or no possibility of directly monetizing their products as they lacked the CCs to do so. This makes these firms very risky endeavors. The ones that are acquired, however, as the YouTube and Instagram acquisitions certainly illustrate, can make the founders of these firms very wealthy: Both were acquired for over $1 billion (Arrington, 2006; Constine and Cutler, 2012).

Appendix B   Elicitations and persona development

Business model discovery requires hypotheses to be built and tested. Both require information to be gathered. Obtaining information, particularly information on the market, involves breaking the whole down into finite elements. This is the zooming-in and dissection process that will uncover specific needs. Elicitation will be an important tool in the discovery of these specific needs. Your firm, however, cannot customize an offering to the unique needs of every single individual. After the dissection, you will therefore need to do some integration; to regroup subsets of the disintegrated whole. These new subgroups of the whole will be based on common needs. This zooming-out and assembly process will define specific market segments. In the creation of new offerings, particularly if your customer is also an end user, it can be helpful to envision how your customer will engage with your product. To do that, it is convenient to personify the market segment, to create an image of a person. The imagined person will represent a market group that makes decisions based on specific needs. Elicitation and persona development are the two topics of this appendix.

PRIMARY RESEARCH TECHNIQUES

The information you seek will be obtained through primary and secondary research. The secondary research will involve reading industry and association reports in addition to market reports. Hypothesis building often comes from secondary research, while hypothesis testing is typically done via primary research, although there are exceptions to both. From the research you do you will start to formulate beliefs. You will have beliefs about the industry, the market, your proposed product, your collaborators, and the end users. These beliefs make up your hypotheses. These hypotheses may be purely speculative, conjectured from some preliminary understanding, or fact-based, understanding that is rigorously supported by evidence. In other words, you will have things that you know, things that you *think* you know, and things that you would like to know. Those conjectures that we think we know may turn out to be more fantasy than fact. As Figure B1 illustrates, we want to move from items we want to know to data-supported understanding by creating and testing hypotheses.

265

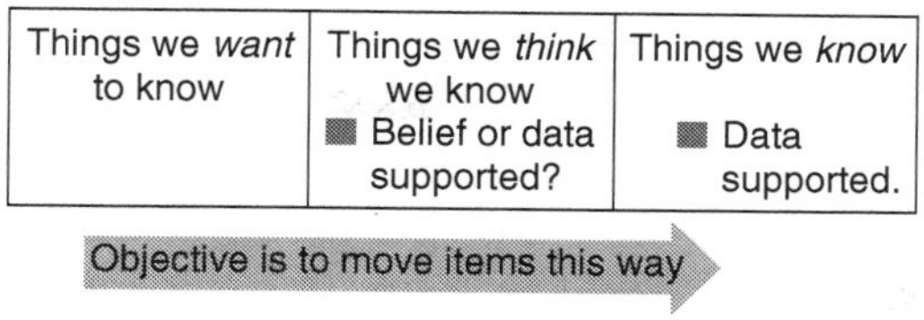

Things we *want* to know	Things we *think* we know ▦ Belief or data supported?	Things we *know* ▦ Data supported.

Objective is to move items this way ▶

FIGURE B1 Hypothesis-directed discovery

In addition, there are items that may turn out to be important of which, as of this moment, you are completely unaware. As a former United States Secretary of Defense stated at a press conference (Rumsfeld, 2002):

> [T]here are known knowns; there are things we know we know.
>
> We also know there are known unknowns; that is to say we know there are some things we do not know.
>
> But there are also unknown unknowns – there are things we do not know we don't know.

About these unknown unknowns – the "things we do not know we don't know" – we need to obtain information and to uncover them (Khosla, 2002). That is to say, we seek information that provides insight into the questions we know we do not currently have answers to, as well as uncovering the questions we do not yet know to ask. In short, we seek tacit knowledge. Tacit knowledge is not easily shared. Tacit knowledge often consists of habits and culture and know-how that we may not recognize in ourselves. The next time you find yourself at a club laughing at a comedian, ask yourself why one joke was funnier than another. Odds are you will have a difficult time articulating the difference, yet you *know* the difference. Tacit knowledge is buried deep inside people's heads and must be teased out. It is the opposite of explicit knowledge that has been codified. You can perform an online search for explicit knowledge. You can read explicit knowledge. Tacit knowledge must be coaxed into the light.

ELICITATIONS

Discovering what people think and know, revealing their tacit knowledge, is critical to testing your hypotheses and an important part of the business discovery process. It is how your known unknowns become known knowns, and how the unknown unknowns become known unknowns. Uncovering what is in people's heads is a key component to testing and reshaping your hypotheses. A questionnaire will not uncover this understanding; what would you possibly ask to uncover unknown unknowns? You need to engage in a discovery-driven dialogue with people to uncover what they may not even realize they know. Such dialogues achieve three objectives. First, they offer the chance to meet and talk to people who can deepen your perception and understanding of the issues. Second, these dialogues create the opportunity to learn and mutually explore specific needs and frustrations. These are not sales calls in which you are promoting your conceived solution; rather, they are hypothesis-driven learning opportunities. While people enjoy conversations where they get to tell you their expertise, they generally dislike being sold to. Finally, these dialogues offer the opportunity to discover and log the people that will eventually become your customers, collaborators, or end users. When you eventually have a product to promote, it is so much easier to return to someone you have previously talked to and say, in effect, "recall when we had that conversation and you told me your biggest issue was such-and-such? I'd like to talk to you now about a product that I believe will address that issue for you." To achieve all three of these objectives, your dialogues will need to extend beyond potential customers, collaborators, and end users. You will additionally need to talk to potential competitors, industry experts, and other thought leaders in the field.

Before engaging in such dialogues you need to be prepared. While this conversation is not a sales pitch you still need to bring something to the table. It should be a conversation, albeit a directed one, and not a rambling soliloquy on the part of the interviewee. To prepare for this dialogue you need to do your homework. You need to research and read and uncover as much explicit knowledge as you can. You need to document your beliefs and hypotheses. You cannot test and reshape something that you have not explicitly described in the first place. You also want this to be a dialogue, not an inquisition.

Be wary of asking direct, specific questions. Answers to these questions can be misleading, as they may not be the "right" questions to ask. If you ask someone whether manufacturing is a problem, they may say "yes." Manufacturing is always challenging. However, the big issue may lie in the distribution of the product, which would never be revealed by such a specific question. Elicitations are a process of discovery that will uncover issues. It is not a true–false test. The objective is to evaluate, to readjust your hypotheses using information gathered in this dialogue. This is the essence of the scientific method. You hypothesize, experiment, evaluate the data, readjust the hypotheses, and repeat the process. The "experiments" in this case are the elicitations. You are looking to uncover the issues and general problems. You want to drill down to a root-cause issue and understand the potential to create value in solving that issue. You want to know how potential customers think and choose so that you can understand the reaction even before a prototype is created. You want to understand customer and collaborator motivations for future decisions.

During this discovery process you must be aware of your own biases. You may have a particular problem in mind that you think is the root-cause issue. You may even have a particular solution in mind. You will have hypotheses, but remember that this is all that they are until you uncover the data that confirms them. Many an entrepreneur has been misled by disregarding the data if it is inconsistent with their hypotheses. Doing so is cognitive dissonance. Be aware of that trap. Write down your hypothesis and if you discover information that is inconsistent with your hypotheses, change the hypothesis. That is the scientific method. The scientific method will lead you toward a potential business; cognitive dissonance will lead you to a mirage.

The success of these dialogues in advancing and refining your hypotheses begins with your attitude toward them. The objective is to learn, not to sell. Internalize the world of the person you are talking to. What do they do day-to-day? What have they gotten used to, so they do not even see it as part of the problem? Most of us are apologists or survivors (Cooper, 1999, Chapter 2). We quickly adapt to our environment and accept it, limitations and all, as fixed. We are unable to fix problems we cannot even "see." How does the person you are talking to consider alternatives? Who do they look to in making decisions and tapping the outside know-how? Do not assume you know already know the answers. You do not, you simply have hypotheses that you are testing. Be curious about what you hear. Follow up with questions to find out more detail about things you hear that surprise you. As Tom Kelley says, "think like a traveler" (Kelley, 2008). When we travel to a new place we are often in this hyper-aware state in which we see things anew, like a child.

These dialogues are best conducted with one person at a time. Groups, like a conversation, can be dominated by a single individual. If that occurs, the tacit knowledge of the others will be drowned out by the loudest voice in the room. Although interviewing a single person, you may want to have a partner with you. That way you can keep in the flow of the conversation, while your partner records the information. Elicitations with a partner allow you to obtain two perspectives on the non-verbal cues. If you do take a partner to an interview, it is important that one guides the conversation. You should also introduce your respective roles to the interviewee before you start so that there will be no confusion as to who is leading the conversation on your side.

Engaging in deep, one-on-one conversations with people you do not know may sound intimidating. Like any other skill, you will get better the more you do it. You will be pleased to find that generally people are very open and responsive to such engagements. People love to be listened to; they love that you are interested in their perspective. They equally get annoyed and shut down if they sense you are secretly trying to sell them something, which is why cold sales calls are so difficult. Understand that the first interview may not always go that well and may not be with the right person. Also, you do not want to hold your first dialogue with one of the world's experts, or with the CEO of the key company in your value system. You need to work up to these vital individuals by building knowledge and understanding as you go. You do not want your first dialogue about physics to be with Stephen Hawking! Take copious notes. Organize these notes using mind-mapping techniques or other methods that will help you integrate the elicitations.

Always end your engagement by asking for recommendations to others to talk to.

Always start the conversation by stating what you are trying to accomplish. For example, you may say "I would like to have a twenty-minute conversation with you about current products in marketing communications." It sets expectations in terms of time and content. It tells your interviewee that you are really interested in their opinion and their insights, and are not going to be selling them a new idea. Always introduce yourself and provide your motivation for the conversation. If you are a student play the "student card." People love to help students, especially students from their alma mater. You can say "I'm a student studying business at the University of Michigan and I'm doing a research project related to consumer demand for iPhone applications and would like to spend twenty minutes talking to you to gain your insight into this topic." Your responses will be surprisingly fabulous.

Since we are after information that people do not necessarily even know they have, how do we uncover these root issues? One technique for doing this is to observe them. The behavior you see may be different to their response to a direct question. Observing people fuel their vehicles revealed that an incredibly high number of people spill fuel on themselves during the process, but in a survey the same people answered that they had "no problem" fueling their vehicles (David Kelley, 2001). Observing people in the real world, while ideal, is time-consuming and generally impractical. That means we need to devise a method to do the observing virtually. Ask your interviewee to explain their day and explain the things they do. Allow yourself to observe them in their virtual world. Look for annoyances during this virtual observation period (Schmitt, 2006).[1] These annoyances may be revealed through non-verbal cues as much as verbal communications. Listen for an increase in the cadence of the speech, increased volume, as hints that you have hit upon something interesting. Once you have found something at this wide-focus level, zoom in to elucidate a deeper understanding of this high level with a series of "why" questions to learn more detail. In the car-fuelling example, we could perhaps have obtained the same result as obtained by direct observation through this conversation:

Q. When do you typically fuel your car?

A. Typically on the weekend or on the way home from work.

Q. Why you fuel on your way home from work, but not on the way there?

A. I don't like to smell like fuel when I get to work.

Q. Why would you smell like fuel?

A. For some reason, I often end up spilling fuel on myself during the process.

During a dialogue you have to be keenly aware and read between the lines. Show empathy with your interviewee. Tacit knowledge is difficult to communicate. Of communication, 55 percent is non-verbal (Covey, 1989). Watch for signs of excitement or discomfort in your interviewee. How we say the words is 38 percent of communication. Listen for high-energy intonation that indicates passion. Annoyances are the tip of the iceberg of opportunities. Listen for the energy that reveals an annoyance. When you have hit upon an issue or annoyance it is time to drill deeper with a series of open-ended questions, to get further understanding. Asking such questions too soon, however, before an important issue or annoyance has been identified, will take the conversation to an uncomfortable dead end. Zoom out with virtual observations, zoom in with open-ended questions. Think of the process as exploring for general issues and annoyances through observation. Once the high-level observations have uncovered a hot-spot, drill down to find the specific issue or underlying motivation through a series of open-ended questions. The best way to think of these questions is to think like a 6-year-old. Some questions that can help in this pursuit include:

- Why?
- Please tell me more.
- How does this story begin?
- Then what happens? What is next?
- What are you thinking?
- What are you feeling?
- Why is that a problem for you?
- What do you spend time on?
- What don't you seem to have time to do that?
- What is preventing you from doing what you want?
- If you had a magic wand . . . .

While observations, real or virtual, are revealing, asking your interviewee to be an innovator typically is not. You are the innovator, not them. Most people will only see incremental improvements to what already exists; they do not envision break-through products. Henry Ford famously said that if you asked people what they wanted they would not say an automobile they would say a faster horse (Ford, n.d.). You are not looking for product concepts; you want to uncover issues, annoyances, needs, wants, and desires. Further, be aware that context creates bias and that experts are highly contextualized. If you are talking to the world's expert on diesel combustion, they will not likely lead you to believe that the future power source for personal transportation lies in solar, natural gas, or any potential automobile power plants other than diesel. That does not mean you should not engage with experts; quite to the contrary. These experts are great sources of knowledge, including the limitations of the current approaches.

My last caution in seeking understanding through dialogue is to be patient. Noise comes before illumination. You will need to perform many elicitations. Do not expect all the information you gather to lead you on a direct path to an offering that addresses a high-valued issue. This process is also an iterative path forward. Hypothesize, gather data, assess the data, rehypothesize, and repeat. Be diligent, you will get there.

PERSONA DEVELOPMENT

Through your elicitations you will find many specific needs or wants or desires. Once you have gone through this dissection process you will have to search for patterns in the information you gathered. This is the assembly process that follows the deconstruction process. You have zoomed in on the individual. You now need to zoom out slightly to put that individual into a group. You are looking to aggregate people that make decisions based on similar needs. How would you describe them? Personas can often be helpful.

A persona is an archetype of a customer. It is specific. It aggregates those with similar decision-driving needs, wants, and desires. The goal is identify those that think and choose alike. Build a picture of that representative person. What effects do they value? Make sure to include both rational and emotional effects. How do they make decisions? Geographic, demographic, psychographic, and behavioristic characteristics can be helpful. What are their desired outcomes? Note that saving money (outcome) is different from having a low cost (product attribute). What are their annoyances? Are they a mash-up of people that you interviewed?

It is often much easier to understand which attributes of a product resonate with particular customers if you can personify them; see them interacting with the product. Construct a story of their engagement with your offering. What is their situation, their annoyance? What will they experience with your offering? How is the outcome for them? Try to visualize it.

Naming your personas can also be helpful in making these personas real. Would "player Paul" and "soccer-mom Mary" base purchasing decisions on the same automobile attributes? Doubtful. "Paul" is more interested in image, where "Mary" is more interested in the safety features. What is the feeling each achieves from his or her desired product? Their decision-making needs are completely different although their base need – "requiring transportation" – may be the same. The objective is to define a user-group, yet keep the description specific enough to be useful. It is a challenging balance to maintain but, like other skills, this one too will improve with practice.

NOTE

1. The VOCA technique was derived from the LOCA (Latent Observation, Constant Annoyance) technique developed by The Inovo Group, www.theinovogroup. com, founders Larry Schmitt and Steve Schwartz.

Appendix C Implications of investment type for the founders

Step 2 of the business assessment methodology outlined in Chapter 4 was to determine the type of capital that aligns optimally with the proposed new venture. This assessment was made from the perspective of the financier. The type of financing also has significant implications for the founders. It is therefore worthwhile to flip the perspective and examine the implications of various types of investments for both the venture and the entrepreneur since, in the end, the financing structure has to be good for all involved. This section will take the perspective of the entrepreneur. That examination will start by looking at the entrepreneur's eventual exit from the firm.

EXIT OPTIONS

The entrepreneur's exit from their business probably sounds like a strange place to start a discussion on how to build the financial structure for the launch of a new business. New business founders are usually superfocused on what they can accomplish through their business if only they could obtain financing. The last thing on their minds is how they personally will exit from the business one day. But think about it they must, for no single factor has a greater impact on how the founder may operate and leave the company than does that company's financing. It is therefore extremely important that the financing be congruent with the goals the founders have, both for the company and for themselves.

Venture capitalists are often unjustly criticized for focusing on the company's exit, but VCs fully understand that, unless the founders are on the same page with them on that issue, the parties will struggle against each other on many, many company decisions going forward. This is because the financing of the company has so many consequences for the business. As unexpected as it may seem, the place to begin, as Habit 3 from *7 Habits of Highly Effective People* states, is to begin with the end in mind (Covey, 1989).

Four general factors motivate the owners to exit a business (Faley and Porter, 2005a):

- personal ambitions and interests change: It may be time to move on
- desire to cash out the equity they have built in the business
- desire to pass the company along to family/partners, and
- desire to raise more capital for the company.

While the fourth item on this list is not strictly a motivation to exit their new business, since founders often end up selling all or parts of their business in order to raise capital for the company, it needs to be included.

When founders "exit" the business they have started, the founders are ceding control of one or both of two distinct aspects of the business:

- operation of the business, or
- ownership of the business.

The aspects of their business the founders are willing to cede, and their motivations for doing so, will impact the type of exit options they may desire in the future. These exit strategies will, in turn, impact their choices of company financing options now.

There are generally three options for owners that would like to exit their business:

- sell their company to another company or individual
- transfer the company to family or partners, or
- take the company public – offer company equity for sale on the public stock exchanges (i.e. have an initial public offering, IPO, of stock in the company).

The IPO option is driven by many factors, including the size of the business, and is not simply a choice the entrepreneur can arbitrarily make. That being said, each of these exit options has different implications on the founder's future operation of or ownership role in the company. Figure C1 summarizes how these three exit methods affect the transfer of ownership and founder's control in addition to how positively they align with the various potential motives an owner may have for exiting their business.

	Sell	Transfer	IPO
Founder's cessation of:			
Operational control	Yes	Yes	No
Ownership	Yes	Maybe	Yes
Founder's motives:			
Time to move on	Yes	Yes	No
Desire to cash out	Yes	Unlikely	Yes
Need to raise capital	No	No	Yes

FIGURE C1 Impact of company exit options

Sell

Selling the company, which is vastly more common than an IPO, usually involves both a transfer of ownership and a transfer of operational control. When a company is sold, the role of the previous owner is usually negotiated along with other terms of the sale. After the entrepreneurial company is purchased, the current operating team may be asked to stay on during a transition period, but after that the new owners will most likely want to put their own stamp on the venture or integrate it into their other businesses. In addition, in most cases the acquirer will want the selling founders or managers to execute some kind of "not to compete" provision to discourage the seller from forming a new company that could compete directly with the new owners.

Transfer

The second exit option, transfer, is the most common exit option for family businesses. Countless reasons motivate the company founders to personally step aside from a leadership position and transfer operational, but not necessarily ownership, control of their company. Maybe they desire to start something new, retire, or take on a different role in the company. No matter what their motivation, as long as the founders retain some ownership in the company, they will want to ensure its future health. Succession planning is therefore critical for entrepreneurs contemplating this exit route. Chapter 7 discussed the three primary aspects of growth, including corporate and personal. As a founder's company continues to grow, skills such as strategic planning, systems and controls, and delegation become increasingly important. When founders are sizing up a successor, therefore, they need to realistically consider the needs of the company today and tomorrow. While the founders may be tempted to hire younger versions of themselves as their successor, the rubber band theory discussed in Chapter 7 suggests that doing this is a poor choice for the future of the business. Original founders need to realistically assess what skills are needed at the current and near-future stage of their company and hire someone that has those skills (Brown, 2009). In the case of family businesses, however, the successor may have to be drawn from family members.

IPO

An IPO is more than a liquidity event for a privately held company. It is definitely a liquidity event, since the previously private shares of stock are transformed to publicly traded – and therefore more liquid – shares of corporate stock. (The owners of the formerly private shares of stock usually agree, as part of the IPO, to refrain from selling their shares until after some designated "lock-up" period – typically around 180 days.) However, in addition to being a liquidity event for the owners of the formerly private company, an IPO is also a financing event for the company. In addition to transforming shares of stock that were once privately held into publicly traded ones, many new shares are also created and sold to investors during the IPO. The selling of these new shares to the public generates capital for the company. As such, pursuing an IPO only makes sense for companies that can benefit from a substantial infusion of cash. While the IPO transfers ownership of the company, the management team in place before the IPO will typically still be in charge of the company after it. Founders pursuing an IPO therefore need to be aware that they will still be responsible for running this company; but it will not be "theirs" any longer. Among other things, more disclosure requirements will bind them as a public company than ever did as a private one. Not every firm can choose to be listed on the public markets. All the major listings have significant requirements, meaning an entrepreneur does not simply choose to become a publicly traded company. Among other conditions, for example, NASDAQ requires companies to have a market capitalization over a half a billion dollars (Investopedia.com, n.d.).

EXIT PROBABILITIES FOR VENTURE CAPITAL-FINANCED BUSINESSES

Not all exit options are equally probable. How the company is financed, as will be discussed in the next section, has a significant influence on the probable exits for successful companies. The vast majority of successful VC-financed companies are acquired by larger companies rather than going public on their own. Size is a major determinant of this circumstance, timing being the other. These companies have to grow large enough to be traded on the major exchanges within the period within which the VCs are willing to keep them private companies. During the past decade (2002–12) IPOs made up just slightly more than 10 percent of the exits of VC-financed businesses. These IPO percentages oscillated during this ten-year period from a high of 21.2 percent of exits in 2004 to a low of 1.6 percent of exits in 2008 (NVCA website, n.d.).

FINANCING SOURCES

There are numerous potential financing options for new entrepreneurial companies. Among these options are:

1. *Non-equity financing:*
   Government grants.
   Friends and family.
   Bank loans.
   Crowdfunding.
2. *Equity financing:*
   Angel investors.
   Venture capitalists.

Non-equity financing

Someone that pulls themselves up by their bootstraps is a description given to a self-reliant person. Bootstrapping a company is a euphemism for creating a company from virtually nothing. While the methods used for bootstrapping companies are as varied as the companies themselves, in most entrepreneurs' minds bootstrapping encompasses any technique outside of selling equity in the company to outside investors.

Bootstrapped companies usually begin with the founders pooling their financial resources. These resources may range from personal savings and second mortgages on the founders' homes to taking on credit card debt. Direct bank loans, discussed later, may also be involved in a bootstrapping strategy. Creative bootstrappers are ingenious at getting company financing from wherever they can. This may range from government programs to pre-payment of advanced product orders through Kickstarter and other crowdfunding sources. Some creative bootstrapping technology companies have been known to license their technology in fields beyond those being planned for use by the company. The downside to such a tactic is that the company must be certain of the areas in which it plans to develop products. Licensing away its own technology will limit the company's future growth possibilities. For many entrepreneurs, however, the tradeoff is well worth it.

The clear advantage to non-equity financing is that the founders retain ownership and control of the company. While this method works easily for low-capital or niche businesses, the disadvantage is that company growth can be slowed by the limited resources that founders can align. Companies with high growth potential that attempt to bootstrap often perform under their potential due to their limited financing. This often creates opportunities for other "fast follower" companies to fill the market need the original startup identified, ultimately marginalizing the potential of the startup. The details of the funding sources for non-equity financing can be found in Chapter 6.

Equity financing

Selling a portion of your company in exchange for cash is known as equity financing. Unlike loans that can get paid from the cash generated by the profitable operations of the company, a private company's equity – an illiquid asset – can only be turned into cash or some other liquid asset by two means. One is to sell the entrepreneurial company to another entity for cash or publicly traded stock. A second way is to take the private company public through an IPO on a major stock exchange (NYSE, NADAQ, etc.). IPOs, as previously discussed, are much rarer than acquisitions. To be considered for an IPO, a company must be quite large (typically with revenues over $500 million and growing quickly). Growing a company to such a size can take much longer than the time the investors are willing to keep their investment illiquid. This is one of the main reasons why the vast majority of startups financed via equity financing are acquired, as was discussed in the IPO section of this appendix.

Angel investors and VCs are the two primary groups that make equity investments in nascent private companies. Each is described in detail in Chapter 6. Investor groups that are interested in taking an equity stake in an entrepreneur's company will not want to have their investment tied up forever; "forever" may be as little as three to ten years. As a result, the entrepreneur seeking this type of financing should anticipate the sale of the startup in well under ten years. The exception to this timing is some government-supported equity investors that aim at economic development. Since the government interest is usually tied to job creation rather than IRR, the exit timing may be extended. This is why it is sometimes referred to as "patient capital." Patient capital or not, an exit is in an entrepreneur's future once equity capital is accepted. Entrepreneurs can also expect any group taking an equity position in their firm to perform proper due diligence on the firm before investing.

Whatever the form of financing the company pursues it must be congruent with the investment potential the company has and the aspirations of the founders. This appendix focused on the implications for the founders. Appendix D, the investment potential framework, focuses on the alignment of the financing source with the new venture's potential.

Appendix D   Investment potential framework

The financial sources used to capitalize new companies can range from the straightforward (credit card debt) to complex investment agreements crafted between these companies and venture capitalists. As convoluted as the entrepreneurial company's funding may become, it is critical the financing structure of the company be completely aligned with two things:

- the company's needs and
- the founder's desires.

Funding the initial financial needs of entrepreneurial companies is challenging as most of these nascent organizations have no collateral to leverage for a traditional bank loan. As a result, these companies must seek alternate forms of financing, which often include selling equity in the business. Selling company equity creates additional company owners whose desires must also be aligned with future funding decisions. The founders, however, are the ones that from the onset must make sure that the financing path they take the company down delivers both what the company needs and what is consistent with their personal vision for their new company. This appendix discusses the financing from the perspective of the financiers. Appendix C discusses the impact the various type of financing option will have on the founders.

The type of funding entrepreneurs can seek for their new venture, if they desire, must be consistent with the business that is being created. The investment potential framework (shown in Figure D.1),[1] indicates the type of funding that could be attracted to the firm as it is currently designed. Of course, the simple fact that the firm is potentially equity investable (upper right-hand quadrant) does not mean that the founders desire that type of funding. It simply means they are creating the type of business that would be attractive to that type of investor. On the other hand, a firm that finds itself in one of the other three quadrants would not be attractive to equity investors even if the founders desired such investment. Few firms even have the potential to be equity investable. Indeed, in 1999, at the height of the VC investment bubble, only 6.3 percent of Inc. 500 companies had equity investments (*Inc. Magazine*, 1999). Today the percentage is less than half that level. This is despite the fact that the Inc. 500 represents the top privately held companies in the United States.

279

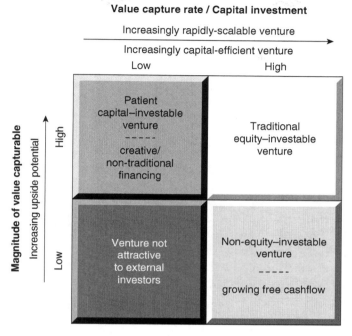

FIGURE D1 Investment potential framework

Successful businesses capture a healthy share of the value their firms create. Clearly, a new firm must create value in the marketplace, but though a necessary, that is an insufficient criterion. What new entrepreneurs often fail to realize is that your business can fail, even when providing goods for an exceptionally attractive market, if the business is not able to capture any of the value it creates. The PVC framework reviewed in Appendix A indicated the chances of a firm being able to capture the lion's share of the value it creates in the market. The vertical axis of the investment potential diagram (Figure D1) represents the magnitude of the value the new firm could potentially capture. A large market in which the firm can capture large EBITDA (earnings before interest, taxes, depreciation and amortization) margins represents the top of this axis, while a small market in which the firm can only capture small margins represents the bottom of this vertical axis.

The horizontal axis of the investment potential framework represents the relative rate at which the value represented on the vertical axis could be captured per unit of capital investment. This axis measures both how rapidly scalable the firm is and how capital-efficient it is. A firm on the far right-hand end of the horizontal axis would be quickly scalable and very capital-efficient. A software company that is producing a product for which the market demand is such that the company could grow very quickly would meet both the scalability and capital-efficiency criteria, assuming that the software could be easily distributed electronically over the internet. That is attributable to the fact that once the product is developed it takes relatively little additional capital to increase production and distribution capacities. This is very different from, say, a chemical manufacturer that, even if it could grow rapidly, would require significant capital investment for each block of new volume it would need to produce. This is because costly new production plants would need to be built for each significant volume of new market demand the firm would need to satisfy. Restaurants are similar. A restaurant can increase its volume somewhat by increasing its table-turns, but at some point, if the company wants to continue to grow its revenue and market share, it will have to construct a new restaurant, which is a significant capital expenditure. A firm's fixed assets ratio is an indication of how much revenue a firm produces per dollar of PP&E (property, plant, and equipment). That ratio, combined with the expected EBITDA margin, provides a good indication of the capital-efficiency of the firm's ability to capture value.

The upper right-hand quadrant of the investment potential framework would be attractive to traditional equity investors such as VC and angel investors. Firms in this quadrant are targeting large markets, have the ability to capture a significant portion of the value created, and can also scale quickly with limited need for additional capital. These firms have the potential to grow quite large and are capital-efficient in their growth. This is the traditional target of VCs. Venture capitalists typically target companies where growth can be rapidly accelerated through an infusion of capital, but that do not need continued additions of significant capital to sustain that growth. High-margin software firms or electronic hardware firms where the manufacturing can be readily scaled or outsourced are their traditional targets.

Firms in the upper left-hand quadrant of the investment potential framework are also targeting large markets from which they can capture a significant share of the value. However, these firms either scale more slowly, relative to the firms in the traditional equity quadrant, or need continual capital influxes to grow. Green energy companies often find themselves in this quadrant. The slower growth, or the need for additional, follow-on investment, or both, will reduce the return rate for investors as well as the timeframe for that return; hence the label "patient." Traditional equity financing with its relatively short investment-to-return targets (three to five years) will not typically operate here. Government economic developers, with longer time horizons, are attracted to this quadrant, but must be creative in financing firms here, including the creation of public–private partnerships (DeWulf,

Blanken, and Bult-Spiering, 2012). Entrepreneurs finding their firms in this quadrant must address the challenge of raising large amounts of capital with long pay-back horizons.

Firms in the lower right-hand quadrant will scale quickly and will be capital-efficient, but not much capital is required to launch them. Since these firms are targeting relatively small markets, they do not have the potential to become extremely large. These firms will not be able to raise funding from VCs as the potential payoff is just too small. However, because these firms do not require nearly as much capital (perhaps as much as 1,000-fold less) their return rate to potential investors will be at the level that the VCs are targeting. Entrepreneurs whose firms show these types of high ROI potential are often puzzled by the fact that they are "too small" to attract venture capital. Since these firms have the potential to generate a significant amount of cash flow, their long-term growth can easily be supported by debt financing: Hence the "non-equity-investable" label for this quadrant. The challenge these firms face is in finding the capital they need to get started. These firms often need to scale back from their initial vision to a firm that they can start with self-financing or monies from friends and families. These firms need a clear strategic path to continue expanding to the firm they dream of creating or they will be in danger of slipping into the lower left-hand quadrant of Figure D1. These "bootstrappable" firms will increase their equity value due to their rapidly increasing cash flow. Accordingly, the founders may one day find a buyer for their firm at a valuation significantly greater than the capital it took them to start the business.

The firms in the lower left-hand quadrant of Figure D1, unlike those in the lower-right-hand quadrant, do not have the potential for rapid growth. Indeed, firms located here may not have the potential for much growth at all without significant, additional, capital infusions. Once up and running, these firms can often produce enough cash flow to provide a nice financial life for their founders. As a result, these types of firm are often labeled "lifestyle" companies, since they are not attractive to outside investors but may provide a very healthy lifestyle for the founders, so long as they can find the patient debt financing required to get them started. At exit, these firms often sell for just slightly more than their PP&E values. The quintessential example of this type of firm is a singular convenience store. It requires significant capital to launch (purchase the building, stock the shelves), will generate a decent cash flow (depending on the location), but will likely sell for the PP&E value when the owner eventually decides to exit. The value of the business is not in its escalating equity value, but in the cash it generates for the owners: Hence the quadrant label "not attractive to outside investors."

The investment potential framework is not a judgment on the quality of the business. It is simply a question of alignment; alignment of the business's potential with the type of investment the entrepreneurs could reasonably expect to obtain. Knowing the type of funding will also allow you to perform the appropriate financial assessments, as those assessment methods are dependent on investment type. Equity investors, for example, are interested in the equity growth of the firm. The assessment of those firms will involve estimating the value of the firm over time. On the other hand, the main interest of debt financiers is in your ability to pay back your loan. Your firm's equity growth is irrelevant to them. Instead, loan agents want to understand projections of your free cash flow. If the firm is viable after the financial screens, a sensitivity analysis can be performed to determine the venture's key economic drivers; its critical success factors. Since all the analysis starts with knowing the type of financing, understanding how to determine that quickly is key to quickly understanding the financial viability of your firm.

NOTE

1. This framework was co-developed during the collaboration of Timothy L. Faley and Peter Adriaens at the University of Michigan between 2008 and 2013.

Appendix E   Product development and the Entrepreneurial Arch

Product development is a part of the overall business development process. The example listed below offers one view as to how the product development steps could overlay and synchronize with the business discovery, development, validation, and launch phases of the Entrepreneurial Arch.

Historically, the challenge of product development was that it was out of sync with the ideal business development de-risking. In a typical product development scheme (product concept → prototype → beta product → commercial product), no direct customer feedback was obtained until after the beta product had been created. This meant that, for many products, a significant investment was made before it was known whether the product would resonate with a customer. There were a couple of exceptions. One was software, where the development costs are low. The other exception was devices that create the same user experience as current products, albeit in a differentiated way (faster, cheaper, better). This classic product development schema created a disconnection between product development and business development, since the significant resources available for beta-product development are not generally available until the resource phase of the Entrepreneurial Arch. This meant that on the product development side entrepreneurs tended to leap from product concept to prototype development. In other words, entrepreneurs were leaping from the opportunity identification segment of the Arch to the resourcing segment, where financing was available. In turn, this leaping legitimately called into question the value of the business planning activities, since these plans were often being completed with little or no customer feedback. However, the real issue is not the value of assessing the feasibility of one's business or of determining how to operationalize it before resourcing and launching it; rather it is the re-synchronizing of the business's development processes with the product development process.

Eric Ries, in *The Lean Startup* (2011), suggested that some aspects of customer risk could be mitigated earlier without taking on significant financial risk through the development of a "mock" or "simulated" or "minimum viable" product (MVP). This approach minimizes the trade-off between mitigating customer risk and increasing financial risk. Most importantly, it holds the promise of re-synchronizing the business and product development schemas and getting the business and product team members back on the same page. The list below illustrates how, by using the MVP concept, you can re-sync the product development with the business development segments of the Entrepreneurial Arch: The product development activities that can and should be performed at each segment of the Arch are listed below.

- *Opportunity identification:* Identify a solution (an approach to addressing the identified issue).
- *Business design:* Develop an offering concept (a product concept that targets a specific customer).
- *Business assessment:* Create a simulated or "mock-up" product. Doing so will create a customer experience with a pseudo-product. Such an experience provides the user with a sense of the experience of the product without the expense of having to create an actual product. The approach provides significant insight into whether the product concept would be valued by the customer.
- *Operationalization:* Develop a product prototype. (These activities could also take place early in the resourcing segment of the Arch, depending on the development costs.) The prototype's aim is to realize the functionality of the final offering (demonstrate that the offering will work), but not necessarily the form factor of a commercial product. Typically, the prototype is not operable by those other than "experts." The funding source for this development could be government grants such as the SBIR and STTR programs in the United States.
- *Resource:* Given this segment covers the first five years of your firm, the product development activities performed during this time can extend from beta product development to the minimum viable product (MVP) to the development and sales of a commercial product. The beta product is the first offering that you can put into customers' hands for their use and feedback. It will likely not have the manufacturability nor the final form factor of the ultimate commercial product, but should have all of its functionality. The MVP is the first product that you can sell, but may only be attractive to the early adopters. The full commercial product is a manufacturable product with the functionality the target customer desires.
- *Growth:* Alter the offering as needed as you grow into capability and/or market adjacencies.

References

3M Corporation website, "History". Retrieved December 21, 2013 from http://solutions.3m.com/wps/portal/3M/en_US/3M-Company/Information/Resources/History/.

Afuah, Allen (1999). "Strategies to turn adversity into profits." *MIT Sloan Management Review*, January 1999.

AllBusiness.com. "The five basic methods of market research." Retrieved December 1, 2013 from www.allbusiness.com/marketing/market-research/1287-1.html.

Angel Capital Association (2012). "ACA, angel groups and angel-backed companies." Retrieved November 19, 2013 from www.angelcapitalassociation.org/data/Documents/Resources/ACAandAngelGroupBackground09–12.pdf.

Arrington, Michael (2006). "Google has acquired YouTube." *Techcrunch.com*, October 9, 2006. Retrieved December 21, 2013 from http://techcrunch.com/2006/10/09/google-has-acquired-youtube/.

Blank, Steven G. (2006). *The Four Steps to the Epiphany: Successful Strategies for Products that Win*. San Mateo, CA: Cafepress.com

Brophy, David (2000). Unpublished Entrepreneurial Finance lecture for the Center for Venture Capital and Private Equity, Ross School of Michigan, University of Michigan.

Brown, Paul B. (2009). "And the next CEO will be..." *New York Times*, August 5, 2009.

Brummer, Chris and Gorfine, Daniel (2013). "The JOBS Act isn't all 'crowdfunding.'" *Forbes.com*, October 8, 2013. Retrieved November 18, 2013 from www.forbes.com/sites/realspin/2013/10/08/the-jobs-act-isnt-all-crowdfunding/.

Bund, Ian (2006). Plymouth Venture Partners' presentation at the University of Michigan, February 7, 2006.

Burlingham, Bo (2005). *Small Giants*. New York: Penguin Group.

Caddell, Bud (2009). "How to be happy in business – Venn diagram." *Whatconsumesme.com*, Posted June 3, 2009. Retrieved February 18, 2013 from http://whatconsumesme.com/2009/posts-ive-written/how-to-be-happy-in-business-venn-diagram/.

Camp, Justin J. (2002). *Venture Capital Due Diligence*. New York: John Wiley and Sons.

Catlett, Charlie (2009). "Technology adoption rates: Historical perspective." *International Science Grid This Week*, May 6, 2009. Retrieved January 14, 2011 from www.isgtw.org/visualization/isgtw-image-week-technology-adoption-rates-historical-perspective.

Centers for Disease Control and Prevention website. Retrieved November 18, 2013 from www.cdc.gov/cancer/dcpc/resources/features/WorldCancerDay/.

Chesbrough, Henry (2003). *Open Innovation: The New Imperative for Creating and Profiting from Technology.* Boston, MA: Harvard Business Review Press.

Chesbrough, Henry (2006). *Open Business Models: How to Thrive in the New Innovation Landscape,* Boston, MA: Harvard Business Review Press.

Christensen, Clayton M. (1997). *Innovator's Dilemma.* Boston, MA: Harvard Business School Press.

Churchill, Neil C. and Lewis, Virginia L. (1983). "The five stages of small business growth." *Harvard Business Review*, May–June, 1983.

Collins, Jim (2001a) "Good to great." *FastCompany*, October 2001. Retrieved December 22, 2013 from www.jimcollins.com/article_topics/articles/good-to-great.html.

Collins, Jim (2001b). *Good to Great.* New York: HarperCollins.

Constine, Josh and Cutler, Kim-Mai (2012). "Facebook buys Instagram for $1 billion." *Techcrunch.com*. April 9, 2012. Retrieved December 21, 2013 from http://techcrunch.com/2012/04/09/facebook-to-acquire-instagram-for-1-billion/.

Cooper, Alan (1999). *The Inmates Are Running the Asylum: Why High Tech Products Drive Us Crazy and How to Restore the Sanity.* New York: Sams.

Covey, Stephen R. (1989). *The 7 Habits of Highly Effective People.* New York: Simon and Schuster.

Cuban, Mark (2010), "Product v. feature: The story of Xmark." September 30, 2010. Retrieved June 9, 2012 from http://blogmaverick.com/2010/09/30/product-vs-feature-the-lesson-of-xmarks/.

Davila, A. and Foster, G. (2012). "How to structure companies for high growth." *IESE Insight*, September 15, 2012.

DeWulf, G., Blanken, A., and Bult-Spiering, M. (2012). *Strategic Issues in Public–Private Partnerships.* New York: Wiley.

Drucker, Peter F. (1985). *Innovation and Entrepreneurship.* New York: Harper and Row.

Einstein, Albert. Quote retrieved November 13, 2013 from www.brainyquote.com/quotes/quotes/a/alberteins103652.html.

Eisenhower, Dwight D. Retrieved on December 21, 2013 from http://en.wikiquote.org/wiki/Dwight_D._Eisenhower.

Eller, Karl (2005). *Integrity is All You've Got: and Seven Other Lessons of the Entrepreneurial Life.* New York: McGraw-Hill.

Enterprise Ireland website. Retrieved November 19, 2013 from www.enterprise-ireland.com/en/About-Us/.

Ernst & Young (2001). "Guide to producing a business plan." Retrieved on November 11, 2013 from http://group27.narod.ru/ucheba/files/EY_Business_Plan_Guide.pdf.

Ernst & Young (2012). *Growth Actually: Ernst and Young's 2012 European Attractiveness Survey.* Retrieved December 20, 2013 from www.ey.com/Publication/vwLUAssets/Attractiveness_2012_europe/$FILE/Attractiveness_2012_europe.pdf.

Evans, Phillip B. and Wurster, Thomas S. (1997). "Strategy and the new economics of information." *Harvard Business Review,* September–October, 1997.

Faley, Timothy L. and Porter, T. S. (2005a). "Making your exit." *Inc. Magazine,* March 15, 2005. Retrieved October 21, 2010 from www.inc.com/resources/startup/articles/20060301/tfaley.html.

Faley, Timothy L. and Kirsch, Paul, (2005b). "Creating your business plan." *Inc. Magazine,* November 3, 2005. Retrieved December 20, 2013 from www.inc.com/resources/startup/articles/20051101/bplans.html.

Ford, Henry. "Henry Ford's quotations." Retrieved December 21, 2013 from http://blog.thehenryford.org/2013/03/henry-fords-quotations/.

Gallimore, Alec (2010). Presentation to a student entrepreneurship club at the University of Michigan on September 30, 2010.

Gatewood, Elizabeth (2003). Entrepreneurship presentation, University of Michigan, October 16, 2003.

Hamermesh, Richard G. (2002). "Note on business model analysis for the entrepreneur." *Harvard Business School Case 9–802–048.*

Inc. Magazine (1999). "Almanac: A statistical look at 1999's Inc. 500 companies and the CEOs who run them." *Inc. Magazine,* October 15, 1999.

Inc. Magazine (2008). "How the 2008 Inc. 500 companies were selected." *Inc.com,* posted November 15, 2008. Retrieved December 22, 2013 from www.inc.com/magazine/20080901/how-the-2008-inc-500-companies-were-selected.html.

Investopedia.com website. Retrieved December 21, 2013 from www.investopedia.com/ask/answers/121.asp.

Isaacson, Walter (2011). *Steve Jobs.* New York: Simon and Schuster.

ITCandor. com (2012). "Apple and Samsung – 2-horse leaders of the handset race." *ITCandor.com,* September 18, 2012. Retrieved January 10, 2013 from www.itcandor.com/smart-phone-q212.

Kawasaki, Guy (2004). *The Art of the Start: Time-tested, Battle-hardened, Guide for Anyone Starting Anything.* New York: Penguin Group.

Kawasaki, Guy. (2013). "How to create an enchanting pitch." January 9, 2013. Retrieved November 26, 2013 from http://blog.guykawasaki.com/2012/01/how-to-create-an-enchanting-pitch-officeandguyk.html.

Keating, Peter (2002). "Biotechnology valuations are finally making sense." *Red Herring*, March, 2002.

Kelley, David (2001). Presentation at Stanford University, October 10, 2001.

Kelley, Tom (2008). Presentations at Stanford University, November 12, 2008.

Khosla, Vinod (2002). Presentation at Stanford University, April 24, 2002.

Leung, C. H. (2007). "Evolution of the business model." MSc thesis presented at Technische Universiteit Eindhoven. Retrieved February 3, 2013 from http://alexandria.tue.nl/extra1/afstversl/tm/leung2007.pdf.

Merrick, Amy (2006). "Asking 'What would Ann do?'." *The Wall Street Journal*, September 15, 2006.

Middleton, Len (2010). University of Michigan Multidisciplinary Action Project (MAP) summary personal correspondence.

von Moltke, Field Marshal Helmuth. Retrieved on December 21, 2013 from http://en.wikiquote.org/wiki/Helmuth_von_Moltke_the_Elder.

Moon, Youngme (2002). "Inside Intel Inside." *Harvard Business School Case 9–502–083.*

Moore, Geoffrey A. (1991). *Crossing the Chasm.* New York: HarperCollins.

Moore, Geoffrey A. (2005). Presentation at Stanford University, April 6, 2005.

Mullins, John W. (2003). *The New Business Road Test.* London: Prentice Hall Financial Times.

Nagel, Thomas T. and Holden, Reed K. (1987). *The Strategy and Tactics of Pricing: A Guide to Profitable Decision Making.* New York: Prentice-Hall, Inc.

National Venture Capital Association (NVCA) website. "Industry stats by date." Retrieved December 20, 2013 from www.nvca.org/index.php?option=com_content&view=article&id=78&Itemid=102.

National Venture Capital Association (NVCA). "VC exits." Referenced December 20, 2013 from www.nvca.org/index.php?option=com_docman&task=cat_view&gid=58&Itemid=317.

National Venture Capital Association. Retrieved November 15, 2008 from www.nvca.org/aboutnvca.html.

Osterwalder, Alexander and Pigneur, Yves (2010). *Business Model Generation.* New York: John Wiley and Sons.

Pagliery, Jose. (2012). "JOBS Act opens fundraising doors for small firms." *CNN Money*, April 6, 2012. Retrieved December 21, 2013 from http://money.cnn.com/2012/04/05/smallbusiness/jobs-act/index.htm.

Paul, Mark (2003), *The Entrepreneur's Survival Guide*. Portland, OR: Cedar Mill Publishing.

PNC, "Financing for your future – the five C's of credit." Retrieved November 18, 2013 from www.pnc.com/webapp/unsec/ProductsAndService.do?siteArea=/pnccorp/PNC/Home/Small+Business/Financing+Your+Future/The+Five+Cs+of+Credit.

Porter, Michael E. (1979). "How competitive forces shape strategy." *Harvard Business Review*, March–April, 1979.

Porter, Michael E. (1980). *Competitive Strategy: Techniques for Analyzing Industries and Competitors*. New York: The Free Press.

Porter, Michael E. (1985). *Competitive Advantage: Creating and Sustaining Superior Performance*. New York: The Free Press.

Prahalad, C. K. and Hamel, Gary (1989). "Strategic intent." *Harvard Business Review*, May–June, 1989. Retrieved December 21, 2013 from http://www3.uma.pt/filipejmsousa/ge/Hamel%20and%20Prahalad,%201989.pdf.

PricewaterhouseCoopers website. Retrieved June 8, 2012 from www.pwc.com.

Reisinger, Don (2011). "Android widens smartphone market lead over iOS." *C|Net*, October 6, 2011. Retrieved January 22, 2013 from http://news.cnet.com/8301–13506_3-20116599-17/android-widens-smartphone-market-lead-over-ios/.

Ries, Eric (2011). *The Lean Startup: How Today's Entrepreneurs Use Continuous Innovation to Create Radically Successful Businesses*. New York: Crown Business.

Rogers, Everett (1995). *Diffusion of Innovation*. New York: The Free Press.

Rumsfeld, Donald (2002). Statement made at a press briefing, February 12, 2002. Retrieved on December 20, 2013 from http://en.wikipedia.org/wiki/There_are_known_knowns.

Schmitt, Larry (2006). LOCA technique presented in "Driving the innovation process", a graduate class at the Ross School of Business at the University of Michigan, Winter term, 2006.

Shane, Scott (2008). "Top ten myths of entrepreneurship." Retrieved December 21, 2013 from http://blog.guykawasaki.com/2008/01/top-ten-myths-o.html#ixzz0ea35EGW5.

Shleifer, A. and Vishny, R. W. (1997), "A survey of corporate governance." *The Journal of Finance*, 52.

Sullivan, Arthur and Sheffrin, Steven M. (2003). *Economics: Principles in action*. Upper Saddle River, NJ: Pearson Prentice Hall.

Sutton, Robert I. (2007). *The No Ass-hole Rule: Building a Civilized Workplace and Surviving One That Isn't*, New York: Business Plus Publishers.

Teece, David (1986). "Profiting from technological innovation: Implication for integration, collaboration, licensing and public policy." *Research Policy* 15(6).

Tenner, Daniel (2011). "Product vs. business vs. company." Retrieved December 20, 2013 from http://swombat.com/2011/10/24/product-business-company.

Treacy, Michael and Wiersema, Fred (1995). *The Discipline of Market Leaders.* Boston: Perseus Books.

US Small Business Administration website. Retrieved November 29, 2008 from www.sba.gov/.

Wikipedia. History of McDonald's Corporation. Retrieved December 21, 2013 from http://en.wikipedia.org/wiki/McDonald's.

Wikipedia. History of Microsoft's Encarta (1993–2009). Retrieved December 21, 2013 from http://en.wikipedia.org/wiki/Encarta.

Zingerman's Community of Businesses website. Retrieved on October 11, 2013 from www.zingermanscommunity.com.

Zygmont, Jeffrey (2001). *The VC Way: Investment Secrets from the Wizards of Venture Capital.* Boston: Perseus Publishing.

Index

Made in the USA
Lexington, KY
20 April 2016